I Think I'm Going to Be an Airline Pilot

To Jenny

I Think I'm Going to Be an Airline Pilot

Ken White

I Think I'm Going to Be an Airline Pilot
Author – Ken White
© Ken White 2023
Email: jwhi3413@bigpond.net.au

This book is sold with the understanding that the author is not offering specific personal advice to the reader. For professional advice, seek the services of a suitable, qualified practitioner. The author disclaims any responsibility for liability, loss or risk, personal or otherwise, that happens as a consequence of the use and application of any of the contents of this book.

All rights reserved. This book may not be reproduced in whole or part, stored, posted on the internet, or transmitted in any form or by any means, electronic, mechanical, photocopying, recording, or other, without permission from the author of this book.

Editing by www.TamaraProtassow.com
Design and publishing support by www.AuthorSupportServices.com

ISBN: 9781922375254

A catalogue record for this book is available from the National Library of Australia

Contents

Introduction		1

Part One: Early Days

Chapter 1	Growing up in Greenwich	7
Chapter 2	How we lived back then	11
Chapter 3	Portrait of my family at the time (AKA: the people in our house)	21
Chapter 4	School days	29
Chapter 5	Jobs and girls and cars	37
Chapter 6	Apprenticeship	43
Chapter 7	Becoming LAME (that stands for 'Licensed Aircraft Maintenance Engineer')	63
Chapter 8	Learning to fly	71
Chapter 9	Scholarship and beyond	81

Part Two: My Move to Melbourne to Become an Airline Pilot!

Chapter 10	Melbourne-bound	97
Chapter 11	Finally flying... well, almost	103
Chapter 12	Finally flying... properly!	111
Chapter 13	Viscounts, a risky business	117
Chapter 14	Boeing school	125
Chapter 15	Flying Fokkers	133
Chapter 16	Stormy flying, of a different nature	145

Chapter 17	Flying freight in an Electra	153
Chapter 18	Finally, the DC-9!	159
Chapter 19	The B737	169
Chapter 20	More change on the home front	187
Chapter 21	Some time in New Zealand	195
Chapter 22	The pilots' dispute	205
Chapter 23	Singapore days	219
Chapter 24	Singapore-based, multi-country fun	229
Chapter 25	Flying the B-744	247
Chapter 26	Round the world for retirement!	265

Part Three: Retirement

Chapter 27	Keeping up with fast-paced life	271
Chapter 28	Cars and planes	277
Chapter 29	9/11	283
Chapter 30	A stint in the Rotary Club and becoming a 'Collins St farmer'	285
Chapter 31	St Andrews	291
Chapter 32	Money matters	295
Chapter 33	More boating and a return to the canals	299
Chapter 34	SarsCoV2 or Covid19	307
Chapter 35	Some advice and opinions	309
Epilogue		315

Introduction

At any age, but especially as one gets older, memory is a wilful dog. It won't be summoned or dismissed, but it cannot survive without you. It can sustain you or feed on you. It visits when it wants to, not when you want it to. It has a schedule all of its own that you can never know, it can capture, corner, or liberate you. Hopefully you can smile with it, and be dismayed without it. It's easy to argue that without memory, you can't be human.

Being human, my memories are of the good times; those times that were not so good perhaps are better off being forgotten. However, I will note some of those down here too because life is not just sunshine and roses, but the shadows too.

An early mantra for me was, "Do the difficult things first, because whatever it is that comes after that will get easier." Mantra is a funny word, I'm not at all sure where it came from, but sometimes it's an easy way to understand difficult things.

I think that doing difficult things first is something I learnt as an apprentice. Most of the tasks that were given then were not the sort of jobs that were very enjoyable. However, there was no escape so the best thing to do was do the hardest thing first, and then you could hope that it would get easier after that.

Looking back on the last 80 years, that was pretty good advice that I gave myself, all those years ago.

Effectively, this is some sort of history. History after all is the perceived story of everything from the point of view of the observer, which in this case is me. Everyone has a story, and each of them are quite different. This one is mine.

Knowing our own story helps us to know ourselves, others, and the world around us better than we did before. The miracle of existing at all is always individual and worth sharing.

To that end, this is an outline of my life 'so far'.

My generation didn't take much notice of our grandparents' backgrounds, where they came from, what they did etc. Hopefully if I make an attempt to describe my life as best I can remember the details, someone will find it of interest in the future. Every person ever born has a story, and every story is different depending on that individual's character and experience. Indeed, it's reasonable to think that the only reason mankind is on earth is to tell stories.

When all's said and done, stories are the only thing that are left after a full and hopefully productive life. The marks you got at school, the promotions, (or not) at work and the loves made and lost all become part of the story. Some stories are more interesting than others, but they're a story nonetheless. It takes a lot of faceless people to make up the essence of a story, but seeing that this story is about me, I'll talk about myself a lot. Many will be hovering in the background, and I hope that their stories are remembered too.

Obviously, like picking apart a piece of fabric, much of the warp and weft will be left out of this story but I'll try and end up with some sort of overview from beginning to hopefully not quite the end, as even at 82 I like to think that I've got quite a while to go yet!

The events themselves might become dim, but the story endures and becomes a tiny part of the huge tapestry that makes up humankind, and as time goes on, is history.

Essentially, I'm writing this in the hope that my grandchildren, and perhaps their children when they grow up will be interested in 'what went before' and will find this story 'of the olden days' worth reading. Hopefully, my much-loved grandchildren and perhaps their children will read it one day and get an insight into my life, which is sure to be vastly different, in ways that I can't imagine, to theirs.

PART ONE

Early Days

CHAPTER 1

Growing up in Greenwich

In March 1940 Australia was at war. The adults all thought it was a phony war, as it was far away on the other side of the world, and by then had had little effect on Australia. But Robert Menzies the Prime Minister at the time had declared war six months earlier to support Britain, the so-called 'mother country', in its war on Germany. Australia then had a population of just over 7 million, who were called British. Australian citizenship wasn't introduced until 1949, and even then, people called Britain 'home'.

Australian Professor Howard Florey had just invented penicillin, too. This probably makes him the most important Australian ever born when you consider the number of lives saved by antibiotics ever since. Imagine, all those lives saved, starting with mouldy bread.

And the other significant event of the year 1940 was that I was born.

I was born in Maitland NSW, a place that, other than a drive-through once, I have no knowledge of at all. My father George was a National Roads and Motorists' Association (NRMA) guide/mechanic there at the time, answering callouts from distressed and stuck motorists.

Our house and the bay

After my start in Maitland, I grew up in Greenwich which is a harbourside suburb of Sydney. It was working class then (though it's quite gentrified now) and for some reason the population of children was mostly boys and not many girls. Mind you, maybe the girls were off having their own adventures and avoided us boys. Who knows?

Being born in 1940, my first five years were war years, of which I don't have much memory. Dad being a trained mechanic, was conscripted into the Air Force and therefore spent the war in a propeller maintenance shop at Mascot. I do recall him coming home in uniform on leave occasionally.

There were not many cars in those days and the streets were just a strip of paving down the middle, with dirt at the edges. Cars weren't common enough to worry about what happened when they met someone going the other way, and they didn't drive that fast either. At the time, most streets had a sign nailed to a power pole proclaiming, "This is a war bond street". War bonds were money that people lent to the government to help pay for the war.

Our house was at the end of the street, with quite a spectacular view across the harbour to the Harbour Bridge and the city. It was marred a little by the oil storage depot in Berrys Bay, but to see the oil tankers come and go added to the interest. Berrys Bay had a wharf where the oil tankers docked. I remember the tanks being huge, but then everything is big to a kid.

I Think I'm Going to Be an Airline Pilot

I do remember all the old Navy ships tied up next to Berrys Island in the bay. American liberty ships I think they were. They were mainly derelict so didn't go anywhere at all. As I got older, I also remember seeing the cruiser *Shropshire,* which was on loan from the British. They moored her over at the other side of the harbour, and I'm not sure what she did really.

We had quite a large block of land on Vista St with a chook yard right at the back, but more on that later. From the end of the street in front of our house down to the water was bush, and the end of our street was a council dump. It's hard to imagine now with all the health and safety regulations that such a thing would be allowed. It was a 'hard rubbish' dump, which made a great playground for us kids.

I remember a big pile of unfired pottery which made great chalk for drawing on the road. We drew the court markings for hopscotch, ball games or whatever we felt like.

A lot of our free time was spent playing in the bush, which ran from right in front of my house down to Berrys Bay. There was a creek and mud flats at low tide, so a lot of fun could be had playing 'hidings' or building mud houses. Even though there were supposed to be sharks in the harbour, we would fashion rafts and canoes out of driftwood and paddle about near the mud flats. A broomstick with a raincoat on it made a good sail if the wind was behind you. We made quite a few punts out of driftwood and would float around the bay. Generally, we just went home when we got hungry, or when it got dark.

We played in the bush, went to the local primary school, and had a normal life for the time. I was in the Cubs, but for some reason didn't progress to the Scouts. My parents didn't have much money, so they probably couldn't afford the uniform.

The currency was pounds, shillings, and pence. Distances were in statute miles (different to nautical miles), feet and inches. There were 20 shillings to the pound and 12 pence to the shilling. Sometimes, prices were quoted in guineas, which were one pound, one shilling for some reason. All this was known as the 'Imperial system'. The UK uses pounds to this day, albeit with 100 pence now making a pound and shillings no longer in use. Australia changed to the Metric system in 1964. It's a much more sensible system, but it took a long time to stop thinking in Imperial. Some older people never did.

CHAPTER 2

How we lived back then

Our place in the world

Australia was quite an inward looking and Anglo-centric country back then. We didn't know it, but the whole world was developing and moving on, while Australia was being left behind socially, culturally and economically. Australia just wasn't developing as much as everywhere else. Everything was government controlled or owned – it wasn't socialist, but it also wasn't privatised – including the board of works, education, transport, power companies and airlines. It was very conformist and regulated.

The pubs closed at 18:00 every night, leading to a phenomenon known as the 'six o'clock swill'. Crowds of men, pushing and shoving to get to the bar, would 'swill' as much beer as possible before being thrown out at six o'clock, all in the name of social harmony. Women weren't allowed in the general drinking areas of pubs, they had to use the 'Ladies' Lounge'. It's not hard to imagine how much 'harmony' there was from crowds of drunks on just about every street corner at six o'clock!

The Labor government took over in 1972 and spent significant money on the Arts and reduced trading tariffs and business regulation in general. This made access to the world for the average Australian much easier. However, the changes were so numerous and so quick that the population just couldn't cope, and the Whitlam government ended with the well-known constitutional crisis in 1975.

But back when I was a child, there was no weekend trading, so if you wanted anything from the shop you just had to wait until Monday. For those people who worked the normal working week and couldn't get to the shops, it was too bad. Other than plentiful standard food, good restaurants were very few and far between, and way outside the price range of most families. There were such high customs tariffs on any imported goods that the price of anything out of the ordinary was just about impossible for the average person to afford.

Ice chests were the norm. An ice chest looked like a normal 'fridge but the top would have an ice block in it which cooled the bottom section. Accordingly, food wouldn't last very long, so our diet while basic, was mostly fresh food. We did eat some stuff out of cans too.

The ice man would come around twice a week in an old truck. He'd carry the blocks of ice into the kitchen wrapped in hessian bags to stop it melting. In Summer, us kids would run along behind the ice truck, and as he hacked his pick into the ice block, bits would break off and we'd pick them up and suck on them.

The milk man had a horse and cart, and he'd leave the milk in a billy that Mum would hang on the back gate. Unfortunately, when the sun rose early in the Summer, the milk would warm up and taste more like chalk than milk. But that didn't matter; you either drank it or went without. Milk was considered good for your bones. It's amusing now to see the number of young people insisting on 'dairy free' diets, for what reason, I can't imagine.

Also, the 'rabbit-o man' was a regular. Rabbits were cheap fare then, and the 'rabbit-o man' would walk around the streets with a long stick with dead rabbits hanging off it, shouting, "Rabbit-o!" which is where he got his name.

Mothers would do the family washing in a copper with a gas ring under it to heat the water. It was coal gas then, before natural gas. The smell was awful. The clothes would be stirred with a stick, then wrung out by being passed through a wringer which was turned by hand, then hung on the clothesline. It was very hard work.

Clothes lines were long lines of wire strung from a post with a cross piece at each end, with a long stick to hold them up in the middle. A man would walk along the streets calling, "Clothes props!" at the top of his voice. As the props would regularly break, he always had plenty of customers. There were regular power outages too, so the idea of electric clothes dryers was a long way in the future.

Bathrooms had a gas heater for water. It was quite an event to turn on the cold water, light a match, turn on the gas, and hold the match under the heater. If you didn't get it right there'd be a flash and a burnt hand. It took some time for the water to heat, so showers were not a pleasant experience in the Winter. Gas leaks in the heaters we used to warm indoor rooms were not uncommon, so it was very dangerous to leave the doors and windows closed with the heater on.

The insurance man would knock on the door once a month to collect the life insurance premium. I don't know what happened to it when my parents died. I've spoken about insurance with a couple of old blokes lately who remembered their parents taking out a policy for them when they were born. They thought that the policy was worth about $1,500 now, hardly worth the trouble.

Not many homes had a phone, and we had no car until I was about 11. We lived in a rented home until I was five or six. We moved then to Vista Street, which I described in Chapter 1. That house was a bit of a wreck. It had borers in the floor inside the house, and a dirt floor in the kitchen and laundry out the back. Dad bought an old house for the lumber once. He pulled it down, borrowed an old pre-war truck and brought the salvaged materials to Vista Street. He stored the timber in the back yard, as building materials were hard to get after the war. I think the idea was to one day build a holiday house, but like so many good ideas, it never came to anything!

Credit was scarce, and raising the money to buy a house on a tradesman's wage was very difficult, even for a house considered a 'wreck'. Renting was the norm for many people, and for newly married couples just a room in a widow's house was most often the best they could manage.

There are always a lot of complaints now as to how bad society has become. Even though people don't feel any richer, people take it for granted that they'll have a car each, a couple of TVs, mobile phones, etc. It took quite a long time for my family to have a car, house phone, or TV. And this was pretty normal for the other Greenwich families too. It was taken for granted then that it was the father's duty to work, and for mothers to stay home and look after the kids. A family living on just a tradesman's wage wasn't very well off at all.

Cultural values at the time

I assume because of our English heritage, most subjects were considered unmentionable. In my opinion, this led to a lot of outrageous behaviour that was swept under the carpet. Life was a lot harder and crueller than it is now.

For example, there was no contraception back then and when nature took its course, girls were sent away or put into a home and then the babies taken off them and adopted out. The girls would never be mentioned again.

Money also couldn't be mentioned, and neither could religion or politics. Domestic violence was nobody's business and drugs were unknown. However, it was standard fare for women to have a Bex powder in a cup of tea each afternoon which was quite addictive, and very destructive to the kidneys. And no wonder: Bex in the 1940's was a mix of aspirin, phenacetin and caffeine. The phenacetin was linked to kidney cancer in the 1970's and the caffeine was probably the addictive part.

Alcoholism or 'cupboard drinking' as it was known then, could never be mentioned. As I've said before, pubs closed at 18:00 and men would come home from work broke and drunk.

Even so, most mothers didn't work, and one wage was enough to buy a house. That's quite out of the question now with today's incredibly high house prices that have not been matched by wage growth.

All of us kids were sent to Sunday school: St Giles Church of England for the Protestants, and the Catholic Church for the Catholic families. We were Church of England, so my brothers and I were sent to St Giles Protestant church. My father wasn't at all interested in religion, but my mother was. Mum insisted that we went to Sunday School, but I don't remember her going to church every Sunday. She'd do the flowers for the church every now and again. My father never went to church at all.

In general, the families from different religious backgrounds didn't mix much. I remember asking if I could go with my Catholic mate to his Sunday school, but I received a very firm no, with no explanation at all. It wasn't considered necessary to explain things to kids then, especially about religion or politics. We were expected to just accept what adults said, no matter what we thought about it.

Whether it was generally known or not that priests regularly interfered with altar boys at Catholic institutions, it was a standing joke amongst us teenagers later. It has been a hideous revelation from the Royal Commission in 2018 that this was indeed the case. It makes me think that perhaps it wasn't only prejudice that stopped Protestant parents from allowing their kids to frequent Catholic institutions.

My auntie Doris, (Mum's sister) had married a Scotsman, Uncle Duncan. He remains a mystery to me, as my mother didn't like him much so his background was never discussed. He was supposed to be on a 'shell shock' pension from the war. He and Doris lived in an historic cottage in the Sydney Botanical Gardens in Camp Cove. Camp Cove was the site of the first European settlement in Australia. Uncle Duncan's only duty was to open and close the gates of the Botanical Gardens to the public each day. When we went there to visit Aunty Doris, Uncle Duncan would give us a coin if we'd sit with him and listen to him attempt to play the tuba. Otherwise, we had the run of the gardens which were, and still are, beautiful and historic. The giant Moreton Bay fig trees were ideal climbing and hiding trees for small boys.

At this time (2023) attempts are being made by some radical activists to erase the so-called bad parts of European history in Australia. As Camp Cove was the site of the first settlement in Australia, one can only hope that the so-called 'politically correct' group don't want the gardens' name changed to Invasion Site, or some such.

A smattering of Aboriginal folk stories were taught to us in primary school, but the First Peoples' ownership and mastery of the land was, in general, dismissed. The only history that mattered was that of the first settlers and the 'discovery' of Australia by the British. There's a significant resurgence of interest now of First Peoples' culture, which seems, often as not, by people whose original link to First Peoples appears tenuous at least.

Australia Day (currently the 26th January), the day that Captain Phillip landed at Camp Cove, has become very significant to Australia as a turning point in the nation's history. I think it's important to have a special day when all Australians can come together to celebrate the things that this country has achieved in a relatively short time, historically speaking. However, if it's offensive to the antecedents of the First Peoples then personally, I'd be quite happy to have it on another date. Which date to choose seems to be the question. Unfortunately, if the date is changed at some point down the track, there will always be some group that'd be offended.

Roger, Rover, and my first flight

My best friend back then was Roger Evans. His mother Mary was wonderful to me and provided me more mothering than I ever got at home. Cuts and bruises were fixed with a hug and a kiss, and if available, a little treat that was most definitely never offered at home. She loved me as much as a friend's mother can, and I loved her also.

Mr. Evans was a health inspector, and one day the family were posted to Bathurst in NSW, so it became a special event for me to travel there in the school holidays. They'd invite me up to stay and I'd have a wonderful time. Roger and I were free as birds. I remember the frosts in the morning, and roaming the countryside far and wide across farmlands in search of adventure. Explosives became our great passion. We made a gun out of water pipe and would fill it with gunpowder from penny bungers and a ball bearing with a wick out the end. We'd light the wick, point at a target and with a very satisfying bang we'd usually miss whatever the target was. Completely not politically correct (PC) now, but great fun with no adults anywhere nearby!

It was a long trip in a steam train over the Blue Mountains to Bathurst, and it seemed to take forever. The last time I went to visit Roger, it was arranged that I'd fly there. I took a train across the Harbour Bridge to the airline terminal in the city, then a special bus to Mascot.

I flew in a Butler Airlines DC-3. It was my first flight. The pilots sent back a note to passengers with our time of arrival and the weather on it. The bumps over the Blue Mountains weren't pleasant, and I couldn't understand why the pilots didn't just fly smoothly. Compared to the six-hour journey by steam train it was just great. Little did I imagine that one day as a DC-3 co-pilot I'd be writing out our Estimated Time of Arrival (ETA) for the passengers too.

Roger went on to become an Electrical Engineer, in charge of a section of a steel mill at Wollongong. After many years of not being in touch, Roger's mother Mary Evans found me and used to ring me on my birthday every year. I was thrilled. Once, Mary came to Melbourne where I was living at the time, to visit her sister in Moonee Ponds. We arranged for me to come and meet at her place, but I locked myself out of my apartment and so couldn't get back in to find the address. I took a taxi to Moonee Ponds and drove around the streets trying to find her, but couldn't. Apparently, she sat on a bench outside the address, waiting for me all day on the footpath. We ended up not meeting. It was a terrible mishap!

I had a 'bitzer' dog, Rover. He was a beauty. He followed me to school, and nothing would dissuade him from trying to come into the classroom. He was so persistent that eventually he had to be tied up at school time. He was a bit psychotic in that he'd chase cars and bark and bark forever, nothing would stop him. I was very sad when he died of tick poison.

Sadly, all my dogs died this way. The bush in front of our house was full of ticks, and once one got into a dog's skin, the dog was a goner. The theory for saving dogs from ticks was that you put 'metho' (methylated spirits) on the tick to kill it, then looped a bit of cotton around the tick and pulled it out. Unfortunately, by the time you found the tick, it was usually full of the dog's blood. If the head of the tick was broken off and still under the dog's skin when you pulled the body out, the dog died. There wasn't enough money around to ever call a vet.

It wasn't unusual for a kid to also get a tick from playing in the bush. The same method was used to remove it, but I don't remember anyone getting particularly sick from them, luckily.

CHAPTER 3

Portrait of my family at the time (AKA: the people in our house)

Mum, Dad and my place in the family

There didn't seem to be much fun in my house: we didn't get many visitors, there was no drinking, and no playing cards. Card playing was 'of the devil', and drinking was unmentionable, as I've said. Censorship by the government was alive and well, as was the abuse of children in institutions. For example, there was a Palestine Girls' Home attached to the church. The girls would sit at the back of the church on a Sunday and no one would have anything to do with them. It's only with the Royal Commission a few years back that their terrible treatment was made public. I can only assume that society was being protected from stuff that the powers that be thought would lead to moral degradation and social breakdown, so hypocrisy was rife. A case of 'don't do as I do, do as I say'.

Unauthorised relations between the sexes was prohibited most strongly, never mind relations between the same sexes. Unfortunately, the very people that were making the rules were working to cover up horrific institutional abuse that as I mentioned earlier, is just being exposed now.

My mother did like to go to the art gallery in the city, and would drag us kids along with her for a bit of 'culture'. One time she met a dapper little man there, called Mr. Friend. She invited him home. As she wasn't at all social, I don't know why she did this. She insisted that my brother Robert and I go with him for a walk. I can't remember how old I was, but he sat me up on a rock and put his hand up my trouser leg. Robert pushed him away, and we ran home. Nothing was said by Mum, but we didn't hear anything of Mr. Friend after that. And thank goodness.

Mother's spinach

As I got older, unfortunately my mother and I didn't understand each other very well. We just seemed out of step like two records set to play, but at slightly different speeds. As best as I can recall, she suffered badly during menopause, and before that had been considered too 'delicate' to be sent out to work as a young adult. Not that I knew of such things then. Her behaviour was quite erratic, which might explain her decision to invite Mr. Friend to come to visit.

She had a very strong belief in the value of eating spinach. It's not a bad vegetable, of course it's not. After all, Popeye gorged on spinach and look what he became: all those muscles and the adoration of his girlfriend Olive Oyl. I never believed spinach built those muscles, but I guess I will never get that answer.

Sadly, Mum didn't wash spinach properly so there was always grit in it that would get between your teeth and crunch as you chewed. It was like eating sandpaper, absolutely horrible.

I Think I'm Going to Be an Airline Pilot

One night at dinner, I refused to eat my spinach.

"Eat your spinach or you will spend the night in the chook house," Mum said.

It was the ultimatum that really did it. I hate ultimatums about as much as I hate spinach and have never responded to them in any sort of a positive way. Now, the chook house was not all that appealing to a ten-year-old and a night is a long time, but I thought about that gritty spinach and decided it was time to make a stand. So I did.

It became a standoff. I flatly refused to eat my spinach, Mum wouldn't back down, and so off to the chook yard I was sent. They were a bit surprised to have me join them and created a bit of a stir but we all finally sorted out our pecking order and settled down into a sort of mutual unease.

It was a terrible night. Why I didn't go back inside and beg forgiveness is beyond me. In those dark surrounds while thinking of fleas and other deep thoughts I began my plan of revenge. I would get my own back. Those chooks and my parents would pay.

I was full of resentment and decided to enact a terrible revenge. One of my jobs was to clean out the chook yard before Sunday school. There was a large mulberry tree in the yard and the chooks would eat the fruit, which made their droppings very messy. It was a job I hated with all the fibre of my being, so I hatched a plan. One Sunday I put weed killer from the garage into their food, which we called 'pollen', then went off to Sunday school, another activity that didn't fill me with pleasure. During the sermon I felt awful remorse as I was convinced that God was watching me, and I'd be punished for chook murder.

I rushed home to find the chooks eating their pollen; I pushed them aside and tipped the pollen out where they couldn't reach it. I hoped I'd been quick enough to save them, but later in the day, my father, who was always mild-mannered, came inside very angry. One of the chooks was dead, and the others were pecking at it. They were also collapsing and dying. My plan, even though I'd wanted to stop it, was working.

My father assumed that I'd hit the first dead chook with the shovel. Of course, it was the poison that did the trick, but fortunately I was never discovered as the murderer. I guess I was sent to my room without tea, which was the usual punishment. But even though I really was remorseful, the victory remained: as the chooks were all dead, there was no more chook yard cleaning for me.

It's hard to imagine now, but chicken was a very big deal in those days, and it was eaten only rarely. Dad would wring its neck or chop its head off. It would then run around the yard until it died. Then it would be gutted and plucked and roasted for Christmas dinner.

As far as I recall, my Dad was a very good husband and father. He seemed to be very easygoing and friendly. He did have some strange quirks though. He hated fish and would put on quite a performance if fish was being served at a meal. I think that scared me when I was little and that's where my killer fish nightmares came from. I'm just reluctant to pick up anything squirming or flapping, like fish do when they're caught.

As you might have guessed, I was the middle child with a good dose of 'middle child syndrome'. Robert was older than me by three years, and John was four years younger than me. We really just didn't have much to do with each other. I was kept back a year in primary school and Robert was already doing his apprenticeship when I was in high school. Robert and John went to a tech school whereas I went to the local high school. We all went to different schools in essence, and by the time I got to leave school at 15, my older brother was 20 and got married at 21. Even though I felt like we weren't that close as kids, we're content now. Robert lives in Port Douglas and John lives in Nelson Bay. We speak on birthdays, but that's about it really.

My mother and I never really related. Every middle child knows what I mean. You aren't the gorgeous firstborn with all the photos in every album you look at and in almost every picture frame in the house. You aren't the youngest and the last-born who is spoiled rotten by your mother and doted on by all. No, you are just the middle blob in the family that nobody recognises or even wants to know. Even worse than 'middle child syndrome', my mother and I just didn't like each other which is not good for any parent/child relationship. I believe that generally the middle child grows up exhibiting quite a bit of attention-getting behaviour, it's not very nice to admit it, but I guess that explains a lot of my later actions.

I understand now that I must have been precociously judgmental! My mother was not a bad woman at all; my brothers had a sort of normal relationship with her, so I guess it had something to do with me. Now, as a grandparent myself, I can better understand what was really going on in the family dynamics area and what the problem could possibly have been. Looking back, I'd say I was a pretty horrible child. Being a bit dyslexic didn't help, given it made me not care particularly much for school, but that was only part of the equation. I was a bit of a reject: I was no good at sports, was short-sighted and just didn't fit in. I mean it wasn't my fault entirely – my mother was also a bit of a case and my Dad didn't want to get too involved.

George the mechanic

My father, George, had been in the Air Force during the war. I can remember him coming home in his uniform, which was khaki in colour, and consisted of shorts, shirt and an Air Force cap. He did his training at Wagga Wagga, and he was also billeted at Essendon in Melbourne for some time in the home of a couple of elderly ladies. He remembered it was very cold in their house, they never liked to use the heating as they couldn't afford it – and when they did use it, it wasn't very good.

He recounted that when Japan bombed Pearl Harbour, he was stationed on the edge of the airfield in Wagga with a machine gun. An unlikely story I would think, given he spent the war at De Havilland, the English aircraft manufacturer, in the 'prop shop' (the propeller maintenance workshop).

However, there was nothing defensive in Australia at all at the time. When Singapore fell, it was a disaster, and the country was wide open. And when Macarthur came and set up HQ here, Australia had nothing with which to help fight at all. Everything was manufactured in England and sent over here. In return, we sent food over there. All those who were called up had nothing: no uniforms, only about 20 rifles between them, and they trained with broomsticks. It was the most remarkable transformation when Australia readied itself, by all accounts. Nobody knows whether the Japanese intended to capture Australia, but there was definitely nothing to stop them if they suddenly did.

I Think I'm Going to Be an Airline Pilot

Years later when I was an apprentice, I also spent some time in the 'prop shop'. I can't remember doing anything very productive there, however.

After he was de-mobbed, my Dad returned to his job as a motor mechanic. He was a road patrolman for the NRMA, who at the time were called 'guides'. The guides' job was to help country people coming to town find their way into the city and to fix breakdowns of members. My first memory of his work was that he had quite a flash uniform with leggings and gloves, and a Harley Davidson motorbike with sidecar for his tools. Later on, he got a jeep and then a van.

He'd spend a lot of time at home, waiting to be called out to a breakdown. On school holidays he'd be rung to go to a breakdown and I'd go with him sitting on top of the sidecar. I didn't wear a helmet or anything, and the sidecar was more like a box with a wheel attached. Health and safety obviously wasn't an issue then. Cars weren't as reliable as they are now, either. It always looked like magic to me that Dad always seemed to know what was wrong before we got to the breakdown. He told me the secret later: if the car had just stopped, it was probably out of petrol. If it wouldn't start, it probably had a flat battery. Anything other than that would be a component failure that would require a tow truck. Simple really! That's probably where I got my interest in mechanical things. Dad also hated going into the city, so he'd refuse to attend breakdowns where it required him to cross the Harbour Bridge into town.

As time went on and Mum became more difficult, I think Dad withdrew more and more from family life. Probably about then he formed an association with a woman called Joan, which of course I didn't know anything about until much later after Mum died and he married her. Along with the trials of menopause, Dad's involvement with Joan was probably what caused much of Mum's unfortunate behaviour.

Occasionally, the owner of the car Dad had fixed would be very grateful to him for getting the car started and would try to give me some small change. After the fuss with Mr. Friend, we'd been told never to take money off strange men, so when a man who Dad had helped offered me some change, I refused the offer. The driver said, "Suit yourself," and put the money back in his pocket. I was mortified, though I'm not sure exactly what I thought would happen when I refused. It wasn't the last time that my shyness worked against me, but more on that later.

CHAPTER 4

School days

The attention seeker

In 6th class, my last year of primary school, I had quite a crash on my bike.

After Sunday school, my older brother Robert wanted to use my bike. He said he'd double me home. There was a steep hill by the church, so we raced down it. As we were riding along, the dynamo on the front wheel slipped down into the spokes, and over we went. Robert went straight onto the road, but I went high in the air and landed on my head and hand. Robert got all the attention, the bike was wrecked, and in the end I felt that I was ignored! There was a polio scare on at the time, so I 'milked' my injuries for all they were worth and stayed in bed for some time. I was mostly ignored, so I guess that I was desperate for attention.

Sometime later I was swinging between the table and a chair, when they collapsed and resulted in a full faceplant on the floor for me. My front tooth went through my lip, and there was lots of blood everywhere. Rather than admit that I'd been foolish, I said that my legs had collapsed out from under me. I was once again put to bed and left there alone for ages.

Eventually some doctors came. After they examined me, they mentioned polio, and with my vivid imagination I was sure that I heard them say that I wouldn't last the night. I shared a bedroom with Robert, so when he came to bed I told him, "I'm going to die!" He said, "Don't worry, it won't hurt!" I tried to stay awake waiting to die, but eventually must have gone to sleep. I remember waking and looking at the cream wall beside my bed and thinking that this must be how it was to be dead. Obviously, I was a very dramatic child.

As a result of my long bed rest after the bicycle accident and then the chair collapse debacle, I had to repeat 6th class, so didn't go to high school for another year.

High school hijinks

The norm at the time was for the local kids to go to a 'tech school' as my brothers did, but for some reason, I was sent to Mosman Intermediate High School. This was an academic high school. I think I was considered pretty smart but too 'delicate' for the rough and tumble of a tech school!

The teachers were a mixed bunch, and the Principal was a very austere and distant figure, unlike the friendlier school experiences students have today. Heaven help you if you were called to his office, because it almost certainly meant a caning. My fingers have always been very sensitive, especially on cold days, so even though I was only caned twice in my school career, the pain was almost unbearable. It was something worth avoiding at all costs.

Looking back on my time at Mosman High, I think my behaviour was not bad enough to be punished, but just bad enough to be ignored and left at the back of the class. I was probably just crying out for attention, if I'm honest.

One thing I do remember about the Principal Mr. Dixon is that he was a big man in a dark suit and waistcoat, who had some sort of prejudice against water pistols. One was discovered in the school once, and the school was called to assembly. He threw the water pistol on the floor and jumped up and down on it in a rage, smashing it to bits. It was an incident that's seared into my memory – it was also very strange behaviour.

You could leave school after intermediate, which was three years of high school. The smart or rich kids went on to another high school to do Leaving Certificate, and some went to university. University didn't figure in our family vocabulary at that time, so it wasn't something we thought of pursuing.

My father's attitude then, and time has shown it to be very wise, was that boys had to have a trade. Remembering that they had lived through a depression and a war, he'd say that a tradesman was the last to go if workers were being laid off. This is as true now, as it was then; depending on the trade of course.

I didn't do very well at Mosman High. Unknowingly, I was quite myopic so the blackboard was never very clear to me. The result was that I got further and further behind in almost every class. You'd think that I might have made up for it by being sporty, but I was also no good at catching and throwing a ball so was rejected by the other kids in the playground. Try as I might, I was never any good at sport at all. This meant that I was never picked for any teams, so I had a pretty lonely time of it. I guess I was quite a 'wuss', which means not very brave or daring, but there was just no place then for someone who couldn't keep up.

I remember being taken to an away school cricket match and given the job of scoring. Unfortunately, nobody thought to show me how to fill in the scoring sheet so I made quite a mess of it. I was never taken to a match again. I felt mortified, but I don't think anybody cared about kids' feelings then. We were just left to it.

Another thing I remember was that our class was to go to another school for some sort of performance. My voice was judged to be quite peculiar, so I was left behind even though I was desperate to be included. I think that being a 'reject' as a child explains a lot of my attitudes as an adult. I'm hopeless at being part of a group, but am very keen not to be just ignored. I've often been accused of talking too much if you can believe it. I try to moderate myself, but I suppose it's just part of wanting attention.

Being an attention seeking boy and no good at sports, I resorted to being naughty, just trying to get noticed I guess. As a result, I started in class 1A and ended my school career in 3C.

It was made pretty clear at the end of 3rd class, after I'd passed the Intermediate Certificate, that there was not much point in sending me on to further schooling. This decision turned out to be pretty lucky for me, as if I had gone further at school, I wouldn't have been an apprentice and would never have gone on to become a pilot.

I can remember one teacher from high school. He was a youngish man, teaching maths. He was reputed to have been a pilot in the war. Remember, I was at high school in the early 50's, so the war wasn't that long over. I idolised him, and used to follow him home from school until he got sick of it and told me to go away. His name was "Basher Barnett".

I Think I'm Going to Be an Airline Pilot

Recently, I saw a newsreel about the RAAF in New Guinea. One of the pilots featured was called Basher Barnett. I'll never know if it was my old idol, and I guess he'll never know his part in leading me toward aviation as a career.

Trams were still running in Sydney then. I'd walk to the top of Greenwich Road, about two kilometres, and then catch the tram to Mosman Junction, which was not far from school. The trams were the type we called the 'toast rack'. The compartments were separate, with the conductor moving up and down the outside of the tram on a running board, collecting tickets. There was a canvas blind to pull down at the side to stop passengers from getting wet if it was raining. If we didn't have enough money for the fare, we'd climb out onto the board on the other side of the tram and move to another compartment when we saw the conductor approaching.

It was the conductor's job to pull the pole from the overhead wire with a rope at the end of the track and extend the pole at the other end of the tram and attach it to the wire for it to travel in the other direction. If he was friendly, sometimes he'd let us schoolboys do it for him. That was a real treat.

On special occasions I'd get to ride in the driver's cab. I was fascinated with controls, and I was quite capable of moving the tram and bringing it to a stop. There was a pedal on the floor for the bell, too. Being allowed to ring the bell was really something; a highlight for the day.

There was a lot of fun to be had with trams too. We would steal saltpetre from science classes, wrap it in the silver paper from a cigarette packet and put it on the tram line. It would make a loud bang when the tram ran over it. It meant a certain caning if you were caught, but we didn't let that stop us. Putting a penny on the track was another thrill; they'd be squashed wafer thin by the tram's steel wheels when they got run over.

Once I was on a tram on my way home from school when the driver and conductor got off, presumably to change the tracks or direction of the tram. I hopped into the driver's cabin and set off down the road, driving the tram by myself. There was hell to pay over that when they caught me. I only moved it 100 metres or so up the track, then stopped. There was a lot of shouting, but I don't remember any other punishment from school or parents for this; it was just a bit of fun.

After three years, I was glad to see the end of formal schooling and I think formal schooling was glad to see the end of me. I don't ever remember there being much contact between the school and parents, not like there is now.

I often wonder now, with all the emphasis on leadership and 'moving forward' what happens to the kids like me who are left behind. I think now, without the luck of fine mentoring, or falling into a vocation that they're naturally good at, they'd have no hope. I think that kids who are unable to develop a vocation early on in life are at a great disadvantage later on. It seems that young adults are trying to compete with many other well-educated but unskilled people for fewer and fewer jobs.

The call of the sea

Most of the Greenwich boys belonged to the local sailing club, The Greenwich 12ft Sailing Squadron. It was a grand name for a club that had unfortunately seen better days. The 12ft skiffs were open boats, 12ft long with a large bumpkin out the front, and a gaff-rigged sail. They'd have a crew of three men and a bailer boy. The bailer boy was me.

As there was no decking on these skiffs, it was very easy for them to take a gutful of water. Then it was the bailer boy's job to use a bucket to toss the water back over the side. Sometimes it came in faster than it could be bailed out. In that case, a capsize was inevitable. Down we'd go, and as there were no buoyancy compartments, the boat would lie on its side mostly under water and the crew would have to float in the middle of the sail. There we'd wait until a motorboat came along to tow us back to shore. We'd always hope that they'd tow us back in to a sandy spot. The skiff would then have to be unrigged, righted, the water bailed out again, re-rigged, launched and then sail home. All while hoping that another capsize wouldn't happen before we got back to the club.

It was an exhausting and at times quite a scary way to spend Saturday afternoons. It was especially so for me as I was never a strong swimmer. It was never even considered necessary to wear a life jacket then, so it's no wonder I was scared most of the time.

Eventually, I teamed up with another chap from the club who had a VJ. This was a decked-in small boat for two. It had a leaning plank, for the crew to slide way out to windward to balance the tipping pressure of the wind in the sails. I always ended up with the skin worn off my bum after crewing with him, which was very painful for the rest of the week. My time at the sailing club also explains why my legs were covered with skin cancers later on in life. There was no sunscreen back then, and getting 'a touch of sun' was considered healthy for all.

It was from my time 'mucking around with boats' that I developed an enduring interest for anything to do with the sea. I consider myself very lucky to be living on the waterfront at Port Melbourne in retirement, where I can watch the comings and goings of the boats and other watercraft.

CHAPTER 5

Jobs and girls and cars

A working chap

I remember I had two jobs while I was at high school. My Dad got me a job at a panel beater's for a Saturday morning. My main duties were to sweep and tidy the workshops. I think my work ethic was pretty lax though. Also, having never had any money before then, I didn't handle my pay very well and would spend it on lollies on the way home.

I liked hanging out with the men at the panel beaters. I was told not to go into the paint shop on my own or be alone with the painter. I couldn't understand why at all back then, but I did what I was told. It's only now that abhorrent stories are surfacing about child sexual abuse that I wonder if it was to avoid such incidents that I was told that. Such things were never talked about then, as I've said. We were also told not to go near the Haymarket area near Central Station in Sydney, because apparently a lot of what were called back then 'deviant men' hung around there. No one would explain exactly what that meant, but it frightened the devil out of me. One day the boss at the panel beater's told me he was letting me go. I didn't know what he meant, but he made it pretty clear I was sacked.

My next job on the weekends was at Golds Caltex service station on the Pacific Highway at Artarmon, a Sydney suburb. My duties were serving petrol and general cleaning. I was as keen as mustard, so without being told, I decided to wash a customer's car that had just been painted. I went ahead with the detergent that was used to clean the floor. Unfortunately, it was caustic soda, so my car wash ruined the paint job. It was amazing that I didn't get sacked, even though it was an honest mistake.

The owners of the service station, Mr., and Mrs. Gold, had an Austin Healey sports car and a Messerschmitt runabout, they were super cool. The runabout was a cross between a motor scooter and a car. It had three wheels and a bubble Perspex canopy, with seating for two in tandem – one behind the other. Mr. and Mrs. Gold gave me a Maltese Terrier, the pup of their dog, it was a cute little thing. But as happened with all my dogs, it sadly died of tick poisoning.

While I was working at the service station, one of the men took me out on a Harbour Board work boat for the day, delivering the pay to work sites around the harbour. I loved it but was a bit scared that he'd head out through the heads to sea. I feel now that if I hadn't gone into the air, I would've liked to have gone to sea. At this remove, it's probably a fantasy though.

Girls, girls, girls

Before I talk about my early loves, I'd like to set the scene. I've always had a very strong interest in girls, which I put down to my fractured relationship with my mother, as well as the natural order of things. I genuinely like the female of the species and find chatting with sensible women very satisfying. I would consider myself one of the original feminists, even from before they were invented.

One of the side effects of having to go to Sunday school was that I had my first love affair, one-sided though it was. I was about 14 at the time. She was a beautiful blonde called Pat Russel. I would hang around waiting for her after Sunday school finished so I could walk home with her. She didn't seem to mind, but I could never raise the courage to hold her hand, or ever dare to ask for a kiss. One of the tough guys from the local tech school was after her, and he very positively warned me off talking to Pat. As I was – and still am – a bit of a wimp, afraid of broken bones and black eyes, I reluctantly took his advice and left her alone. So, it remained an unrequited first love affair.

As I mentioned earlier, there were very few girls around Greenwich, and none at the QANTAS workshops when I became an apprentice later. This was standard for a trade at the time, though it's different now, of course. The only reliable venue for meeting girls was the town hall dance at Lane Cove. Because we were very poor, I usually had the arse out of my trousers and no car, except when I could borrow Dad's – when he finally got one, that is. That meant that except for the odd cuddle, my success rate for any girl-related action was quite low.

The dances were the usual affair: the girls would sit on seats along the side of the hall, and the boys would gather near the door. You'd have to walk the gauntlet of everyone lined up to ask a girl to dance. If she said no, you'd have to sidle back to your spot. I'm told that if the girls weren't asked, it was murder for them too – they got called wallflowers, because they just stayed sitting next to the wall. If you liked a girl, you'd ask if you could take her home, but without a car that was impossible. That's why, whenever I could, I'd borrow Dad's car.

Getting about in cars

It was some time before my family could afford a car, but we got one eventually. It was a pre-war Chrysler (1939, I think). It was square like a box, and it didn't have a boot but instead had a rack on the back which folded down to put a wooden trunk on. Post-war cars were coming in then, and how different they were to the pre-war boxy ones. They were streamlined and shiny with chrome, the epitome of the modern age. It was mortifying for me, being far too judgemental a child for my friends to see us in our old-fashioned clunker.

We'd fill the box on the back of the car with our supplies, and we'd set off to Avoca, which was north of Broken Bay, for holidays. It was long before there were any freeways, so we drove a very twisty and bumpy road to get there. This, combined with very hard suspension, and we kids would be suffering from car sickness before we were even halfway there. A stop at Mt White for a bit of a chuck and a drink of warm soda water was the only remedy.

Sometimes we made the trip to visit Pop and Nana White at Narrabeen, a Northern Beaches suburb on a coastal lake. These trips weren't regular, as far as I can recall. Driving there was a treat in the back of the old car, apart from the car sickness, of course. We'd drive through Frenchs Forest in the dark. Sitting in the back of the car was lovely at those times; cars didn't have heating in them then, so we'd be in the back under a blanket with the dark all around, snug as anything. It was really good.

After heavy rains the lake usually flooded, and water was right up to their doorstep. Robert and I would dream of using one of the old-fashioned wardrobes that Pop and Nana had in their bedrooms as a boat and paddling around the lake in it. While it probably would have taken on water straight away and sunk, the wardrobes just looked like they'd have been terrific lake-going vessels to us.

One day though, something happened and Mum wouldn't go up to Pop and Nana White's any more. The visits just stopped. There was no discussion with us kids as to why, of course. We just didn't go there any more.

That Chrysler did have its uses though. My Dad taught us boys to drive in it – at least, he taught my brother Robert and me. He'd probably got rid of it and had something else to drive by the time John got old enough.

Automatic transmission hadn't been invented at that point, so all cars on the road were manual. Because ours was pre-war, it didn't have a Synchromesh gearbox. This meant that double declutching was required for all gear changes. Double declutching is when you push in the clutch pedal to move the gear lever out of one gear, release the pedal and then push it in again and move the gear lever into the next gear. Learning to double declutch was very run-of-the-mill and expected at the time, though it's very rare to find someone who knows how to do it now. I was across it pretty quickly, as I recall. We also learnt reverse parking with no power steering, and no reverser warnings or cameras, never mind auto-parking which is a feature of most modern cars today.

The Chrysler also had mechanical brakes with very limited stopping power, so we quickly learnt the value of significant spacing between cars to avoid running up the back of the car in front. It seems like every morning now, a rear-ender is reported on the traffic bulletin on the radio. I believe that this high rate is mostly due to driving too close to the car in front. Most people learn to drive cars with automatic transmission now, so manual transmission, never mind double declutching, is a mystery.

Dad must have been a good teacher, as my driving record to this day has avoided any major collisions or disasters.

My family didn't really know what to do with me after I finished Intermediate, but luckily for me, my father knew someone, who knew someone, who knew the master of apprentices at QANTAS. And that's how it happened. I had pictures of aeroplanes pinned up on my cupboard door, and I loved watching the flying boats on the bay after they'd taken off, climbing over the Harbour Bridge. So, Mum and Dad decided that I'd go for a QANTAS apprenticeship.

CHAPTER 6

Apprenticeship

Real work begins

The entrance exam for the QANTAS apprenticeship was pretty testing. It was held at Shell House in the central business district in Sydney. It was a big deal to go into the city. I caught the train, which meant a walk through the bush to the station, then found my way to Shell House from the station. The exam included a lot of mechanical aptitude questions. Luckily for me I'd been with my Dad to his old garage workshop, where all the machines were belt-driven from an old diesel engine out the back. This meant that I had a pretty good understanding of gears and drive ratios etc, which is just as well because those were covered on the entrance exam.

For a change it was a subject I was interested in, so I did well and was accepted. I did feel that it just showed that if I was interested, I could apply myself and get good results. Recognising and nurturing a young boy's interest was the hard bit for everyone around me, it seems. My older brother Robert had done an extra year at school which included a pre-apprenticeship (Like the VCAL now, in Victoria). He was at school up to Leaving, then started an apprenticeship as a 2nd year, training as a carpenter. Me as the next child, it was made quite clear by my parents that I'd have to do a trade. They'd been through the depression and the war and knew that trades were the last to be laid off if cuts were made. It was a given, and I also think they didn't know what else to do with me. It was very different to the conversations that young kids have with their parents about careers now! Because I'd shown interest in planes, I was lucky they noticed that and pushed me in that direction. When the letter arrived to say I had a place, I don't remember any specific reaction other than, "Good. That's what you're supposed to do."

I was signed up for the apprenticeship for five years, after which I was set to graduate as an aircraft mechanic. The apprenticeship start date was January 1956. There were a total of 80 boys accepted, and we became known as the class of '56. As a first-year apprentice, I was kitted out with a Gladstone bag to carry my lunch in, and a rudimentary tool kit.

I set off on my first day of 'real work' early on a January morning. Start time was 07:40 which meant I had to get up about 05:30 to get to work on time. Fortunately it was Summer, so it got light pretty early, but that sort of schedule was daunting for me as a 15-year-old. Getting to the aerodrome required me to walk through the bush to Wollstonecraft station, take the train to Central or Redfern stations, then catch a bus to Mascot aerodrome. And I had to repeat the procedure at night to get home, but in reverse.

We were taught all sorts of practical skills, as well as several hours of theory subjects in the classroom. We spent one night a week, from 17:00 hours to 20:00 hours in night school at Sydney Technical College (Now called the TAFE New South Wales Sydney Institute). It was very scary, coming home from tech in the dark after night school. There was a long walk through a tunnel under Central Station. All sorts of 'undesirables' as they were called back then, would camp there and it very much felt like running the gauntlet until you got to the other end.

The walk from Wollstonecraft station to home was on a path through the bush. There was the odd streetlight every now and again which threw more shadows than light, so my imagination would run riot, convincing me that all sorts of monsters were hiding, waiting to jump out and get me at any moment. Fortunately, nothing ever happened although I do remember seeing a possum on a lamp post once and trying to pat it. I got severely scratched for my trouble. Needless to say, I was always glad to make the safety of my bed on the veranda at 29 Vista St after night school.

We also spent one day a fortnight at Sydney Tech College in the aircraft trades section.

As an aside, the original Sydney Powerhouse which was part of the tech' buildings, was the Powerhouse museum. It held many of the amazing machines that helped make Australia the agricultural powerhouse it was at the time. We weren't an industrial country, but looking at how much really isn't made here now, it's remarkable what was made in Australia from scratch back then. The frigate in the Williamstown Museum is one of the ones that was made from scratch, for example. Another example is a fighter aircraft that they made at Fisherman's Bend in just six weeks. It had a DC-3 engine and Wirraway fuselage, and was called a Boomerang. It was made just in case we needed it when they thought Darwin was going to be invaded.

For some strange reason as I write in 2022/23 the NSW government now is closing the Powerhouse museum in Sydney down and building a much smaller museum at Parramatta.

This means that much of Australian, and the world's, industrial history will have to be put in storage and never seen again, which is a great shame.

There were numerous old aircraft and engines at the tech college I went to, some of them would be priceless now. Spitfire, Vultee Vengeance and Puss Moth were some of the ones I can remember seeing.

The first task us boys were given was to hand-shape a block of steel so that one side was a perfectly flat surface. Try as I might, I couldn't get rid of the lumps and bumps in mine. And rather than work at it some more, I decided to bribe one of the other more dexterous boys to finish it for me. I don't recall exactly what I did, but I suspect I might have just used someone else's and passed it off as my own when the teacher came around to see what we'd managed to do. To test the quality of our work, we'd have to put blue stain on our surface and then put it face down on a machine block so any imperfections would be seen in the print it made.

We did a subject called 'tech drawing' with a teacher called Mr. Penny for two years, and try as I might my offerings were always smudged and wonky. Drafting wasn't my calling, I'm afraid. Neither was turning on a lathe which was one of the practical components we were taught. The chucks of the lathes weren't self-centring, so try as I might, I could never get the piece to centre so it always came out oval rather than round.

With hindsight, I wasn't taking it all as seriously as I perhaps should have done. But at the time I think there wasn't a great deal of discipline. We were there, and were required to be there. You either did the work or didn't – not like being at school. They'd set the task and give you some basic instruction and you'd figure it out from there. It was pretty laissez-faire instruction when I look back on it.

As the years went on we apprentices played a lot of practical jokes on each other. We'd go around stealing each other's jobs, welding up the welding booth, hiding tools from each other, etc. It was all in good fun, and seemed to be expected by the teaching staff, who turned a bit of a blind eye to goings-on. I found the classroom lectures very heavy going, but some of the theory must have stuck as I've still got a pretty good grasp of how things work.

I recently met a chap whose first job at about the same time was as Reg Ansett's office boy. He said that his pay was only about $12 a week. As a first-year apprentice got about $7 per week, that gives a fair indication of how much trades fitted in to society's pecking order. Apprentices' pay increased each year as the apprenticeship went on. For the first few years, we apprentices were circulated around the different departments, so that eventually we had experienced most of them. The duties we had to do were mostly cleaning and painting, sometimes being allowed to pass a spanner or hold a torch.

My first department at the QANTAS maintenance base was electrical overhaul. As its name suggests, components from the aircraft were sent there to be refurbished. The job I was given was testing Fenwal switches. These were metal tubes with a metal strip inside them. They were located inside the engine cowl, and the idea was that when a certain temperature was reached the strip would bend, touch the side of the tube, make a circuit and set off the fire alarm. My task was to insert the switch inside a metal casting, turn it on to heat up, then check that a light came on at the required temperature, to show that the switch was working properly. Very time consuming and very boring. I was always looking for short cuts, not realising how important a reliable fire warning is.

In between, the apprentice had to clean down the work benches, and collect the morning tea and lunch orders. After the orders were collected, it was a trip to the canteen, a lot of pushing and shoving to get orders in before the other boys, so one could get back in time. Unfortunately, a lot of mistakes were made, and quite a few clips around the ear, and trips back to the canteen had to happen to get the correct order. One small advantage, was, if there was the odd cent left over, you got to keep it. That was no small thing for a very poor apprentice.

Other than line servicing, Repair and Overhaul Shop (ROS) was the biggest department. This was where the engines were overhauled and I just hated it. It was like a big dark factory, with constant routine tasks. After clocking on at 07:40 the first task was to sweep the floor, then go around the work benches and get the lunch orders. After morning tea, the boys were not allowed to sit on the benches as the tradesmen did, but had to clean all the benches, then paint them until it was time to collect the lunch orders. After lunch there was more cleaning, then into the degreasing station, full of noxious chemicals, to clean engine parts. Very little work on the engines was allowed.

Once, I was given the job on a new motor to remove the blanking plug on top, and install a new spark plug. I turned the blank too quickly, and it broke off in the cylinder. The whole cylinder had to be removed to get it out. I wasn't too popular after that and don't remember being given any more 'proper jobs'.

I Think I'm Going to Be an Airline Pilot

Dirty jobs

One job that I didn't seem to mind so much was paid more and was called 'confined space money'. This tells you what we got for doing the job. A skinny boy (I.e.: me) would be sent into an empty aircraft tank. We'd have a torch and a pot of soapy water with us. We'd paint the soapy water onto the joints in the tank, then air would be pumped in, and any leaks would show as bubbles visible to someone watching on the outside. An awful putty stuff would be handed in, and we'd have to jam it into the join that was leaking. The smell from the pockets of leftover fuel plus the putty was awful. Never mind the danger if anything happened and you were stuck in there. It'd take about half an hour to get in, do the job and get out. We'd do all this for about threepence an hour extra – and it was worth it on our apprentice's wage. At least when I was in the tank I was left alone and not chased around to do other noisome jobs that I didn't like, such as painting and cleaning.

A particularly revolting job that was left for us apprentices was checking under the floor of the DC-4. The Salk anti-polio vaccine had only just been invented and monkeys were imported from Malaysia to provide the basis for the vaccine. Of course, they would make quite a mess on the flight as they were flown into the country in cages and quite a bit of their wee would escape from the cage and seep through the floor.

It was the apprentice's job to take the panels down from the ceiling of the baggage holds so the engineers could check the structure, control cables and other bits and pieces for corrosion. Monkey pee was very corrosive when in contact with aluminium, which is what the structure was made of. Unfortunately, there was no way to lower the panels without them tipping and spilling whatever was leaked onto them, so we always ended up covered in monkey piss. It'd smell for weeks in our overalls, which obviously made us incredibly popular.

Speaking of vaccines, as I'm writing this, the world's in the middle of the SARSCov-2 (Covid-19) pandemic. It has many similarities with polio as far as I can make out. There's no treatment and no cure, it spreads like wildfire and a lot of people recover, but a lot of people are affected forever, or they die. There are various vaccines, but unlike the polio vaccine, they don't provide protection from catching the virus. Rather, they prevent serious illness and/or death. We hold out hope for a vaccine to be developed that does prevent transmission of this serious virus.

Extra apprenticeship time

I was outside one day painting an engine stand, but mostly watching the aircraft landing on runway 25. Trans Australia Airlines (TAA) had Viscounts as part of their fleet then. Little did I know that the V 700 would play a large part in my life later, but at that point I just loved watching them come and go.

The boss, Mr. Upex, happened past. He was an Englishman of the old industrial school and wore a suit and tie. He was short, which meant that I was taller and seemed to look down on him. His attitude to us apprentices was severe; he thought we needed a firm hand. Anyway, Mr. Upex caught me watching the planes and slacking and he scolded me most severely. Apparently, my attitude while being told off was insolent, and I was sent home in disgrace. Because of my supposed insolence and being sent home, I became the talk of the apprentice ranks. As a result, my time as an apprentice was extended by the same amount of time I spent suspended.

There was a tradesman who worked at the Repair and Overhaul Shop (ROS) who lived in Greenwich and offered to give me a lift to work each morning. He charged me for the ride, which was a substantial amount from my meagre pay. Unfortunately, by the time he dropped me off and I walked to the hangar and clocked on I was always a few minutes late. The apprenticeship was timed to the minute, so my five years of apprenticeship was extended by several days' worth of minutes by the end of my time there. When questioned, I blamed him for my lateness, so he refused to give me a lift anymore. It was back to the early train and bus for me after that.

Working with a crew

Eventually, I was drafted to the DC-4 hangar (hangar 85) to do maintenance on airframes. I was allocated to a crew. Generally, a crew consisted of a leading hand, who was a licensed engineer, an assistant leading hand, several tradesmen and one or two apprentices.

I was lucky with my leading hand, who was a man called Merv Mason. He was very tough, but must have seen something worthwhile in me as he'd give me jobs that required a bit more nouse and involved quite a bit of responsibility. This was right up my alley, as up 'til then I'd been a bit of a 'hard case'. I didn't really understand the requirement to 'do as you're told and don't answer back'. Mind you, if I didn't come up to Merv's high expectations, he was not backward in letting me know that I was a disappointment. This was very good for me as it made me work hard not to disappoint him.

Strangely enough, I've always liked being responsible and usually rose to the occasion when required. Quite often throughout my life, people would say of various positions I achieved, "That's a lot of responsibility!" But I never thought of it like that, I was just grateful to be considered capable of a position of responsibility. If it hadn't been for Merv, I don't know what would have happened to me. I'm guessing I'd have been kicked out for some sort of insolence, probably.

As well as airframe work on the DC-4 we were sometimes 'sold' to other departments, such as when we were sent to work on 1049 line maintenance. The 1049 was the Lockheed Super Constellation, an icon in its day. It was the international airliner de jour! It was a beautiful looking thing, but a brute to work on, especially looking after the engines. They were the Wright DA series of motor. Eighteen-cylinder radial, turbo compound, supercharged engine that was probably the most advanced piston engine in service before turbines came in. I would sometimes be allocated to an engine crew on the 1049, and us apprentices always got the worst jobs.

Every time the engines were run, the filters had to be checked. This was a foul job, which always resulted in skinned knuckles, burnt fingers, and being covered in very black oil. This happened because the engines were very dirty so when the cowls were opened, used oil would spill all over us.

When the engines were run, I'd usually be allocated a spot at the bottom of the movable stairs, ready to push them in if the engineers running the engines wanted to get out quickly. The noise was deafening, and I'm sure this particular job had a lot to do with my poor hearing in later years.

The Constellation was the front-line aircraft in its day. It was a big event when QANTAS got the traffic rights to fly the Constellation across the US. I remember watching when two aircraft took off from Mascot, flew together over the city and one turned left to head for London and the other turned right for the USA. It was a huge deal at the time. Australia had traffic rights to fly to England, but that was about all. It was only comparatively recently that airlines could fly over the USA. That means it was a big deal when QANTAS got the right to fly over America with the flight I watched take off being the first to be allowed to do so. These two planes flew right around the world in opposite directions and then met again in Sydney.

It's hard to imagine that these planes only carried about 54 passengers, and had beds that pulled down from the ceiling for the First Class travellers. They used to take more than two days to get to London, with multiple stops along the way, including Darwin, Singapore, Calcutta, Karachi, Cairo, Castel Benito and Rome. The services also stopped in Frankfurt, Zurich, Belgrade, Athens, Beirut, Tehran, Bombay and Colombo at times. Flying at the level they did at about 220 knots without radar must have been a very arduous undertaking. The wet season weather over the Bay of Bengal at night, and the Winter weather over the Alps at the level and speed they flew at would have had to be experienced to be believed.

The engines on the Lockheed Constellations were very unreliable. It seemed as often as not they would arrive at their destination with one engine shut down. When the first Boeing 707 jets arrived, the engine failure rate dropped from seven failures per 1,000 hours down to one per 1,000 hours. I would guess now it'd almost certainly be none. I flew for almost 20,000 hours on many different types of airliner, and didn't have one engine failure. I guess that while statistics show us that things do indeed happen, it doesn't mean we'll have it happen to us.

One notorious tale that was the talk of the maintenance department at the time was about the time Queen Elizabeth II was touring, and was travelling on an airline that wasn't British. The planes in question were QANTAS Constellations. An engine failed every single leg of the trip. QANTAS ran out of spare engines and British Airways had to send a flight out to India to collect Her Majesty to take her home. It was very embarrassing indeed for our national airline.

Postings to Narromine

A sought-after detail (posting) for all of us apprentices was to go with an aircraft, either a DC-4 or a 1049 (Constellation) to a country aerodrome at Narromine in Western NSW for crew training. Each crew training required an engineer and apprentice to go with them to look after the aircraft on the ground. We all wanted to be chosen to go, as it was considered a bit of a bludge. Once we'd arrived, we'd be given a canvas wind shelter, a box lunch and would sit at the end of the runway watching the plane come and go. Every fourth landing or so we'd go and check the tyres and brakes, then retire to our little shelter to doze in the sun again.

An extra special treat on those trips was the lunch boxes that were put on board to sustain us. They were full of good things that we could never afford with our meagre wages, like peaches and cream, smoked ham and suchlike. But the most prized item for me was the chocolate Freddo frog. I was sitting quietly down the back one day, when one of the pilots came down and started rummaging through the lunch boxes. He was taking out the

Freddo frogs! He made some comment about how his kids liked them, and pocketed all that he could find. Naturally, due to our very low rank, we couldn't comment or make a fuss but I was outraged at the loss of my treat. I think that incident coloured my view of QANTAS pilots forever.

The Constellation was notorious for brake fires. The brakes were bag types; that is they consisted of a circular bag, like an inner tube, inside a steel drum. When the brakes were applied, hydraulic pressure would expand the bag, forcing pads against the inside of the drum, which would slow the plane. There was no cooling apart from the air rushing past, so if the brakes were overused the bag full of hydraulic fluid could overheat and burst the bag under pressure. The fluid would then spurt onto the hot drum and catch fire. This was never a good situation.

One day, I was sitting in our wind shelter, watching the aircraft landing. As I watched, I thought it looked a bit fast and lo and behold, as it rushed past me smoke started pouring from the brakes. It eventually stopped with smoke billowing out from its tyres. I picked up the fire extinguisher and started a very awkward run towards the aircraft with the extinguisher tank banging against my leg. I gradually became aware that a lot of people were running the other way. The crew had shut down, extended the escape ladder and were leaving the scene, quickly.

I slowed to a stop, undecided whether to continue towards a blazing machine full of high-octane fuel, or to drop the fire extinguisher and join the departing crew. Fortunately, while I was hesitating, the brakes cooled down and the fire went out of its own accord. I continued on to the wheels and struck a heroic stance, holding the extinguisher at the ready.

Another incident that happened in front of our wind shelter was an aircraft landing long. This meant that the aircraft couldn't stop and ran off the end of the strip quite slowly and got bogged in the dirt. When this happened, it was called an 'overrun'. We had to dig a trench, lay wooden ramps in them then taxi the aircraft up the ramps onto the hard stands. Luckily it didn't happen often, as it was a very major event.

A chap called Chick (proper name Charles) Williams became a good friend of mine. One of our great finds while we were at Narromine was that when the DC-3 came back from a training exercise, the catering for the pilots would be left down the back of the plane. As we were always hungry, being broke and growing boys, we'd sneak into the DC-3 after the crew had left, and pig out on peaches and cream, the prized Freddo Frogs, chicken legs etc. We got caught once, tried to run away to escape but were too bloated from excess food and were caught. We were both put on cleaning duties for a month as punishment, but somehow it was worth it anyway.

Yet more training

As well as our time at Ultimo Tech, QANTAS had its own training centre. There were classrooms tucked up under the roof of hangar 58 at Mascot airfield where our classes were held. It was always freezing cold in Winter and unbearably hot in the Summer.

We were lectured for what seemed like hours in such arcane subjects as basic metallurgy, the multi-chambered pressure carburettor, the principles of air conditioning and pressurisation, compass swinging, and a lot of impossible maths including calculating Brake Mean Effective Pressure (BMEP) and many other technical subjects. I can still remember the formula for calculating the bend radius of sheet metal, and the colour range for the temperature of tempered steel, and also, the precession rate for a gyroscope. Did I use any of this in my time as a pilot? Some, yes. All? Definitely not.

We were required to present a practical notebook for inspection in order to graduate from the apprenticeship. It was task that seemed quite beyond me, even though I was threatened with dire consequences I never seemed to get around to compiling one. Just like the steel block whose surface I had to make smooth but just couldn't, so the notebook compilation eluded me. It was a case of 'the dog ate my homework' over and over and eventually I made so many excuses that I think they got sick of asking for it and I got away with not submitting one.

I don't think my attention span did justice to the excellent training we received as apprentices, and I was too young to realise the benefit of it all. But even now, nearly 60 years later, I have a good basic grasp of most things mechanical and mostly only remember the good times I had back then. I'm very grateful for the excellent QANTAS training I received. It's pained me for a long time that the value of trade training has been undermined in favour of marketing and public relations (PR), etc. For a young person to be forced to work outside their comfort zone, accept discipline and learn a skill that they can use for the rest of their life, is a very worthwhile character-building exercise, I think.

The other thing a trade provides is training in a vital role that society can't do without. In fact, the Covid-19 pandemic seems to have created conditions for society to realise that jobs in trades that were at best ignored now can't be done without. Companies are announcing that due to a shortage of fitters and turners, third-generation manufacturing companies are moving to China, never mind all the other skills that a well-balanced society needs. All of these are now considered infra dig and many training centres have been disbanded in favour of Universities. I heard recently that when the huge dump trucks used on the mining sites in WA need repairs they're loaded on to the ore carriers when they sail for China. They're then repaired there and returned to Australia, simply because we don't have the skills to do it here. I find that disgraceful.

At this time on the Federal political scene, the conservative coalition (Liberal and Country party) had held government forever, and it just seemed the natural way of things. The Labor party was split by a Catholic group calling themselves the Democratic Labor Party (DLP). The Catholic bishops had a great deal of political influence, and despite the fact that what was good for the church was not necessarily good for the country didn't matter to them.

In my opinion it could be argued that the Labor party should be the normal party of government, simply as there are more working people in the population than businesspeople. An oversimplification perhaps, and impractical regardless because the Labor party was always split by internal strife, keeping it out of government.

With the benefit of hindsight, the Labor party, led by Prime Ministers Bob Hawke and Paul Keating, brought in much needed economic and social reforms that did a lot to bring Australia into the modern economic world. Of course, I didn't appreciate this at the time at all.

Graduating to shift work – and my first car

In third year, when I turned 18, I was allowed to start shift work. This was very welcome, as it meant we didn't have to get up early every morning, but only every other week. Also, shift allowances meant a bit more pay in our pockets which was always welcome. The shifts were 07:40 to 16:10 day shift and 15:00 to 23:00 night shift. They were alternate shifts of five days each with two days off in between.

Before I could afford a car, it was very difficult to arrive on time especially in the Winter. It was a requirement to clock on when we arrived, and off before we left. However, along with penalty payments added to our very measly wages, I had a bit more money to spend. The bit of extra money meant that I could buy my first car, a pretty tired 1938 Morris 8/40 Tourer. It cost $120 which was a lot, since a week's pay was about $30. I'd been able to top up my driving skills while still below the legal age for a learner's permit by driving a QANTAS jeep around the tarmac. I also drove a 'tug', which was a machine that you stood on. It had a trailer that you popped your boxes etc on and then you trundled around to where you needed to go. If you had a way to go, you drove the jeep.

My fellow apprentice Chick Williams had the same model car as I. Our cry as we left the car park at Mascot for Ultimo Tech was, "No racing!" Of course, we would jockey for position all the way in, cutting in and out of traffic, taking foolish risks just to get there first and get a parking spot. We were lucky not to get booked and lose our driving licences.

Chick was a pretty serious drinker; I wasn't but to my shame we'd often 'wag' classes and repair to the Vulcan pub across the road where he drank heavily. No one seemed to notice, and if they did notice, they didn't take it seriously at all. It was also possible to crawl into one of the aircraft and go to sleep. The fact that this was pretty irresponsible behaviour was quite lost on us.

That first car of mine provided marvellous service, especially when I started to learn to fly. Being able to drive to Bankstown aerodrome instead of catching a train and hitchhiking was quite a luxury. Unfortunately, that car came to a sticky end, and ended up in the scrap yard. A fellow apprentice, Graham Louder, was being interviewed by the Navy selection panel for pilot training in the Fleet Air Arm. Three of us, me, Graham, and Chick, squeezed into the front seat that was meant for two. I was driving, and was travelling merrily along until I sped around an s-bend too fast. The passenger door flew open, and my passenger was deposited on the road, fortunately without injury.

There was a cab double-parked and my out-of-control Tourer cannoned off it, leaving its door and much of its side behind. As I didn't have any money there was no insurance for repairs, and as the car was still drivable, I propped up the roof with a garden stake and continued to use it. It was very cold driving about in the Winter months, so I'd wear an old army greatcoat backwards to keep the wind off me. I must have been quite a sight driving along with no side on the car and my coat on backwards.

In the end, Graham Louder was accepted for the Fleet Air Arm, but sadly it was disbanded so he never became a Navy pilot. Graham was courting a girl at Bankstown in the hope of getting free flying – her father owned an aeroplane. (Graham wasn't that interested in the girl, the rascal.) She required him to go to a ball with her and as he had no transport of his own I lent him my Morris. Graham turning up to pick up their daughter in a hired dinner suit with a car missing a side didn't impress her parents at all, so the romance was short lived. Poor Graham never did get to fly for nothing. He eventually became a TAA pilot though, so all was not lost.

CHAPTER 7

Becoming LAME (that stands for 'Licensed Aircraft Maintenance Engineer')

After five years of apprenticeship, we graduated as aircraft mechanics. To become fully licensed, it was necessary to pass what were known as 'basic licences'. These exams were administered by the then Department of Civil Aviation (DCA) and they were divided into Airframes, Engines, and Avionics. Each exam covered the subject in general, and they were very difficult as there was no way of knowing what you were likely to be asked.

The main aids to study were old exam papers, and ex-Air Force manuals. I spent a lot of time studying and managed to pass Airframes, including pressurisation. I also then passed Engines, including supercharged and fuel injection systems, and later basic gas turbine, Avionics. It took quite an effort and was unusual to have all disciplines covered. Because of my passes in the Basic exams, I was sent to do a course on the L188 Electra airframe, and later the engine and avionics.

The Electra

The Electra was a medium-range turbo prop aircraft, an airliner built by Lockheed. It was used on regional routes to Asia and domestically in Australia. The Electra was put into service in Australia in the early 1960's. They were very popular in Australia because we had shorter runways which were not suitable for jets at that time. Also, the pavement strength was too low for the higher tyre pressure of jet aircraft. Electras provided very good service until they were replaced by smaller jets. Once they weren't used for passengers, they flew on as freighters in Ansett until the late 70's.

The Electra had very complicated systems and was quickly overtaken in popularity and usage by the jets that were coming into service then. QANTAS used the Electra on regional services, and also to fly to Asia, Japan etc. Sydney to Japan took about 20 hours with two stops for fuel along the way. They weren't a great success, as other than Cathay Pacific in Hong Kong and the Australian/NZ airlines none were sold outside the US. It's a bit different now with extra-long-range twin engine jets. It's less than ten hours direct at this point in time. Australia then didn't have many airports with runways that were long and strong enough for jets, so the Electra was considered a suitable fill in.

Lockheed used a completely different and innovative manufacturing system to build their planes back then – the late 50's. Instead of a wing spar with the wing built around it, large billets of metal were machined to make the skin of the wing, with a very light structure inside the wing. This was supposed to weigh less and be stronger. Unfortunately, in turbulence the big propellers created a gyroscopic effect, which set up a harmonic vibration in the wing. This risked the whole wing coming apart and several aircraft fell out of the sky in pieces in the US.

Why this happened was a real mystery for a long time. Investigating engineers decided to cut an escape hatch into the cockpit roof and some very brave test pilots flew that plane at high speed in severe turbulence to discover what was happening to the structure. If it had come to pieces like the planes in the US, they were supposed to bail out through the escape hatch in the cockpit. Fat chance that it would have worked, I'd say. Modifications were carried out on the design and there were no more problems with them. Unfortunately, this delayed the Lockheed's entry into service, and the jets replaced them.

We had a trip to Boston a few years ago, pre-pandemic, and there was a lookout on top of one of their highest buildings that had a view over the bay and airport as well as the rest of the city. Once an Electra had crashed there on take-off. It ran into a flock of seagulls and three of its engines failed, causing it to dive into the bay.

Working as a LAME

After I'd completed the airframe course, I took a couple of courses at the Allison Engine School, including avionics, so I became a licensed Aircraft Maintenance Engineer, or LAME.

Because I was the only one licensed on the engine, airframe and avionics, I was detailed to work at the International terminal helping to handle the arriving and departing aircraft. I found that this was pretty easy work. It involved marshalling the aircraft in with a pair of red ping pong bats to their parking spot (well before air bridges), and standing by while engines were started for departure. When he was about eight years old, I got quite a buzz out of showing my grandson Oliver how to marshal a jet to its parking spot at the Sunshine Coast airport once. We go there yearly for holidays, and it's always a fun time. This particular time, we stood watching the planes come in, him in front of me, and I held his arms and waved them in the signals just as I used to do as the planes taxied in.

The serious bit of being LAME was that I'd sign the maintenance release for the Electra before departure, which certified that all required work had been done and the aircraft was safe for flight. Looking back, I realise that was a big responsibility for a 22-year-old at the time.

QANTAS, as a government-owned airline, was very hidebound and structured back then. Promotion was slow and wages were nothing to write home about. A few of my fellow workers had applied for and got jobs in Hong Kong. The pay and conditions over there were very good. I decided to go to Hong Kong to ask about a job. When I presented myself at the offices there, I was given a pencil and a form, and that was about it. I filled it in as best I could, but then heard no more about it.

Being young and impetuous I indulged in occasional bad behaviour while I was in Hong Kong. I was out on the town with friends one night and we were challenged by British military police. (Hong Kong was under the control of the British then). I've always recognised my British heritage, but also strongly identify as Australian and not British, so I told them they had no right to challenge me. There was probably a bit of alcohol involved if I'm being very honest. A chase ensued, the police with batons drawn, and I only managed to escape by hiding under a parked car while my friends escaped into side alleys like rats up a drainpipe.

The start of my travel for work

At about this time in my career, I started to travel for work. A report would arrive that an Electra was stuck on the ground somewhere with a fault and I would be sent to fix it. It was my job to diagnose the problem and tell the local staff what to do to rectify the malfunction.

My first trip was to Fiji where an Electra was stuck with all the warning lights coming on at once, and there were a lot of them. I didn't have a clue what was wrong, but everyone was looking to me for an answer, so I guessed what the problem might be, and ordered them to change the diodes. Diodes were the predecessor of the transistor. Miraculously, it worked and I was thereafter looked on as some sort of a guru. I don't know what I'd have done if it didn't work, just tried things until something did, I guess.

Other trips followed, including to Singapore, Hong Kong, and a short stretch on Cocos Islands. When I was on Cocos Island, I went to see the wreck of the *SMS Emden*, a German cruiser that was dominating the area around Direction Island. The *Emden* was sunk by the Australian cruiser *HMAS Sydney* in a very one-sided battle, as the Sydney was a lot faster and had greater range than the *Emden*.

There's a rumour that the *Emden's* First Officer and the surviving crew sailed all the way back to Germany in a lifeboat, one of the most epic voyages ever. Of course, it may not have happened and even if it had it would not have been publicised at the time as the people involved weren't British.

The most memorable trip of all for me at the time was to Tokyo, along with two colleagues, also ex-apprentices. My colleagues were Terry Wood, who went on to become the principal of Sydney Tech, and Spud Murphy, who later became an Ansett pilot. In 1962 there were very few Westerners in Japan, because tourism as we know it now hadn't happened yet. Airfares were out of reach of most people, and consequently so were foreign adventures.

In Tokyo we stayed in a traditional Japanese guest house, slept on the floor on a futon, wore kimonos 'at home' and were looked after by a 'Mama San'. It was a truly wonderful experience! A regular haunt of ours was the Albion Club. It was very high-tech for the time, which is what Tokyo still prides itself on. The end wall was covered with old car taillights, which would pulse to the very loud music. The hostesses were lovely, and I was very taken with them. It was then that I guess I developed an enduring affection for Japanese girls.

We went on a ski trip to Sapporo on the North Island. I'd been to the snow once or twice before, but the others had never seen snow at all. Of course, being young and silly, we were well fortified with sake, Japanese rice wine. I remember Terry performed various stunts that amused us all. He would sit on the tail of his skis and come straight down the hill screaming random Japanese words, leaving bewildered Japanese scattered in his wake. To stop, he'd just fall over at the bottom of the hill, a tangle of skis, legs and sake fumes.

I Think I'm Going to Be an Airline Pilot

The communal unisex baths at the hot springs – the onsen – were especially memorable. I did suffer a well-deserved embarrassment at the local onsen. The three of us were in a public bath which was mixed sex, and everyone was naked as was usual for Japanese communal bathing. I was well fuelled with Sake, and instead of sitting quietly as decorum demanded, I decided to swim underwater and pop up next to random poor innocent women.

When it came time to get out of the pool, I was overheated and collapsed stark naked onto the ground. I had to be carried out into the cold to recover, which was mortifying. I was fully conscious, but unable to move a muscle. Lying immobile and naked on the footpath, surrounded by curious strangers, was not an experience that I ever wanted to repeat, I can tell you. And I can almost hear anyone reading this saying, "Serves you right!"

We also spent some time at a Japanese resort town on the coast some distance from Tokyo. It was a spot that was famous for having 1,000 bars, some of them only big enough for just two or three customers. Of course, we did our best to try them all. We thought that we were pretty cool, but we must have looked very silly in our kimonos and traditional-style clogs staggering from bar to bar.

CHAPTER 8

Learning to fly

I got the flying bug

While I was still an apprentice, my old friend Chick Williams was saving every penny he could from his meagre apprentice wage so that he could start flying training. He was very athletic, so would jog to work at Mascot along the railway track that carried coal trains to Bunnerong power station at Botany Bay. There was a trestle bridge over the Cook River at Milperra, and it took a lot of judgement and a fair swag of courage to judge the time it would take to jog over the bridge before a train came. If he got it wrong, the only choice would have been to hang from the sleepers under the bridge while the train went over.

His target was to save $200 before he could start taking flying lessons. Sadly, I lost touch with Chick, so I never knew whether he succeeded in learning to fly. And I have just learnt too that sadly in 2021 he died of lung cancer.

Even though I was keen to learn to fly too, I decided to wait until I was further into my apprenticeship and earning a bit more money before I started. So it was in about 4th year that my friend Herb McFarland started having lessons just for fun, and he convinced me to come with him. I began having lessons a couple of times a month, but Herb didn't persevere and soon gave it up. I decided to just keep going with the lessons, even though at that stage there was absolutely no chance of my making a career out of it. As I got further into flying training, I got a weekend job washing cars. The extra money I earned allowed me to do an extra hour or two of flying lessons per month.

A stint as a salesman

Later, I saw an advertisement for encyclopedia salesmen, with what appeared to be a very large wage. Little did I know that the wage information was all based on commission only, no standard or regular amount would be paid at all. I was all set to resign from QANTAS and go out into the world as an encyclopedia salesman to make my fortune and therefore accelerate my flying training. Fortunately, my wise leading hand suggested that I take my accrued leave to see how I'd go, which meant I could always come back if need be.

We were sent on an intensive sales and marketing course that consisted of one day that we spent sitting in a room while someone told us things. I'm not sure I listened very well at all. I was given my territory, which was the foothills of the Blue Mountains, and a box of books and sent on my way. That area was very poor working-class area, with workers who had a long commute to the city to work. Many of their wives were isolated at home and had no money to spare. My reception when I knocked on doors with my sales pitch at the ready wasn't great, to say the least.

Morale was not helped by the cold rain that just never seemed to stop, either. If I was allowed into a house, it was just to be regaled with sob stories of desertion, abandonment, and worse. Being of a sympathetic nature, I would often as not pay the deposit myself after getting promises that it would be paid back later when the husband came home. Unfortunately, when I returned at night to get the promised money, I would be threatened with violence by an angry husband, or had the dogs set on me, and I'd usually just scrape an escape by jumping the fence. All that, plus sleeping in my car as I couldn't afford a hotel, pretty quickly convinced me that I had no future as a travelling salesman. It's no surprise then that I returned to my LAME position after my leave was over.

First flight

I wasn't adept at many things, but I just had a feeling that I'd be able to fly, and it turned out that I could! My first flight was called a Trial Instructional Flight (TIF). My instructor was the Chief Flight Instructor (CFI) of Kingsford Smith Flight School and his name was Joe Somerjay. He was Hungarian-born, and quite a character. The flight was in an Auster Archer, a venerable British trainer plane. Many different models of Archer had been built during and just after the war. It was very basic, with two seats, a tail wheel, no flaps, what was called a 'high wing', and had a Gypsy Major 90 horsepower motor.

Joe taxied out, lined up on the grass then said, "You take off, boy!" So I did. I took to it like a bird to the air, and it felt like I was really doing something. That's not to say there weren't plenty of areas that I had to work hard at to learn, but in general I just somehow knew how to do it.

Various small planes were available after that, following quickly along behind the Austers. There were Piper Colts, The Victor air tourer, and of course, the Cessna. I very quickly discovered that flying was a very expensive pastime. Out of my income of about ten pounds a week, a one-hour lesson cost six pounds. I found if I really scrimped I could afford a lesson a week. But obviously at that rate it would take a long time to get the 200 hours minimum that was required to get a commercial flying licence.

At that time, aviation was in the doldrums and the chance of getting an actual flying job was very slim. I was happy to do it just as a hobby though and content to let the future look after itself. As I was a sports 'reject', it was a good thing to fill my time if I wasn't at work.

I liked to go down to Bankstown airport, and just hang around. Initially, getting to Bankstown it was a case of just cobbling the trip there together as best I could. That meant a fair bit of hitchhiking and public transport in the mix. I was very fortunate to acquire my Morris Tourer when I did.

Even with my own car, getting to the airport was an adventure. Occasionally, I'd drive the back way to the airport, and quite often there'd be a Ford Customline stopped on the side of the road with the bonnet up and a forlorn looking girl standing nearby. Naturally, I would stop to render assistance, only to find a group of swarthy looking gypsies appearing as if from nowhere. The girl would try and read my palm, while another would siphon fuel from the petrol tank, and still yet another would be trying to sell me some trinket of no worth at all. While it was very entertaining, if you weren't careful, you'd end up with no petrol, no money, and no girl.

However, I was fascinated by the gypsies and can confess that I probably still am. How was I to know what effect those encounters would have on my life years later?

Escapades of the flying kind

The trials of learning to fly were many. The Auster Archer was notoriously hard to land, so there were lots of missteps and mishaps on the way to becoming proficient. On a hot day it'd float along just above the ground, with the throttle closed, then drop like a sack of potatoes, in a very undignified manner to the ground, generally with a bounce or two thrown in.

After a few of us had gone solo – which meant we'd completed a takeoff, short flight and a landing by ourselves – on a hot Sunday, we were sitting around outside the hangar watching takeoffs and landings. We were all watching when one of the chaps, Tich Lever, came in to land. He would get down but then go into ground effect, which was what happened when the airflow below the wing became distorted and then he'd just float along above the ground, unable to land. He'd get right to the other side of the aerodrome and then he'd have no choice but to open the throttle and climb out for another go. This happened over and over… and over. Joe Somerjay, the CFI, came out of his office, and with his colourful turn of phrase, was waving his arms and shouting, "Get down, boy!" Which of course from Tich's point of view was of no assistance at all. Eventually, Tich figured out how to get down without setting off the ground effect, but it was a good long time we watched him try first.

There was a major event about this time with an Auster. Once again, we were hanging around outside the hangar, just looking across the airfield when one of our Austers came in to land. It rolled to a stop, and as sometimes happened, the engine cut out. The student pilot got out to swing the prop to get it started again, as Auster's had no starter motor. He needed the motor to be going so he could taxi to the hangar/parking spot. Unfortunately, he'd left the throttle open too much, so when the engine caught, the aircraft started moving. He jumped out of the way so as not to be mowed down, and the dear old Auster trundled off across the grass. It had enough power to get up enough speed, so it took off on its own and rose up into the sky. Here we were on the ground, after struggling to try to fly the recalcitrant beast for months, and it knew how to fly by itself.

Imagine the scene: the poor student was out in the middle of the grass field, his aeroplane climbing steadily away into the distance. The student had no choice but to plod back towards the hangar. Joe, hearing all the commotion, came out to see what was happening, grabbed a spare control column (an extra set of controls that could be attached to an instructor's side of the plane) and chased after the poor boy, waving the column and shouting, "What you do boy?!" What use the spare control column would have been is anyone's guess.

The dear old Auster climbed happily away, flying in lazy circles, as the fuel burned off, slowly climbing and drifting over towards the city. It was before radar, so the airspace was closed to commercial traffic, and the Air Force was put on alert. A Wirraway was sent up, but the gunner in the back seat's fingers froze and he couldn't move them to shoot the Auster down. A Sabre was made ready, but as it wasn't armed, and the officer who had the key to the munitions store was on his weekend off, so that was a failure too. As the Auster drifted out off the coast, the Air Force was ordered to shoot it down, but also had no luck.

Meanwhile, the Navy at Nowra had a flight of Sea Furies holding off Wollongong, so when the RAAF had to admit failure, the Navy swooped down and shot the poor old Auster down into the sea. The red faces in the Air Force can only be imagined, as there was a lot of rivalry between the different branches of the Defence Forces.

That incident with the self-flying Auster was in itself a good lesson for me. Later, when I was an airline pilot, struggling to fly smoothly and well but generally over-controlling, I had to remember that the aircraft 'knew how to fly'. Over-controlling is when a control input is made before the previous input has had an effect. I learned that if the aircraft was mostly left alone, it'd do quite well with only an occasional input from me.

In the Auster, a group of us would fly down to Camden aerodrome which was bordered by the Cook River. Being and all-grass aerodrome with no tarmac runways, you could taxi right up to the riverbank, take your clothes off and do a bit of skinny dipping. As I said before, the Auster was very hard to land, but we had one student who could do 'wheelies'. In the Auster, the trick to doing this was to fly level, drive it onto the ground just on the main wheels, then speed across the grass to the riverbank, swing around, stop and let the tail drop to the ground.

It was quite a spectacular stunt, but carried a big risk of hitting the ground with the prop, or even of turning right over. None of us were ever game to try it, especially with an instructor around.

I became very fond of my instructor Joe, even though he was quite a distant figure, being a fair bit older than me. He had quite a different instructional technique to most. He'd set the student a task, steep turns say, and if you were a bit ragged, he'd slap the glare shield and shout out, "What you do, boy?" I'd try very hard to avoid the 'what you do's,' so I became able to fly quite precisely and accurately.

This discipline held me in good stead many years later. In particular, I recall when I was First Officer (FO) on the B727-100 I'd often fly with an old-time Captain called John Presgrave, who was quite a martinet. He would demand very accurate flying, and would give whoever he thought deserved it a severe scolding if his exacting standards weren't met. When it was my turn to fly the sector with him, I'd concentrate like mad so as not to give him reason to point out my failures. It was quite beyond him to give praise, but on the other hand he very rarely had cause to criticise me either. Not getting scolded was praise enough from John Presgrave.

About this time the flying school bought a Victa Air Tourer. This was an Australian designed aircraft built by the Victa motor mower people. It was a terrific design, an aerobatic two-seater, and much more efficient than the old American Pipers and Cessnas available then. I really enjoyed flying it.

I was out in the training area just West of Bankstown one day, just flying around, and even though I'd had no formal aerobatic training, I decided to give it a go. Big mistake! I pulled too many G's at too slow a speed, and she 'flicked' over onto her back and started an inverted spin. The control stick was thrashing around and I lost hold of it. The canopy came off its track and my world went completely mad. I had no idea which way was up, nor how to regain any sort of control of the plane. I thought I was really for it this time, and prepared to hit the ground, that's all she wrote. Fortunately, without any input from me the plane's nose dropped, its speed picked up and it recovered by itself. I flew back to land in a state of complete shock, and to make it worse, an instructor in the training area at the same time saw what had happened and gave me a severe talking-to.

Unsurprisingly, that experience put me off aerobatics forever. Although I really admire the people that do displays, aerobatics and formation flying, I'm always glad it's not me!

Progressing through the skillsets

As my flying progressed, we'd practice instrument flying. Instrument flying was when you'd have to use only the instruments available in the cockpit to fly and navigate rather than use visual cues by looking out the windows. I'd moved on to flying a Piper Colt by then. It was an ugly little two-seater which was fabric-covered, with a 108-horsepower motor that gave it a speed of about 90 knots. It had a nose wheel but still no flaps, so was a lot easier to land than the Auster but was still very basically equipped.

To test our instrument flying abilities, a sheet would be tied over the windscreen and we'd have to fly a compass course and keep the wings level on very basic instruments. This suited me just fine, as being a bit myopic I wasn't that good at visual navigation. However, instruments on the panel right in front of me were very clear. As it turned out this was to my advantage later in my career. When I got further down the track towards a commercial licence, I did an eye check with a specialist as was required to get the licence. He told me that I'd never be accepted by the airlines due to my myopia. Fortunately, I ignored his advice and continued on with my training anyway.

When I decided to apply to the airlines for a job as a pilot, Joe gave me a very good reference, especially in relation to instrument flying. I'm sure this was a big help in being accepted by Ansett despite my lack of experience, as the main part of airline flying is on instruments.

Until I had 100 hours in my logbook, I was restricted to flying only in the training area and outside controlled airspace. At one hour a week, obviously it was going to take a long time to reach my 100ours. Eventually I did, and I asked a friend to come with me to fly over Sydney Harbour, which is in the Sydney airport control zone.

It was a lovely day and the fellow student that came with me was significantly more experienced than me – he probably had all of 150 hours. Air Traffic Control (ATC) radar hadn't come into service yet, so ATC gave directions to proceed to different positions by radio to keep you clear of commercial traffic. Use of radio in the air is very procedural, and there are particular phrases for each situation. With practise it becomes quite straightforward, but as a beginner it's very easy to get 'mucked up'. When we entered controlled airspace, I was so nervous that I lost my voice and couldn't speak on the radio at all. I must have gaped like a goldfish. Fortunately, my friend realised what was happening and took over the radio in a very competent manner and we escaped unscathed. It was very embarrassing! I stayed well clear of 'Control Zones' after that.

Obviously as an Ansett pilot flying in and out of Sydney became very routine, along with speaking to ATC on the radio. The approach to the main runway, runway 16, descended past Greenwich, so once I became a Captain, I'd have a good view of Vista St from the left-hand seat in the cockpit. (The Captain flew from the left-hand seat.) I never knew if my mother ever looked up and thought, "That's my son up there," but I used to look down and think about my house and my family being down there.

CHAPTER 9

Scholarship and beyond

The Commonwealth scholarship

Billy McMahon was the Federal Treasurer at the time, and he announced near the end of my apprenticeship that due to an expected shortage of pilots as the wartime pilots retired, the Commonwealth would provide a flying scholarship. This was a revelation to me, as at the rate that I could afford flying lessons, it was going to take a long time to get a commercial licence. I applied, and after a long and nervous wait, was awarded one of the first scholarships to be issued. I was asked at the interview what I wanted to do with my commercial licence. As I was already a QANTAS employee, I replied I wanted to be an airline pilot with either QANTAS or TAA, the government airline. That seemed to be the correct answer.

With the scholarship now paying for most of my flying lessons, I could do a lot more hours each week. I asked a girl to come away on a trip with me, and to my surprise, she agreed. We set off for the country town of Parkes in NSW, but due to my inadequate navigation skills, once we'd crossed the Blue Mountains I became quite unsure of my position. I came across a town with an aerodrome so I landed there, and pretended that that's what I intended all along. Unfortunately, the weather closed in overnight, but I had to get back to Sydney for work, and to return the aircraft, so I had no choice but 'to give it a go' and try to get us home.

Fortunately, the countryside all around us was dead flat. However, the cloud was so low that I was flying around the trees in the paddocks rather than over them, just to be able to see. This was a completely unacceptable behaviour for an untrained instrument rated pilot. Obviously, I got away with it but the girl, whom I was quite keen on, was most unimpressed with my performance and made it quite clear that our relationship was finished after that.

Working my way towards pilot status

The Commonwealth scholarship was for 100 hours of instruction, which would take me through enough training to achieve a commercial licence. The scholarship could then be used either for an instructor's rating, which gave you the ability to teach others to fly, or an instrument rating, to allow you to become a commercial pilot. The instructor rating didn't appeal that much, so I continued on after I got my commercial hours and licence, with an instrument rating. That was pretty unusual at the time, as there weren't many Instrument Flight Rules (IFR) aircraft around. However, the decision stood me in good stead!

I'd passed my commercial theory exams early on, which were done by correspondence from 'The College of Knowledge', which was a commercial training centre. Once I got the hours and did the flight test, I was issued with my commercial licence. I continued on with my instrument practice, but didn't advance far enough to get the rating. I then started the study to do the Senior Commercial or Air Transport Pilot Licence exams. I was very lucky that there was a wonderful retired schoolteacher, Mr.

I Think I'm Going to Be an Airline Pilot

Kelvin Leach, who lived across the road from us at Greenwich. As my parents weren't the slightest bit interested, he took me under his wing and helped me a lot with my studies, especially Morse Code.

These subjects were very difficult, and all that could be done was to practise on old exam papers and study old Air Force manuals. The requirement was to pass an exam in each of Meteorology, Flight Planning, and Navigation. Met was the easiest, so I did that first. I passed, then started on Flight Planning, which due to my lack of schooling in maths was a lot more difficult.

There just didn't seem to be any jobs available for embryo pilots with just a bare commercial licence, so I just kept plugging away, doing the odd flight in the Piper or Victa to keep my hand in. I also kept working shift work at the International terminal. One day my old friend Chick Williams, who had realised his dream and who'd been hired by Ansett Airlines as a junior co-pilot not long after he'd finished his apprenticeship, came past the terminal. He told me that the airlines were hiring junior pilots and I should make an application. I did, and before I knew it, I was on my way to Melbourne on a Viscount for an interview with Ansett Airlines! I remember asking the air hostess if I could visit the cockpit, and was refused by the Captain. I was rejected! I later flew as that same Captain's First Officer, and he didn't have much to recommend him then either.

One of the very senior pilots on the interview board was a Captain Roy Sealy. Quite a time after my interview, I was his regular First Officer, and we formed an excellent close working relationship. He's long gone now, but I remember him very fondly. I'd also applied at the same time to TAA and soon got a letter of rejection from them. The reason was listed as not having enough hours to qualify. I attempted to apply for QANTAS, but they wouldn't even give me an application form, as they only took ex-Air Force pilots. As well as that stipulation, they also required a minimum of 500 hours of jet command time, which was quite impossible for a young civilian pilot.

Outside flying training

What was happening on the social front? Well, I was friendly with a group of Kiwi girls who shared a flat at Darling Point. I teamed up for a while with a Canadian girl, who was a parachutist, hence the flying connection. She was quite unsure of her sexuality, and decided in the end that she preferred girls to me.

One of the Kiwis was quite intense. Her lover had been killed in a crop duster accident. She was keen to run a séance with an Ouija board, to attempt to contact his spirit. I scoffed at such things, but she was adamant it was going to work. So, Ouija board séances became our social group's sporadic activity whenever she could cajole us into it. One night I asked 'the spirits' if I was going to be an airline pilot. The answer spelt out by the letters on the table was Y-E-S! So, reassured by the spirits, I just had to wait for my letter of acceptance to arrive from Ansett which it duly did, much to my excitement. Sadly, that excitement wasn't shared by my family. They just seemed to think things should be happening the way they did, so why remark on them at all.

This was in the middle of 1963, and the next course wasn't until January 1964, so I had a wait before I started on the Ansett training/induction course in January. At about that time I also received a letter from TAA who'd rejected my application earlier due to lack of experience, offering me a position as an Electra Flight Engineer, and a DC-3 First Officer position. I still have no idea how that would have worked, and at the time I had no difficulty in saying thanks, but no thanks. That turned out to be a very wise decision, as TAA stagnated, and Ansett went from strength to strength. Ansett had much faster promotion opportunities and also better aircraft.

Meanwhile the world was changing. I was on a cross-country flight to Orange in NSW from Bankstown one day in November 1963 when I heard the news that the American President, John F. Kennedy, had been assassinated. It was a shocking event, and the ramifications were huge. Often, when big events happen in the US it seems as if it's happened here, mostly because Australia is so closely aligned with America.

Kennedy had sent 'advisers' to Vietnam to keep their President, who was Catholic like the Kennedy family, in power. The Vietnamese regime at the time was very unpopular especially with the Buddhists, who were the majority of the South Vietnamese population. How the Vietnam War would have progressed if Kennedy had not been killed, we'll never know.

The Cold War between Soviet Russia and the Western powers led by the US was in full swing. All sorts of conspiracy theories as to how Kennedy was assassinated circulated, but the inquiry decided that it was the work of a lone gunman. There's plenty of evidence if you go looking that more was involved, but the truth may never come out. Lyndon Johnson took over as president, and the war in Vietnam accelerated to become a huge tragedy for the US and to a lesser extent Australia too. Some 50,000 Australian soldiers served there, many of them conscripts, and a lot of them were mentally scarred for life.

Filling in time with world travel

I had a lot of accrued leave from QANTAS, so I decided to set off around the world to fill in the time until I was due to move to Melbourne. A friend that I'd learnt to fly with, Derek Shearer, came from Vienna in Austria. It made sense to go there first to stay with his family. They were very kind to me, and put me up in an apartment across the road from theirs where an older woman had a spare room. She didn't speak much English, so we didn't communicate often.

I did have one unfortunate event while staying there. I'd been to a local bar and had much too much 'Steerblud', a very strong local wine. I staggered back to my room, collapsed into bed, and vomited. What a mess! I was terrified of the landlady, so spent the night trying to wash the bedclothes. As there was only a hand basin available to me, I spent the rest of the night washing the sheets in cold water and holding them out the window in the snow trying to get them dry. Obviously, this was quite ineffective, so I was discovered next morning, blue with cold, hungover, and quite mortified.

I'd eat with the Shearer family most nights, and the standard meal back then was schnitzel. When I left I thought I'd had enough schnitzel and wouldn't ever eat it again, especially when I'd spread it along with red wine all over my bedclothes.

Derek Shearer had three sisters, and I was rather keen on the younger one, who I remember as being small and dark, but I can't remember what work she did. She led me a merry dance, and played me off against her other local suiters pretty well. I didn't really have a chance, but it sure was fun trying! I can only imagine that she went on to get married and have a family. I hope life was kind to her.

I'm unable to remember what district of Vienna the Shearers lived in, but there was a huge concrete bunker at the end of the street left over from the war that had housed anti-aircraft guns.

I was there at mid-Winter of course, and the Austrians had some sort of celebration which was a complete mystery to me. I was at a restaurant one night with a group of new friends, and all of a sudden the lights were dimmed and a monster burst in, thrashing at everyone with tree leaves. I was absolutely terrified! It was a man in a Gorilla suit, and he was performing some sort of ceremony that was supposed to thrash out the devil. Everyone there seemed to know what was going on, but it certainly scared the devil out of me!

Mr. Shearer, being Austrian, was in the German army during World War II. He had been a Prisoner of War (POW) guard during the war and had been based in Italy guarding Australian POWs. That, plus the fact that his son Derek had moved to Australia, made him have a very nice attitude towards me. Mr. Shearer was a cattle buyer, and he took me with him on one of his trips circulating around farms in the Austrian countryside to look at cattle. As I've mentioned before, it was Winter in the Northern Hemisphere and very cold and snowy. We stayed at a farm, with the cattle downstairs and my room in the loft above the cattle. It was unbelievably cold, smelly, and noisy, I got very little sleep, and it was a long night, but it was an experience that I wouldn't have missed.

After that I took a trip on my own to the border between Austria and Slovakia. The Cold War between the Union of

Soviet Socialist Republics (USSR) and the West was still alive and well at that time. It was very daunting to see the barbed wire machine gun nests, and minefields along that border. As it turned out they were more successful in keeping their poor citizens in than us 'Enemies of the People' (the Westerners) out. Soviet propaganda was continually focused on their people being protected from the decadent West, whose armies were apparently poised to invade at any time.

The Soviet Union eventually collapsed from the economic weight of maintaining huge armed forces and the Cold War was over. Sadly, as I write now in 2022, Russia has invaded Ukraine and their propaganda is once more singing the same song. Russia continues to spread the propaganda that it is defending itself from Nazis and Fascists in Ukraine – which is almost the exact opposite of what is really going on.

In preparation for travel, I had transferred my Australian commercial pilot's licence to an Austrian one, so when I went to Innsbruck in the Alps I was introduced to a flying club known to Derek Shearer. They had Piper Super Cubs that they used to fly skiers and supplies up to ski lodges in the mountains. They let me do a couple of trips, which were really spectacular. We'd take off, climb up the valley, then land on the snow, turn across the slope at the top to unload, then take off down the hill again, fly right over the cliff, and dive down into the valley back to Innsbruck. What an adventure that was!

When I got back to Vienna, it was Christmas time, and in a very casual way, I was told that Mrs. Shearer was in hospital. Language was a difficulty, but from what I gathered, no one seemed too concerned. Mr. Shearer, the sisters and I gathered for Christmas Day, and suddenly the news came that Mrs. Shearer had died. I'd had very little experience of death, so I don't think the enormity of it for them all really struck me. I still have a photo of the family and I gathered around the table with a few presents on it, looking very bemused. It certainly was a memorable Christmas, but for all the wrong reasons. We went to midnight mass at the Catholic Cathedral. I found it very moving, just as an experience – never mind that my friend's mother had just died! My family's religious prejudice didn't seem to mean much then.

On another night, trying to impress Derek's sister, I took her to the Vienna Opera. The Vienna Opera house was one of the premier Opera Houses in the world at that time, so it was a big deal to be in the hallowed halls. The opera being performed was the Mikado, I remember, and as it was sung in Austrian it pretty well went over my head. However as usual with opera it was wonderfully spectacular. Not spectacular enough to get me the girl though.

Frequently, I'd go to the local bars for the Gypsy music. It was wild, evocative music that really caught my spirit and made me feel like adventures were to be had. As I've mentioned, the local drink was called "Steerblud" a very strong red wine/port combination. Quite often it would bring me undone, and I'd leave the bar feeling no pain. I thought I was tired when I was making my way home one night, so lay down in the snow for a rest, just for a moment. Fortunately, someone came along and took me home, as it wasn't unusual for drunks to fall down in the snow and freeze to death. I'm very lucky to have avoided that fate!

After that, it was time for me to move on, leave the grieving Shearer family and the not-so-heartbroken (about me) sister and travel to Rome. For the first time in my life I travelled on an overnight train. For a parochial Sydney boy, it was quite an experience. I shared a compartment with three strangers, slept on a fold-down bunk, rocking and rolling through the night.

Rome wasn't particularly memorable for me, except that I shared an open horse drawn carriage with an American man who I met in the hotel for a tour of St Peters square. It was snowing, so we had a blanket over us. It's a pretty romantic event to sit in an open horse drawn carriage trotting around St Peters square in the snow best shared with a lover or wife. As I didn't have either of those at the time, it seemed to be reasonable to share with a stranger, but when I suddenly felt a completely unwelcome hand on my thigh it didn't strike me as at all romantic. I moved my leg away and gave him to understand his attentions were unwelcome so was again unscathed by the untoward advances of strangers.

Many years later, when I met Judy Ager, my darling wife Jennie's sister-in-law, she thought I might have been gay. I knew that I definitely wasn't, but apparently some people got that impression of me regardless. Perhaps that's why I sometimes encountered men who behaved this way.

After Rome, it was off to London. The Morris 1100 had just come out then and for some reason I was very impressed with it. I see one occasionally now, and am amazed that I thought that it had anything going for it, but it seemed good at the time. I suppose I did the usual things in London, but there really was not much to recommend it. The Morris 1100 is my enduring memory of that time!

The US

Then I flew to New York. There was a chap there who was a friend of my brother Robert, Bill Ashton, who was gaining experience over there as an architect. I slept on the floor of his 'brownstone' in the Bronx. I was there for New Year's Eve, and the big deal was to be in Times Square to see the falling of the time ball at midnight and count the old year out and the new one in.

Unfortunately, it was filmed live on TV, so things were a touch chaotic. Arc lights shone on the huge crowd for the cameras to be able to film, and New Yorkers being an excitable lot, tended to go wild when they thought the camera was on them. People were attempting to climb on top of each other to be seen above the crowd and have their moment on TV! It became a mad struggle for survival just to stay standing and not be pushed to the ground and crushed. I considered myself lucky to escape unhurt as the crowd surged around me, but I've always felt uncomfortable in crowded situations ever since.

From New York I travelled to visit San Francisco. San Francisco is a beautiful town, very like Sydney in character. 'Flower power' was just taking off then so there were a lot of what we'd call 'derros' or homeless people sleeping in the street, and the smell of 'weed' was quite pervasive. I had no idea back then what it was, of course, never having heard of it in Australia. It was in San Francisco that I heard a joke against Australia that I still remember. There were a lot of gum trees in the parks in the city because apparently an Australian entrepreneur had convinced them that they made good building timber. The Americans decided to import a lot of them, only to discover that the wood they harvested was too hard to work easily.

The response to Australians was, "You 'clipt us!"

After a few days in San Fran, I took a flight on a DC-6 to Los Angeles (LA). The new terminal had just been built and it looked like a science fiction space station, very exotic. On the way to LA I sat next to a very nice American, who asked me where I'd be staying, I didn't know, so he invited me to stay with him as his wife was away. (It was a very innocent time then.) He dropped me off at a hire car place next morning. I hired a car and set off!

My first stop was Disneyland. It was pretty new then, and the technology in place for the displays and visual effects was amazing. The simulation of a space ride was just incredible, especially when you remember that actual space shots were still some years away. Sea World was just as mind blowing too. The killer whale, and dolphin shows were something we'd never heard of back home.

At the end of a long day, I dropped the car off, and caught a taxi to go back to my new friend's place. I gave the driver the address, but unfortunately he'd never heard of it. LA was so big that it turned out that taxis only operated in their own area and the drivers didn't know other areas that well at all. I'd made the mistake of leaving my passport at that man's house, as well as most of my money and belongings.

A long and very stressful night ensued. Remember that this was well before the internet, or even mobile phones were invented. Other taxis were called with similar results, and in the end I was in a Police cruiser, with my new friends the Police driving me around the 'burbs in LA looking for the right apartment. We found it in the end, but my new friend wasn't very impressed by being woken by the Police in the middle of the night, so I was asked to leave immediately. Many years later, having been a regular visitor to LA as a B747 Captain, I still have no idea where that apartment might have been!

After being away for about two months, I arrived back at my home in Greenwich having travelled right around the world on one of the first QANTAS 707's. Any hope I had of receiving a prodigal son's welcome was soon dashed. "Where have you been?" my mother said. "Oh, Vienna, London, New York," I replied, expecting to be overwhelmed with admiration. All I got was a shrug, and a cold shoulder. Did I mention before that my mother and I didn't get on very well?

After that big adventure, it was time to prepare to move to Melbourne to join Ansett. I owned a Ford Consul at the time, a 4-cylinder British-made car. It was a reasonable car, but as it only had four cylinders it wasn't really suitable for a long road trip to Melbourne. However, it was the only way to get there, so I prepared for the trip as best I could.

The time had come for me to resign from QANTAS and move to Melbourne. I put in my resignation, and without fanfare, fond farewells or fuss, walked out through the security gate at Mascot for the last time. This was long before freeways, so the time it took to drive from Sydney to Melbourne was well above what it takes now. It's hard to imagine, but at the time I had no idea just how far it was. There were no freeways then. I think it took me just about a full day and a night to get down to Melbourne.

I was lucky that my friend Chick Williams had moved to Melbourne before me, so I had somewhere to stay when I arrived, but my poor old car was pretty clapped out by then. The bachelor flat in Aberfeldie St, Essendon a little way North of the city was an old, dark duplex that was in a pretty poor state. The share house had had many generations of single men renting it, so by the time I took up residence, it was less than salubrious. But it was to be my new home, so I set about making the best of it. Aberfeldie St was where I met Geoff Robinson, who'd come down from Alice Springs to do a DC-6 course. He and I are still firm friends some 59 years later.

Several days after I arrived in Melbourne, I was to report to the Ansett training centre at Essendon airport to be inducted into the company as a trainee DC-3 First Officer. It was January 1964 and I was all of 23 years old.

PART TWO

My Move to Melbourne to Become an Airline Pilot!

Sprog pilot after finishing the DC-3 course, standing with the Ford Consul.

CHAPTER 10

Melbourne-bound

After the long drive down the Hume from Sydney, my poor old Ford Consul was on its last legs. I'd a small amount of money saved up, so under the delusion that I was going to be a rich airline pilot I paid a deposit on a new Morris 1100. There were cries of derision from my flat mates when I bought it home, so my hopes of being a cool dude in a new car were very quickly dashed. Sadly, as my pay for the first year of so was only about $38 per week, I also discovered that I couldn't afford my share of the rent, food, grog and car repayments on top. The Morris had to go, which was a shame as it was my first and just about my last new car.

Graduating class of January 1964. Brand new DC-3 First Officers in front of a Viscount 800. I'm the second from the right.

Training for the DC-3

After I'd settled in, it was time to begin my contract at Ansett. On 26 January 1964 off I went to the Ansett training centre at Essendon airport. It consisted of a group of ex-Air Force wooden huts left over from the war. Stinking hot in the middle of a Melbourne Summer and freezing in the Winter.

Gathered outside the wire fence surrounding the training centre were eight young men, looking suitably unsure of themselves. I introduced myself to one of them, whose name was Bob Placket. "What are you doing here?" he said. "I think I'm going to be an airline pilot!" I replied. "Me too," he said. I caught up with Bob recently. He'd just turned 80. Thinking about us all in the present, I had a mental image of a group of fit smart young men. Now we're elderly, with a huge amount of air miles behind us, amazing to think of it!

We were taken into a hut, sat down and given an introductory talk by the Chief Instructor Ted Rutter. He was a man I found to be most unimpressive. We were going to be trained as DC-3 First Officers. Most of the talk centred on what would kill us if we did anything wrong.

What I remember most, was that if you ate your box lunch on your knee with the window open, the salad would be sucked out, go into the engine, which would explode and you'd be killed. Of course, the DC-3 was slow with a 145-knot cruise speed which is over 250 km/h slipstream. Anything that went out the window wasn't going to go across the slipstream, but rather straight backwards, which would not have led to it being sucked into the engine. His tale was patent nonsense meant to big-note himself and scare us, but it certainly got our imaginations going!

We then started the engineering course proper, with systems instructors who covered different aircraft systems. It was all going along just fine for the first part of the course, until we got to radio. Radio wave propagation was a killer. It was all about the mental arithmetic. A compass is 360 degrees, but the heading that you were flying on was different to the direction the radio station was located. Adding or subtracting from the 360 degrees to get your bearing was quite a mental stretch. It was simple if you had time to work it out, but it wasn't instant.

There were plenty of formula to try to remember, and the instructor had a box on castors with a compass needle on the top. He'd draw a transmitting station on the board then push this box around the room to demonstrate radio bearings, which remained a completely impenetrable mystery to me. The identifying signal from the fixed stations was in Morse Code, which fortunately I'd done at Mascot as part of my instrument rating. I could understand Morse Code to ten words per minute which wasn't very fast compared to a professional operator, but it gave me an advantage in identifying stations that were scattered all over the country.

The other complete mystery was High Frequency (HF) radio. Very High Frequency (VHF) was only line-of-sight, so could only go out to about 100 nautical miles, provided there were no hills or obstacles in the way. Anything beyond that distance had to be the dreaded HF radio. In essence the radio waves bounced off the earth and the ionosphere, so could follow the curve of the earth if the receiver was out of the line of sight of the transmitter. That was the theory, anyway. Unfortunately, I never really got the hang of it, and when it came to hand-tuning the set to pick up the 'beat' of the frequency, especially at night, I was not a success.

I think it's reasonable to explain here, how we navigated from place to place, at all hours, and in all weathers. There were dedicated radio aids scattered around the country then. On the main trunk routes, Visual Aural Range (VAR) sent a beam along a particular direction, towards Sydney say. If you were in the centre of the beam, a needle on the dial would be centred. If you were off track, it would show yellow to one side and blue the other. This would be reversed in the opposite direction. If you were North of the station a Morse Code N would be heard. If you were South of it, you'd hear an A. Obviously, it was important to remember which direction you were travelling in.

Next, and much more numerous, were Non-Directional Beacons (NDB's). Most reasonable sized airports had an NDB. Using a radio compass, the NDB would be tuned in. Its signal was identified by its Morse Code identifier, which was usually named for the place where it was located. It was 'EN' for Essendon and 'MI' for Mildura for instance. The aircraft would then track towards or away from the station on a dedicated track, making allowance for wind drift etc. Sometimes there were large gaps between stations where the signal of one would be lost before the next on the track could be picked up.

Next in our navigational toolkit was a very good Australian invention, Distance Measuring Equipment (DME) it told you how far you were from the station. By using a clock and a circular slide rule, a calculation could be made for your speed, and so how long it would take to reach the next station. Last was the Instrument Landing System (ILS) this would line you up with the centre of the runway so it could be followed down to a minimum altitude, and lined you up with the runway in bad weather. Only major airports had that. Using these systems, we could pretty well go anywhere in the country. Of course, over the ocean was a different matter.

CHAPTER 11

Finally flying... well, almost

Working towards DC-3 endorsement

We were taken over to the hangar for an aircraft tour, and even though I was used to working on the DC-3, it looked pretty daunting to think of flying it. Someone said that the approach speed was 80 knots. I replied that I'd never even flown an aircraft that went that fast. That's not quite true, of course, but it was close!

We had finished ground school within about three weeks, so our next step was the endorsement to have the DC-3 Second Class Air Transport rating on our pilot's licence. This required several sessions in the aircraft, doing both air work, and circuits, under the supervision of a Check Captain. The first session was aircraft handling, turns, approach to the stall etc., then we had to shut an engine down and restart it. One of us had a go in the right-hand pilot seat while the others waited in the cabin. I had worn slip-on shoes that I took off while waiting for some reason. The others who were waiting too found them and hid them somewhere as a joke. When I was called to go to the cockpit I couldn't find my shoes and no one would own up, so I had to climb into the co-pilot's seat with only socks on. It was very embarrassing.

Flying a single engine even at cruise speed took a fair bit of rudder, but I seemed to handle it ok as the instructor made no comment. When I say it 'took a fair bit of rudder', I mean I physically had to push the rudder with my foot. With a two-engine plane, one on each side, if you close the power down on one side and give power to the other, the craft will turn. To stop it turning when you shut one engine down, you need to push the rudder in the opposite direction. So you 'put a fair bit of rudder in' when one engine is off to keep the craft flying straight. With one engine dead, the craft also starts to bank, so you need to balance the rudder with the ailerons to keep the wings level as well. All very technical!

In this particular instance, my only issue was that when it came time to start the motor again, it wouldn't start. This might sound a bit scary or dangerous if you've not flown before, but we were students and ultimately the instructor was in charge, and we were dependent on him. Basically, if the engine didn't start, we just sat there and waited to see what would happen next. Fortunately, the engine did eventually start this time, but the great man who was instructing me looked a bit concerned for a while.

I gave my classmates hell when I later found my shoes hidden under a seat!

On one of the flying sessions, the Captain went down the back of the plane to do some paperwork and left Bob Placket and I on our own in the cockpit. That was very brave of him really, as neither of us had the faintest idea of what we were doing. Bob fortunately was a bit more experienced than me, so when we got to 30 miles from Essendon, he knew that we should call the tower. Unfortunately, neither of us knew how. We were very glad when the Captain came back, took over, sent Bob back and I sat there in the right-hand seat feeling quite lost and stupid as he talked to the tower and did all the necessary things.

Endorsement was what we were all working towards. How it works is that you can't be a crew member until it's in your licence. That's what your licence is: you're endorsed as being trained to fly that particular aircraft, under the guidance and observation of a supervisor. Once we got endorsed, we had to do between 50-100 hours of flying on that aircraft under the supervision of a Training Captain, before being cleared by a Check Captain. Then, we could operate as independent crew members. After we got our endorsement, there was quite a long wait as the company decided what to do with us. I had all day and every day to hang around at the not very salubrious house in Aberfeldie St, Essendon. There were no women around to put a measure of restraint on raucous young men, so there was a fair bit of unseemly behaviour on our part.

At the same time as our DC-3 course started there was also a DC-6 course for more experienced intake pilots. Us DC-3 trainees were less experienced, whereas the DC-6 trainee intake was from general aviation, which was already considered more senior. They naturally carried themselves with a superior air, which only experience and seniority can give you, but it turned out that us sprogs had the last laugh. When a seniority list for Ansett was started some years later it depended on your course start date, and as the DC-6 school started a day after us, my course mates and I were ranked senior to them. However, when we were doing the DC-3 course, seniority depended on your birthday.

One of these DC-6 pilots was Geoff Robinson, a stalwart, handsome, and serious looking young man, who'd been invited to share Aberfeldie St with us. He was already an Ansett pilot so was senior to us in every way. After instructing at Royal Aero Club Moorabbin, he'd joined Ansett and been sent to Alice Springs to fly tourists out to Ayers Rock and back. He turned up one evening with his fiancée Sandra whom he'd met at Alice Springs. We were in the middle of some rather serious drinking at the time. Due to the floor being so scungy from many years of lax housekeeping, I'd got it into my head to clean it with a garden hoe. The other boys were lying around in various states of disarray, so it wasn't a very impressive introduction for Geoff and Sandra who were stone cold sober. In spite of a less than inspired introduction, we became firm friends and have stayed close through thick and thin since 1964.

Training in Brisbane

Eventually we were allocated our line training positions. I was to go to Brisbane to train on the DC-3 freighter that left Brisbane several nights a week at midnight to fly all stops to Cairns, picking up and dropping off general cargo as it went. I found myself lodgings at a boarding house at Ascot, not too far from the airport. It was a very lonely time for me, as I didn't know anyone there, and I only had to go to work once or twice a week, and that was at midnight. The time in my celibate room hung rather heavily as Brisbane wasn't noted then for its entertainment.

My Training Captain was to be Peter Smith, he was probably in his late 30's but to a 23-year-old he seemed pretty mature. He was reserved, but had a very pleasant manner. One of the major duties of the First Officer was to maintain the load sheet for the whole trip. Weight and balance had been a subject we were taught during the ground school and a 100% pass mark was required.

The freight had to be weighed and distributed evenly along the cabin and in the lockers, and calculated along with the fuel, crew etc. to ensure that the centre of gravity and the weight of the aircraft was within limits. When we departed Brisbane the freight would have been loaded correctly and a load sheet filled in properly by the load controller and signed by the Captain. At the first stop, some freight would be removed for delivery and some loaded, and some fuel was also burnt off, so it was up to the FO, (me) to prepare a new load sheet. I was generally ok for the first stop, but after several stops, with tractor parts out of the cabin, newspapers from the front lockers, dogs in cages loaded on the back locker and so forth, any degree of realism between the weight and Centre of Gravity (CoG) of the aircraft was purely an illusion.

Fortunately, the DC-3 was a very forgiving aeroplane, and being dark, I'd hand the load sheet to the Captain for his signature and the light was usually too bad for him to see what a dog's breakfast it was. It certainly wouldn't have received a 100% pass mark back at ground school.

Another of my bête noirs was the dreaded High Frequency (HF) radio. Once we'd tracked about 100 nautical miles (nm) North of Brisbane towards Rockhampton, all en route communication was by HF. A position report was required from us about every 40 minutes. I wasn't to guess that some 30-odd years later, I'd still be struggling with the HF over India, but more on that later.

If I found the HF radio was difficult during the day, at night it was well-nigh impossible. The radio waves would suffer from 'night effect', that is, they would skip off the ionosphere and bypass the station you were trying to call. Try as I might, I could never get the station I was calling. The official procedure was to try to call the nearest station, for example, Rockhampton. If you had no luck there, you were instructed to keep trying further afield.

Once a station was contacted, they would send your position by land line back to Air Traffic Control in Brisbane. That was the theory anyway, but it didn't seem to matter how much I'd try, all I ever got from the mongrel thing was hisses and static. I'd fiddle with the thing for ages, then eventually give up. The Captain would look across at me, and ask if I'd given the relevant position. All I could do was nod affirmative, and hope he wouldn't check further.

However, everything I did wasn't all that bad, as my Training Captain was quite satisfied with me. Flying the DC-3 was a challenge especially from the right hand (co-pilot's) seat. There was only a full set of instruments on the Captain's side, so the FO had to use the AH Artificial Horizon (AH) on the Auto Pilot panel in the middle, so instead of looking at the AH straight on, I had to look at an angle. Since many generations of co-pilots had flown that way since the aircraft was invented, I figured it couldn't have been that bad so I just got used to it.

The DC-3 was taxied on the brakes and by using differential power and when braking with the tail wheel unlocked, it could turn on a dime. To explain: differential power is when you leave one engine at idle and increase the power on the other, which turns the aircraft. On the top of each rudder pedal was another pedal that you rotated which applied a brake on each wheel. So, to turn left, you'd put a bit of brake on the left wheel. Most of the taxiing was done by the Captain, but I got a lot of pleasure out of it when it was my go. The DC-3 was a slow old thing, 145 knots (kts) was its cruise speed, so it took a long time to get anywhere. But in smooth air it would rumble along happily and be quite comfortable.

The standard landing technique that Ansett used was called the 'wheel landing', as opposed to the '3-point landing' that other airlines used. We were taught to fly onto the ground in a pretty level attitude, touching down on the main wheels. We'd hold the tail in the air and keep straight with the rudder and differential brakes if there was a cross wind, then slowly lower the tail wheel at low speed. This was a mechanical thing, where on the top of each rudder pedal, there was another pedal that you rotated and a brake on each wheel, as I've said above. Once I got the hang of it, I got pretty good at it.

Leaving Brisbane at midnight in the middle of Summer, we could get some pretty wild weather at times all along the coast. The cockpit windows would leak, so it wasn't unusual to fly with a raincoat over our knees to keep our trousers dry. Sometimes, we'd descend in heavy cloud and rain, you really couldn't see anything at all. The Captain would sight a well-known feature, like the river mouth or hill, make a steep turn, and wipers going flat out suddenly there'd be the runway right under us, the gear would be down, he'd call, "Full flap!" then we'd land, with my mind usually still back about ten miles behind the aircraft thinking, "What happened?" Other times we'd be taxiing out in the pitch-black night and the battery that powered the landing lights would be a bit low so they'd go out. If you've ever turned the car headlights off at night while driving, that was what it was like: quite a shock!

Towards the end of my training, a Check Captain from Brisbane took over my flight. I was to be assessed to see if I'd attained the required standard to be checked out and cleared for line flying. When we arrived over Cairns, the weather was foul. He had to do an instrument let down and it was very turbulent, so he asked me to help him on the controls. An instrument let down is a landing where you can't see the ground, so you rely on instruments to tell you where you are in relation to the ground, right up until you can finally see the ground and can therefore land. Being so new, I didn't realise the significance of it at the time.

Sometime later, when I met him in Melbourne he remembered me, which was unusual as most junior FO's were very forgettable. He told me then that that particular approach into Cairns was the roughest weather he could remember. It certainly met the criteria of 'ignorance is bliss' for me.

After the Training Captain in Brisbane finished with me, the Check Captain flew with me and approved me. He then sent me back to Melbourne and I was put on the roster to wait to be called to fly. This was called being 'cleared to the line'. So back to Melbourne I went.

CHAPTER 12

Finally flying... properly!

Line flying and romance

I was back in Melbourne, back in the less than salubrious Aberfeldie Street, to wait to start line flying. I spent a lot of time hanging around waiting to be called for my first line flight as First Officer. Eventually the call from crewing came. I was as keen as mustard, signed on very early, went out to the aircraft to make sure everything was in order, checking everything twice. I was in the wheel well checking the tires, when I spied the Captain's legs approaching from under the wing. I scuttled out, drew myself up, extended my hand and announced, "Good afternoon, Captain. My name is Wally Oldcastle!" Of course, that was *his* name. I'd been repeating it over and over in my head, so as not to make a mistake. I immediately collapsed into confusion and couldn't remember my own name. The poor man just looked on in amazement. As a result, my first line flight was a complete blank, I have no memory of it at all.

About this time, I was informed that I'd passed Flight Planning. That just left the hardest one, Navigation, to go for me to qualify for my senior commercial licence. There was quite a lot of promotion then as the wartime pilots were starting to retire, and the fleet was expanding. Quite a few senior FO's didn't have their senior commercial licences, so the company made it a requirement that once you got 2,000 hours of flying time, there'd be no promotion until the subjects were passed. If you still didn't pass, then you'd be let go.

Ansett still had quite a large fleet of DC-3s then; they flew to a lot of regional centres in Victoria, NSW and Northern Tasmania. The DC-3 had a normal crew of two pilots and one flight attendant. The 'islands trip' was a big day: Essendon to King Island, Smithtown, Launceston, Flinders Island and back. The Bass Straight weather was often foul, and my problem with an accurate load sheet continued to haunt me. However, the flying skills required, especially crosswind landings, gave me valuable experience. I look back on my DC-3 flying with significant nostalgia. As an aircraft it was a great part of aviation history, and I count myself lucky to have flown it.

As the Winter turned into Summer, some of the midday trips into the country would be very turbulent and uncomfortable. As the aircraft had no air conditioning, flew low in very hot air, and had a pervading smell of vomit in the cabin, it was hardly first-class travel.

On one of these trips, to Warracknabeal then Nhill in Victoria, with an overnight in Nhill, there was a very pretty Flight Attendant (they were called hostesses then) on board. Warracknabeal was a country airport with no radio aids and a grass landing strip, so it had to be sighted visually. As all the surrounding paddocks were also grass, it was very hard to pick out. We arrived at the expected time, but unfortunately the airport was nowhere to be seen. We circled several times and I wondered what the Captain was going to do, as we could hardly return to Essendon and say we couldn't find the airport. We flew out a bit and turned around to have another look, only to discover that we'd been right on top of it, which is why we couldn't see it!

The next morning we got up early, went out to the airport and found it had been so cold that frost had formed on the windscreen and wings. Naturally, it was my job to wipe it off with my bare hands. My fingers froze and it was a very painful experience. Meanwhile, our hostess sat shivering in the cabin, demanding that I warm the cabin up for her. The aircraft could only be warmed while in flight with airflow over the hot exhaust pipes, but not on the ground, so I was definitely not impressed!

However, when we got back to Essendon, she was standing around the airport and I discovered that she lived in a boarding house near Aberfeldie St, so I gave her a lift home. We began courting. That was the start of a beautiful friendship, and Robyn and I eventually ended up married, but I'm getting ahead of myself. It was quite a tumultuous relationship. Looking back, I had quite a lot of commitment issues, and we nearly broke up a few times when she quite rightly would get tired of my inability to make a decision to tie the knot, but more on that to come. Firstly, there was a lot of life to live!

I'd left Aberfeldie St by this stage and had moved to a shared bed sitter in Royal Park with Chick Williams. I later went on to a shared house in Thomastown of all places, with Chick and another chap. It was a pretty miserable existence, as I wasn't much of a drinker, and my house mates were. My other house mate, John Vormister, was a bit older, a heavy drinker, and quite a misogynist. Sadly, he later lost his licence due to diabetes and I never heard what happened to him after that. He didn't like Robyn staying over, so that was a good reason to get married just to escape. Girls didn't live with boys then unless they were married. It's all a bit different now.

Before we married, Robyn had moved in with a delightful and very attractive girl, Dell Jud. Dell was going out with a very ordinary chap, called Ian. Next door to their flat in South Yarra, lived a group of US air force pilots. Their specialty was Black Russians, a very potent cocktail. Those US air force pilots were great fun. The chap in charge, a Major Pat Halloran, took quite a shine to Dell. He was very keen to take her back to the states with him and to marry her. She declined and decided to stick with Ian. I considered that a very bad choice.

The US Air Force pilots were flying the U2 spy plane on air sampling missions out of Laverton, the same aircraft that Gary Powers was flying over Russia in 1960 when he was shot down, nearly causing World War III. They would take us down with them to watch the takeoffs, and landings. They would fly so high, that the pilots would have to wear a pressurised suit, they looked like astronauts, and would have to be helped into and out of the cockpit of these very exotic aircraft. They would go on very long trips up to nine hours at classified altitudes. Because of their suits, they couldn't see ahead to land, so a car would have to race down the strip when they landed to tell them how high they were. When they took us to Laverton, we'd ride in the chase car down the runway, the U2 would approach overhead and we'd race down the strip behind it. It was all very exciting!

Pat Halloran, who Dell rejected, was a top man. He went on to head up the SR17 spy plane squadrons, and eventually became a General. I could never understand why Dell rejected him in favour of Ian. I recently reconnected with Pat; he was narrating a YouTube video about the SR71 and I saw his name on there. I

Googled his name and all I could find about him was mention of a hospital in Colorado, and when I called there I got put onto a nurse who had treated him. I asked the nurse if she could ask Pat if he'd like to hear from me, and he replied straight away. We're now pen pals or email pals, I guess I should say.

Eventually, after a lot of to-ing and fro-ing on my part, Robyn and I were married at St Giles church at Greenwich, and we had a reception at the Hilton in Sydney. I was very fraught at having to do the bridal waltz in public. I knew that Robyn's parents didn't have much money, but it wasn't until sometime later that I discovered that they'd had to borrow the money to pay for it and afterwards struggled to pay it back. Harry, Robyn's father, had a very low paid job in the church at Bathurst. We were very happy, and Andrew, our first child, came along in 1967. But I'm getting ahead of myself – I'll talk more about family in a later chapter.

Viscount school

While Robyn and I were still courting, I was told that I was down for Viscount school – that meant I was enrolled to learn to fly the Viscount and get my licence for that aircraft. There was an Electra school also scheduled, and I decided I would rather do that, because of my engineering experience. I made the mistake of going to see the Chief Pilot, Arthur Lovell to ask for a swap. He was a very austere and remote figure and made it quite clear that he wasn't interested in very junior FO's (like me) trying to buck the system.

So off to the Viscount school I went. It was a very tortuous process. Yet again I spent all day in the classroom, suffering through all the aircraft systems, with the prospect of exams to follow. As always, my ability to concentrate, (or more to the point, listen) was, and probably still is, pretty limited so I found the school days dragged out, seemingly forever. The school went for about 11 weeks, which is quite remarkable, seeing that a ground school for a modern aircraft now, is just a computer-based few days. It can even be done at home, with multiple choice exams.

Possibilities in Hong Kong

I'd not heard any more about my application for a job in Hong Kong until I was a Viscount FO with Ansett and married to Robyn. Out of the blue, a letter arrived from Cathay Pacific (we usually called it just plain 'Cathay'), ordering, not offering, me to report to Hong Kong on a certain date to train as an L188 'assistant' Electra Flight Engineer (FE) and a DC-4 Flight Mechanic (FM). (The DC-4 didn't have an FE) The wage was extraordinary, at least two or three times more than I was earning as a Viscount FO. Just what a L188 FE 'assistant' did was a mystery though, so I elected to stay where I was.

One day, I bumped into an ex-QANTAS apprentice who was now an Ansett Electra FE. I mentioned the letter ordering me to Hong Kong, and he was interested in the job so he travelled over and turned up in Hong Kong calling himself 'Ken White'. After he'd been employed by Cathay, he admitted he wasn't me, but there was no problem. He went on to become their chief Flight Engineer. Several other ex-QANTAS boys who went there as mechanics learnt to fly there and went on to hold very senior positions as pilots in Cathay.

CHAPTER 13

Viscounts, a risky business

Modern aircraft are so complicated it'd be impossible to learn everything about them, especially the computer programs that have replaced many of their old-fashioned mechanical systems. All that's expected now is that pilots learn how to operate them, and follow the procedures, and they don't need to know how they work. A big selling point for manufacturers now is making different aircraft have the same computer programs, so at least in theory a pilot only needs to be trained on one type, but can be qualified to fly them all. This looks good in the sales brochures for the computer programs, but can lead to all sorts of problems in practice.

After endorsement on the Viscount, I was allocated to Captain Coll Calender for line training. The training went along fine, until I was making a night approach into Canberra. There were two models of the Viscount. An old one, the 700 series, and a newer one, the 800, which was a big improvement on the 700. This particular night I was flying a 700. It had a wartime surplus undercarriage indicator. There were three green lights to indicate safe wheel condition, one for each wheel, and three red lights to indicate an unsafe wheel condition. When the gear was up, the lights were out, and there was a rotating cover to dim the lights if required. I was flying the sector (which is what we called the route we were given to fly) and made a bit of a mess of it, so when we were nearing the runway the Captain took over. Just as he was about to land, I looked down, saw no lights, instantly deduced that the wheels were still up, so I pulled the stick back, and pushed the throttles to max power, much to Captain Coll's amazement. As we soared into the black, he shouted, "What the hell are you doing?"

"Gear's not down!" I replied.

"You never go around at Canberra!" he cried.

You see, Canberra airport is surrounded by hills, so it's very dangerous to do what I'd done. The realisation that we were all going to be killed, and it was all my fault, flooded over me. The gear was down, but the lights had been obscured by the dimmer – the rotating cover. Coll was very good about it, but after we landed he gave me some serious counselling as to when exactly the FO should intervene. However, there is a history that FOs need to be more proactive if they spot trouble and not just sit there while disasters unfold. It's important for safety that FOs are trained to speak up if they think something is going wrong – but grabbing the controls from the Captain is still not right!

The trouble with Viscounts

I eventually checked out ok, and over time got to appreciate the poor old Viscount for what it was, but the 700 was a bit of a dog, whichever way you looked at it. The wing only had one spar, and in flight the upper skin of the wing would buckle under stress like corrugated iron. It was better not to look at it, especially in turbulence.

Many years later, I was visiting Hendon aviation museum in the UK with a couple of American pilots. There was a V700 there, and when I told them I'd once been a FO on them, they could hardly believe it, as they considered it an ancient machine.

Viscounts had a chequered career in Australia. TAA got them first, and the pilots in an excess of hubris attempted a 2-engine-takeoff training flight at Mangalore. Viscounts were 4-engined, so the aircraft veered off the runway, crashed spectacularly and was totally wrecked and the pilots were all killed. In the late 50's while I was still working at Mascot, another TAA Viscount departed Sydney into a thunderstorm, but they didn't know it as aircraft didn't have weather radar on board back then. The wings came off in the storm, and it dived into Botany Bay. There were no survivors on that one either.

Years later, I'd done a flight into Brisbane in a Viscount and the next crew took over. The FO replacing me had been on the Viscount course with me. I went to the pub and turned on the TV to see a news flash that an Ansett aircraft had just crashed with no survivors near Winton in outback Queensland. It was VH-RMI, the Viscount that I'd just been flying. It had had an uncontrollable engine fire which had burnt into the wing and weakened the spar, so the wing fell off before they could get it on the ground.

Earlier, in the same aircraft, I'd landed at Tennant Creek in the Northern Territory. Parked beside us was a survey aircraft, a Lockheed Hudson. I walked over to have a chat with the crew before we departed. Later I learnt that the Lockheed had crashed, killing all on board. The Captain that I'd been with in the pub when we got the news about VH-RMI, Peter, later was driving home after finishing a flight. Witnesses saw him throw his hands to his head, his car veered off the road and hit a pole. He had died instantly from a brain aneurism.

I flew the Viscount for about three years as a FO. The 800s were sold off, leaving just one V700. It had five dedicated crews (I was half of one of them), and mostly flew the triangle: Melbourne, Devonport, Wynyard, Melbourne. VH-RMQ was its name. Eventually, it was sent to Macrobertson Miller, an Ansett subsidiary airline operating in WA. On one of its first flights there, it was on descent into Port Headland when the wing came off, killing all on board. The investigation found that an oversize bush was forced into the spar, (a manufacturing error) and, over time cracks had developed until the spar was weakened enough to fail. As the Viscount only had one spar, there wasn't a second one there to carry the load. Viscounts were banned in Australian service after that, unsurprisingly.

Viscounts, both fun and boring

One of the Captains I flew with on the Viscount was old Hughie Bond. There was a rumour, based on his remarkable similarity to the actor and sharing the same initials, that he was a double for Humphry Bogart. The stories of his antics in the old days were many and varied. He was wonderful to fly with from a FO's point of view. He let you fly the aeroplane without much interference from him. I let him down badly one day. I was doing a long straight in approach to Essendon, and I had the aircraft set up perfectly and didn't have to touch the power or put in many control inputs at all. I think I must have become mesmerised or something, as I didn't do anything to check the sink rate for landing and flew into the ground with an almighty thump. It's a wonder it didn't break something on the aircraft. It was all over too quick for poor old Hughie to do anything, I think he looked at me with a bit of a jaundiced eye after that.

Another time I was flying into Townsville with Hughie at night. The airport is surrounded by hills, so the approach requires some care. We broke off from the tracking aid, and headed for a red light on top of a hill to the Northwest of the field. It was pitch black except for this red light at the bottom of the windshield. As we descended, I casually mentioned that we were heading straight for a big black but unseen hill. Hughie didn't seem to react, (he was a bit deaf) I held my tongue, but as the light was climbing higher and higher in the window, I couldn't help but squeak, "The hill, Hughie! The hill!" Very slowly and deliberately, he leant across, touched me on the arm, and said very calmly, "Never mind, young Ken. I'm supremely confident!" Of course, he'd done it many times before and he turned and landed without fuss at all.

When Rupert Murdoch started *The Australian* newspaper in Canberra (CBR) in the mid 60's, there was a cable to Sydney but not Melbourne, so the paper blocks were made up in Canberra then flown to Melbourne (MEL) for printing, ready to hit the streets first thing in the morning. An Aero Commander from Executive air services at Essendon was chartered to fly each night from MEL to CBR and back each night in all weathers, and an Ansett Viscount and crew were on standby each night in case the charter aircraft couldn't do the trip. That was yours truly. I can tell you that hanging around in CBR with nothing to do was very boring and lonely.

Industrial turmoil

While I was a Viscount FO there was quite a bit of industrial turmoil between the pilots' union, the Australian Federation of Air Pilots (AFAP), and the airlines. At that time the company would put out a roster on Friday which started on the following Monday and lasted only a week. That timetable would also often be changed, too. This meant that there could be no family activity planning that included the husband (there were no female pilots back then), as you never knew if you'd be home or not. Pay was also very low.

A firebrand Captain called Dick Holt from Brisbane became president of the union and started a campaign to bring in the North American bidding system for timetabling pilots' work times. This system was based on seniority, which I've mentioned before. It relied on seniority being decided by date (either birth- or course/qualification date), and then bidding for the slots you wanted.

The flying was divided into blocks of one month with suitable reserves. 'Suitable reserves' meant that they had a number of pilots on reserve that they could call in to fly if needed. If you were on reserve, you had to be available to be at the airport within two hours of the call. Given that mobile phones were not even thought of at the time, you'd have to make sure you were near a telephone to take the call. And the AFAP campaign also demanded pay based on the amount of flying hours you did in the month.

The companies opposed it. They claimed that they couldn't make a roster for more than a week, never mind a month, and that the pay rises would send them broke. Dick Holt didn't blink and pushed the companies to the point of a pilots' strike, until the companies agreed. My seniority number was 182. This meant that there were 181 pilots who'd joined the company before I did in 1964. Bidding on the roster meant that you put in your preferences for the flights on the roster for your fleet. You always flew your own fleet's rosters and didn't swap between them. Each fleet flew different schedules, to different places. If you were number 30 and there were 30 on the fleet who also bid, you got your last preference.

Because I spent a lot of time on reserve while crewing the Viscount, and money was very short, I did some part-time work for a charter company called Executive Air Services, at a hangar at Essendon airport. I just helped out with maintenance tasks on their Aero Commander aircraft. While I was there, I met a very nice Indian pilot called Ken Sing. He'd married a Belgian girl called Mats, and they had a child about the same age as Andrew. We did a bit of socialising together outside of work hours.

After I'd moved on from the Viscount to be a B727 FO, Ken got the job to go to the UK to fly an Aero Commander back to Melbourne. In 1984 it was the 50th anniversary of the great 1934 air race from London to Melbourne, so Ken's company decided to enter the anniversary race. Ken departed from the UK, then reported in over France, disappeared, and wasn't ever heard from again. Aircraft wreckage was discovered in the Alps many years later, and sadly it was found to be Ken. Due bad weather and ice, he'd flown into the Alps and been buried under snow for all those years. I never discovered what happened to Mats, his widow, or his child.

CHAPTER 14

Boeing school

A house and a baby!

As the flying career of the Viscounts was coming to an end, I was told by the powers that be that I was to do a Boeing 727 course. Once again, it was to be a 'chalk and talk' school. It wasn't meant to be as long as the Viscount training, fortunately, but quite long enough for me.

Meanwhile Robyn and I had managed, with great difficulty, to raise a small deposit and buy our first house in North Balwyn. It cost a cool $12,000. Credit was very tight back then; wives' incomes weren't counted and bank loans were hard to come by. I managed to get a loan of $10,000 at 10% interest with AMP, using my Ansett superannuation as security.

Our first child, Andrew, came along in July 1967 and Robyn's mother Marty came down from Bathurst to help. He was a fractious baby, wouldn't settle and kept us awake night after night. It turned out that he had a navel hernia, and would only stop crying if held close, as it took the pressure off his sore tummy. Andrew was a gorgeous child, very highly strung but an absolute delight to be around. I felt a very strong love for him, which made coping with events that were to come very hard to bear.

Due I think to my father's general disinterest in family matters, I had a lot to learn about fathering. I'm afraid to admit that my efforts didn't reach a very high standard. In those days it was a given that men looked after everything outside of the house, washed the car on the weekends, went to work and that was all that was expected of them. Everything to do with children was left up to the mother. Of course, not many mothers worked in those days as it was either frowned upon or just not the usual way things were done.

B727 School

I did the B727 School at the old training centre in Essendon. The most notable event was when a pane of glass fell from the window above where Geoff Robinson was sitting. It crashed to the floor like a guillotine; a few centimetres to the left and it would have cut his head off. He was decidedly unimpressed with the disinterest of the rest of the class!

We had a fair wait before we could be fitted in for endorsement, as it was well before simulators it was to be held in the aircraft at Avalon, Southwest of Melbourne. Eventually, the time came and on a very hot Summer's day with a very strong Westerly wind blowing, which was all cross wind at Avalon. We set off; four new FO's, the Check Captain, who was also the fleet manager, and a Flight Engineer. It was very turbulent, and the aircraft air conditioning couldn't keep up with the high outside temperature so the cabin was very hot. Coupled with the tension of being expected to fly this thing which was my first jet, bigger and faster than anything I'd flown before, I was most uncomfortable. Gradually I got past uncomfortable, to feeling quite nauseous.

My turn arrived, and the call, "Ken White!" came from the cockpit. I went into the toilet, did some retching, but nothing eventuated. The aircraft was stopped on the runway, and as I went through the cockpit door, all heads were turned towards me and I vomited all down the front of my shirt. What was to be done? I quickly ripped off my very smelly shirt and squirmed into the right-hand seat in my singlet, absolutely mortified. I took off, went through all the required exercises, and flew that plane like I'd been flying it all my life. Amazing.

Unfortunately, when we got back to Essendon I had to go through crewing to the briefing room in just a singlet, and I couldn't face it. Another FO lent me his sports coat, but it was a very bad scene for me, showing up in front of people with just a smelly singlet under a jacket. Fortunately, we all survive the odd embarrassing event in our lives, and life goes on, even if it doesn't feel like it will at the time.

Eventually I was allocated to a Training Captain, a wise old bird called Doug Seacome. The technique for landing the 727 was quite different to any other aircraft that I'd flown before. As well as landing very fast because the main wheels were a long way back to support the three engines in the tail, after reducing the sink rate on landing the nose was allowed to drop, rather than being held up in the air. I had quite a bit of trouble with this, so my landings were often pretty rough. Doug would invite me in for a beer after we got back to Essendon, and one day he told me that I was making too many excuses, particularly for my poor landings. I promptly tried to tell him why, and he countered by pointing out to me that that's what I was doing: making excuses! I had to concede that he made a very good point.

About this time there was a scandal to do with a senior FO who had been offered command training. He'd told the company that he'd passed the exams for the senior commercial Air Transport Pilot's Licence (ATPL), but had always had an excuse as to why he couldn't start command training. Next thing we heard was that he'd been arrested at midnight in the Department of Civil Aviation offices. He'd broken in and was trying to modify his file, as he hadn't passed at all. He was promptly fired. Some years later, he was killed trying to cross the Blue Mountains West of Sydney in bad weather in a light aircraft.

All of this was sufficient incentive for me to buckle down and attempt the final exam required to meet the requirements for an ATPL. After much study, I sat the very difficult exam. The pass mark required was 70%. There was one question that I'll never forget: it was for 30 marks, so if I got that wrong it would almost certainly mean a fail. The 30-mark question was to navigate a B707 across the North Atlantic. New York to London with an inflight diversion to Reykjavik in Iceland. It was very complex, and one error in a section would lead to compounding errors in others. There was also a time component to it: spend too much time on one question and you wouldn't be able to finish the rest of the paper, so would fail. I became very confused, and time was running out so I took an educated guess and moved on to the next question. By some miracle, I guessed correctly and passed, but my fellow examinees all failed.

I never went to Reykjavik while working as a pilot, but I'd have liked to, as without it I wouldn't have enjoyed the wonderful career that I had until retirement at 60. I did get my wish after retirement when in 2018 Jenny and I took a trip to Iceland via the UK on a cruise ship that we'd sailed on before. It was very interesting, and I was glad that I'd never been required to divert there on one of my North Atlantic crossings, never mind having to calculate the navigation and fuel requirements for that particular diversion!

Flying the B727-100 and new threats in the sky

I loved the B727-100 except for the Perth return flights at night. There was no way to avoid them, as they'd come up once or twice a month. The flight left Essendon at 20:00, stopped at Adelaide, then continued on to Perth. The problem after that was that we couldn't just turn around and make the return flight, as we couldn't land back at Essendon until 06:00. That was the next morning, so depending on wind speed and direction, the Captain would have to delay the Perth departure. This meant hanging around either in the terminal or in the aircraft for hours in the middle of the night, so sleep was impossible. Then it was a three- or four-hour flight through the worst hours of the night trying to stay awake, before being able to land. I found it nothing short of torture.

At that time the Palestinians had hit upon hijacking airliners and holding them on the runway, full of passengers for ransom, as a way of getting publicity for their cause. Along with the threat of hijack, we also had to contend with bomb threats. They were mostly fake, but seemed to happen quite regularly on the night flight to Perth. Even though all the ones I experienced were fake, it was a very unpleasant feeling that this time it could be real.

In 1971 there was a bomb threat that was very real. A QANTAS 707 departed Sydney for Hong Kong. It was about abeam of Brisbane when QANTAS got a phone call that there was a bomb on board and it was set to explode when the aircraft descended, unless a ransom of half a million dollars was paid. A twin to the bomb was in a locker at the airport, it was found and assessed as real, so the ransom was paid. The criminal then admitted there was no bomb on the flight. The aircraft landed with only 15 minutes' worth of fuel remaining. The extortionist was caught, but to this day only half the money was ever recovered.

Easier flying

As time went on, my seniority increased and I could choose my flying block, ask for weekends off, etc. The most senior Captain on the fleet, seniority no.1, was Captain Roy Sealey. He'd been one of Reg Ansett's first pilots and was the flight superintendent. He'd been on my interview board back in 1963, but of course he didn't remember me.

He was a wonderful man, and over time we developed a firm working friendship. I would choose to fly with him as much as possible and we'd have the most wonderful time. We made up all sort of competitions to have with each other: who could do the shortest leg time from Canberra to Sydney? Who could go closest to the field before slowing down? Who could beat TAA on climb (ascent) to get the best level? Who could touch down closest to the spot on the runway? I just loved it, and it made flying together great fun.

The management pilots, who spent most of their time in the office, were irreverently nicknamed "seagulls" because they wouldn't fly when storms were about. This was a bit unfair, but we found it rather funny. Dusty Lane was one of these big chiefs, and one day I was rostered to fly as his FO. He was rather an intimidating figure, and an ex-wartime pilot. Other than the required courtesies he hardly spoke to me at all. In Sydney he said that there was a new noise abatement procedure being considered, and that he was going to try it on departure. The idea was that at 500 feet, power would be reduced, minimum speed would be maintained, and the aircraft would slowly climb away.

Unfortunately, Dusty was out of practice, and he reduced too much power, over controlled, and at quite a low level we were in a parlous situation. As the speed of the plane drops back, the plane can stall and crash. We were heading for the water! Rather than face Dusty's wrath, I sat there next to him didn't say a word. Obviously, death was preferable to the great man's abuse. Anyway, the realisation that our situation wasn't good hit him, he went to max power, and we flew away. Sometime later it became apparent in our industry that many crashes could have been averted if the co-pilot had just spoken up. 'Human Factors', a course that was designed to avoid the situations I've just described was brought in as an essential part of pilot training. I became quite involved with it in Ansett in later years.

The Captains that I flew with back then were generally very good, but there were some among them that were obviously struggling with the demands of high-performance jet operations. I learnt a lot from the good ones, but I decided that when the day came for me to get a command, I would attempt to model myself on Roy Sealy, who I enjoyed flying with immensely. In my opinion they were large shoes to fill, but a positive example on which to model my own behaviour. The old saying, 'you catch a lot more flies with honey than vinegar' appealed to me. Some Captains were grumpy and aggressive, but Roy was always courteous, friendly and complimentary, even when the FO (me) had done something that wasn't up to standard.

Time moved on with Robyn, Andrew and I living at North Balwyn. I had lots of jobs to do fixing up our house. I had the time but unfortunately not the money to bring our cheap little house to a better standard. Even though it was cold in Winter, and hot in the Summer, it had large windows facing North, so the Winter sun filling the lounge room was always a pleasure.

Another baby, Simon, came along in 1970 and I was away when he was delivered by caesarean section. The days of paternity leave and fathers being present at the birth, never mind home birthing, birthing tubs etc, were a long way in the future then. Simon was a completely different baby to his brother Andrew. Where Andrew was frenetic (and still is) Simon was quiet and conformist. He became very close to his mother, while Andrew had an independent streak right from the beginning.

CHAPTER 15

Flying Fokkers

Training

I continued as a B727 FO until the early 70's, when my seniority qualified me for command training, which would mean swapping seats from being the co-pilot to being the one in charge. The Captain. A command is every airline pilot's aspiration, or at least it should be. Unfortunately, even though the intense training is aimed at getting the trainee up to the required standard, there's always one or two that don't make it, and remain permanent FO's. So, there's a fair bit of pressure to perform. The initial command aircraft in the Ansett fleet was the venerable Fokker Friendship, the F27. Nowadays, airlines just have one or two types of aircraft. Back then they had more – and at Ansett, the Fokker was the most junior type of aircraft, and what we did our command training on.

The Fokker Friendship was a 40-seat regional airliner, built in Holland and very successful in Australian service. It cruised at 210 knots, about half the speed of the jets. The route network covered many fair-sized towns from Tasmania to Darwin, but rarely did it go to the capital cities.

It was very challenging flying, as the pilot would have to provide his own separation from other traffic outside controlled airspace, as most country airports are, as well as cope with a lack of radio aids at many places. This meant that Air Traffic Control didn't have you on their radar, and it was up to you to make sure you weren't in anyone's way, or they in yours. In the Winter most approaches were in the dark as there'd be only an evening service, and in the Summer further North, thunderstorms would always be difficult.

The systems on the F27 were pneumatic, as compared to hydraulic on American-built aircraft. That meant that the brakes, undercarriage, nose wheel steering etc., were powered by air pressure, not oil pressure. Now as most people know, air is compressible, unlike oil. That meant that there was a delay between when the brakes were applied before anything happened, so you'd have to compensate by applying the brakes a little earlier than you needed them. The nose wheel steering was ineffective at high speed, so the aircraft was steered by differential braking. With any significant wind she would tend to swerve all over the runway, and had to be kept straight on the brakes. As there was a delay after pressing the brake pedal which was on top of the rudder pedal, and one foot would be ahead of the other as you used the rudder to keep straight, it was very much an acquired skill, and took lots of practice before you could confidently track down the middle of the runway in any conditions.

Also, when turning onto the runway for takeoff you had to be careful not to turn the nose wheel too far or it would spin right around and you'd be stuck. At a country airport if that happened a suitable piece of timber would have to be found, jammed in the nose wheel and used to lever it back to straight again.

Tea and bikkies

If some sort of an incident happened that was your fault, you would be 'invited' up to the flight department, offered a cup of tea and a biscuit, then given a very substantial dressing down for the misdemeanour. So that sort of event was described as a 'tea and bikkies'. While I might say it never happened to me, it was occasionally a close call.

My Training Captain for Command was a wonderful man originally from Norway, Bjorn Amundsen. He was quiet and professional, but expected a high standard in everything I did. Sadly, he later bought a farm at Benalla in Northeast Victoria and was killed when he fell off his tractor and was run over by the slasher.

Early on in my training with him, we had a 'tea and bikkies' event. There was a small storm window on the Fokker and part of the pre-start check was to make sure that it was properly closed, which I did. It was a night departure, so I just gave it a shove. When we took off there was the most unholy noise. It was air pressure rushing out of the slightly open window! Bjorn took over and we returned to land. The ground engineer came up to the window to ask what's wrong, as soon as I opened the sliding window I could see that the storm window was being held open by new paint. I thought that my command was over before it even began. Fortunately, Bjorn took care of it and 'tea and bikkies' weren't required.

One of my training trips was to Alice Springs via Oodnadatta and Leigh Creek. Being in the middle of semi-arid lands they suffer from excess heat. Remarkably on the one and only time I went there, it was snowing. The poor old locals had no suitable clothes, and were wrapped in old sacks or anything they could find to keep them warm. It was quite a remarkable sight!

Eventually, I was deemed ready for check out by a senior Check Captain. Four sectors were required. I was to do Melbourne, Hamilton, Mount Gambier, and back. Unfortunately, the weather was pretty bad with low cloud forecast at Hamilton. The only radio aid there was a Non-Directional Beacon (NDB). You could do a procedure on this but only down to the circling altitude, at which, if visual, you could then circle and land. If not, you had to go around. 'Doing a procedure' entailed flying to a bearing, descending to a set height, then flying back out to a bearing and back in to a minimum height when, if you became visual, you could continue on and land. If you couldn't get visual then you had to depart for your alternate airport.

I did the procedure, but at the minimum altitude was still in cloud. I knew that it was clear under the cloud, but descending below the minima was definitely not allowed. What a dilemma. I was the Captain (under supervision) for the flight, so was being observed for my decision-making ability. My duty was to safely deliver the passengers to their destination.

Too bad, I could have said, we'll go around and continue on to Mt Gambier. How the passengers got back to Hamilton at night was their problem. Or I could break the rules, (safely) and land. I elected to descend a bit below the minimum, became visual and landed. When we stopped, I expected to be told the check was over, and to get out of the seat and go back to being a permanent FO. The Check Captain's only comment was, "That was very difficult but we're here now, so continue on!" I passed my check and then all that was required was an asymmetric session at Mangalore, in which the Check Captain would fail an engine on one side, and I'd have to do the correct procedures, and then I'd be clear to go out on my own with my own crew. What a dream come true!

Unfortunately, my dream wasn't to last very long. The company decided that there was no vacancy for a new Captain, so back to the B727 I went. It was quite a let-down after passing my check, but at least I could fly with Roy Sealey again with two and a half stripes on my epaulets instead of the normal two for a First Officer. I thought this would give me more respect from the cabin crew, but it didn't appear to make any difference at all. I was still the FO and to be ignored by all and sundry. Surprise, Surprise!

It took about a year before I was back on the Fokker as a new Captain. With hindsight I think the excitement and freedom of being in charge went to my head after all the years of discipline. I did some quite silly things that I was lucky to get away with, but I'm quite remorseful when I think about it now though. On the island trips it wasn't unusual to have no passengers, so I'd divert over to the Coast of Flinders Island and zoom along the beach as low as I could go, sea birds flying in every direction. If we'd hit one it would have been disastrous, but it was very exciting though quite irresponsible. Departing Darwin for Katherine early in the morning I'd divert out to the East and fly down the Katherine gorges. Great fun, but completely unacceptable for an airliner.

One night on the way to Adelaide, empty but for a crew of four, I made the mistake of allowing one of the hostesses to sit in my seat, and I moved to the co-pilot's seat on the right while the FO went to the toilet. The hostess had a go at flying in the dark, got mucked up and we ended up in a spiral dive. The FO rose to the roof of the lavatory with the contents of the can coming up to meet him, while I struggled to recover from 'an unusual attitude' as it was called when the plane wasn't flying level. Fortunately, there was no radar back then so Air Traffic Control (ATC) couldn't note the interruption in our steady flight path, and they had no idea what had happened.

In later years, unusual attitude recovery became a standard exercise in the simulator as quite a few jets were lost after an upset at altitude with the pilots being unable to recover. It was an exercise that held no fears for me as I considered that I'd done it for real so must have been an expert.

The 'track trip'

One of my favourite trips on the Fokker was the 'track trip'. This was a route that took us away for about a week, leaving the wives to cope on their own with new babies. The 'track trip' involved flying all stops to Darwin and back, with several overnights along the way. At the Alice, Jack the hire car man would lend us a car, the hotel would pack us a BBQ, and we'd go out to a local water hole, light a fire, cook our steaks, drink probably more than was sensible, and enjoy the fabulous night sky and desert serenity. Occasionally, nature would take its course and a bit of harmless romance would flare, and then die on return to reality back home.

Many of the world's airlines came through Darwin then, on the way to Southern cities before aircraft had the range to overfly many cities. Crews would 'slip' (spend downtime) there until the next service took them on to other places. The Ansett crews stayed at the original Darwin Hotel. While it was perfectly comfortable, it would be assessed as very low star by today's standards. It still had 'punkers' overhead for ventilation in the dining room. Punkers were used in India in the days of the Raj, to provide air movement in the tropics to cope with the heat and humidity, of which Darwin had plenty. They were large panels hanging from the ceiling moved back and forth by a rope pulled by a servant in the corner. Darwin was beyond servants by the early 70's so they were driven by an electric motor, and they were very effective at moving the tepid air around, but were decidedly old fashioned, even in 1973.

We regularly organised events to amuse ourselves while waiting for our next flights. Hiring a launch to go on fishing trips out on Fanny Bay was very popular. I never liked these fishing trips as they'd try to catch sharks. I never wanted to go near them and was made fun of by the cabin crew who'd say, "He's terrified, look at him!" They were right, flapping fish were very definitely not my thing.

I went off to Fanny Bay with my new FO and a lot of foreign crews one day, and it was very hot, so I stripped off and dived off the stern for a swim. The boat started to drift away from me, and being a poor swimmer, I couldn't catch it. I called for the FO to throw me a rope, but all he would do was shake his head. Between strokes I asked, "Why not?" He said, "You're senior to me, so drown!" As I'd only been a Captain for a short time I was most put out, but he thought it a huge joke. Obviously, I didn't drown, and we laughed about it afterwards.

Later, on the way back South, I gave a Public Address (PA) and noticed him holding the microphone (mic) plug in his hand. I swore at him, and one of the hostesses burst in and said they heard me swearing in the cabin – he was holding the plug of his own mic. He was a great practical joker, and quite irreverent.

He went on many years later to be a very successful Captain for Cathay Pacific in Hong Kong.

Quite early after I'd been checked out as a Captain, I was rostered to fly passengers (or 'pax') to Adelaide, and the next day fly empty to Alice Springs to pick up 40 passengers and return to Melbourne. Unfortunately, the Bureau of Meteorology people were on strike, and no Regular Public Transport (RPT) flights could operate without a weather report. Being super keen to fly as a Captain, I came up with the idea of calling it a charter flight so we wouldn't need to operate inside the RPT rules.

I met the FO for the first time, he was an ex-Army pilot, very aggressive, and he positively declared that as he didn't think we could do the flight within the crew flight time limitations he wouldn't proceed past Alice Springs. What a dilemma! I thought we could make it, so I convinced him to continue. He declared that if we had to land at Broken Hill for fuel on the way back, we'd be out of hours, and he'd go to the pub leaving us all stranded.

We departed for the Alice, and I was very tense. I'd spent years training for this position, and really believed that FOs should be seen and not heard. Shortly after takeoff I noticed that one of the two fuel quantity gauges was slowly dropping. I went back to the cabin to look at the motor out of the window but couldn't see any fuel leaking. What to do? We could continue on, but if it was a real leak, we'd not have enough fuel to make Alice Springs. But if we returned, the FO would get off and we'd leave the passengers stranded in Alice Springs! I elected to quickly turn around to return to Adelaide, and in case there was an internal leak in the motor, I shut it down.

It turned out that it was a lot harder to fly on one engine than I expected after all the asymmetric training that I'd done during my command training. The difference was that the instructor would never shut down the engine, but just set it at zero thrust. This created significantly less drag than a failed engine on one side. As soon as we landed, the fuel gauge returned to normal. Crewing then came out to tell me that Melbourne had cancelled the flight.

I was really reacting to the assertiveness of the FO who was not responsible for anything, instead of using my own good command judgement. It was a good lesson to learn. I expected 'tea and bikkies' but never heard another word, thank God.

I was asked a question about what I thought made good leadership recently. I replied, that to ask everyone's opinion as a group can often come up with better ideas than can one person thinking alone. And once you've heard all sides you can take a decision on the path to be followed and stick to it, even if there's opposition to what you've decided. Being prepared to wear the outcome, regardless of the results is the tough bit. That's the leadership system that I tried to follow for many years, and still do.

Stormy flying

Obviously, I hadn't blotted my copybook too much, as I was asked to be a Training Captain soon after all of these events.

Weather plays a large part in airline, indeed in all flying. The Fokker cruised mainly between 18,000 and 25,000 feet. This is also the altitude that thunderstorms are at their fiercest. At lower latitudes, (nearer the equator) in the wet season they can reach up as high as 60,000 feet, so it's impossible to out-climb them.

The vertical air currents inside them can overstress the aircraft structure, and even break the wings off, so it's very important to fly around, rather than through them. I was North of Alice Springs one wet season afternoon, on the way to Tennant Creek, when we came across a line of huge storm build ups all along our track. I diverted out to the West, but unfortunately couldn't find a way back onto track again. We eventually flew out of range of the available radio aids, and I ran out of ideas. When I guessed that we were some 80 miles West of Tennant Creek on a heading to nowhere, I had no choice but to descend and try to fly under the storms.

I was twisting and turning trying to maintain a generally Easterly heading, without enough fuel to continue on to Darwin, or return to Alice Springs. I was wondering what to do when we turned around a rain shower and suddenly there was the airport. I closed the throttles, called gear down, flaps 40 (the position needed for the landing flaps) and landed. About halfway along the landing run, visibility disappeared in heavy rain. When we stopped on the tarmac, the water on the runway was about 15cms deep. I considered myself very lucky to have got away with that, as that amount of water could have caused us to have quite the spectacular crash. We retired to the Darwin pub and consumed quite a few beers to celebrate having made it.

I learnt another a good lesson about thunderstorms on a later trip. We were flying South of Darwin and there was a line of huge storms with a gap about five miles wide right on our track. The Fokker radar wasn't very good, but it looked as though we could just continue on and fly right through a gap between a couple of formations. Unfortunately, just as we got to the gap it started to close and it was too late to turn around.

The turbulence was extreme: the oil in the engines was lifted from the bottom of the tanks so the engines started to automatically shut down, stuff flew all around the cockpit, and the cabin crew later said a bolt of lightning came in one window and out the other. We were spat out of the gap in a steep bank into perfectly calm air. I never tried to squeeze through a gap between storms again.

Training Captain duties

All airlines maintain a constant training system. The pilot training system for us was, when a vacancy came up on a particular aircraft type it was advertised to all crew. This position was then allocated according to the seniority of the pilot who applied for it. That person, along with others, would then go to engineering ground school. After all the required subjects were passed, aircraft endorsement would come next. This was before flight simulators, so this was completed in the aircraft under the supervision of a Check Captain – like I've said happened to me. The aircraft endorsement would include engine out, stalls, takeoff and landings under emergency conditions etc. Then the trainee would be passed on to a Training Captain who would guide him in line operation of the aircraft on normal route flying. This was my role for many years at Ansett until I left due to the 1989 pilots' dispute – but I'll get to that later.

Ansett owned Ansett/ Mandated airlines in New Guinea, but had decided to close it down. Its pilots were given the option of joining mainline Ansett in Melbourne. I was given the job of training those that decided to take up the offer and move South, to get them up to mainline operating standards. They were very much a mixed bag. A couple took to it like a duck to water, but unfortunately, most of them had been flying just visual, without the discipline and conformity of airline flying.

One particular FO just couldn't get it. Generally, there was no wind on the ground in New Guinea, but the further South one gets, the windier it is. He just couldn't be convinced that if there was no reported wind, he had to look at the windsock to decide the runway direction. After several attempts to land downwind or crosswind when there was a perfectly suitable into-wind runway on an island trip to the Bass Strait Islands, I got frustrated with him. I noticed that into Flinders Island he was just going to land straight in, so I told him to go 'round and overfly. Once again, he didn't look at the windsock. I made him overfly again, and told him we weren't going to land until he made a proper assessment of the wind.

The people on the ground were gazing skyward at the poor old Fokker aimlessly wandering every which way above the field and were quite puzzled as to what we were doing. I think he scraped through in the end, but he stayed a junior FO for the rest of his career.

As I've said, I stayed a Training Captain with Ansett until 1989, when I left for greener pastures.

CHAPTER 16

Stormy flying, of a different nature

New directions at home

Meanwhile, when I was still a Fokker pilot, a Hungarian woman called Piroska (who I later called Piri), her husband and her parents had moved in over the road from our house in Balwyn. Almost by accident, a relationship developed between us. She and her parents had been refugees and they had spent the years between the end of the Second World War and 1949 in a refugee camp in Bavaria, in Southern Germany. As a result, she was quite a Germanophile. She was multi-lingual, a fortune teller, an excellent artist, and a great entertainer. Given my earlier attraction to Gypsies, I found her quite irresistible.

She had decided to leave her husband and I'd decided to leave Robyn, so we set off on a new life together. Naturally, it was a very traumatic time, full of guilt and tortured emotions. Hardly a day goes by when I'm not grateful that my two boys grew up into decent and worthwhile citizens despite the trauma that they went through in those early years due to me indulging myself. It was a big price to pay for everyone involved. However, when I make an overall assessment of my life, I wouldn't have missed the experience for anything.

Society has moved on a lot since then. There were quite a lot of restrictions on how you could live your life. Homosexuality was illegal, the Catholic, and indeed all churches, had a lot of political influence. The 10 o'clock closing for pubs hadn't been in long, there was no Sunday trading for shops (a man actually went to jail for opening his hardware shop on Sunday), and no such thing as café tables on the footpath. Abortion was illegal, there was quite strict censorship and in all of that, it was also quite difficult to get a divorce.

It was necessary to prove in court, that there was one or more of: desertion, adultery, drunkenness, cruelty, insanity, or imprisonment. Piri's husband decided to divorce her on the grounds of adultery. That required proof, so private detectives broke into our very cheap flat in St Kilda late one night to take photos of us in bed. Later, she had to stand in the witness box in court and admit to her amoral behaviour. That, alongside all the struggles that come with starting a new life together, were very traumatic.

I'd been given a slot on the Electra freighter, and had to do the endorsement out over Bass Straight and at Avalon airfield under extreme emotional pressure, dealing with my guilt at leaving Robyn and attempting a new relationship. Compared to many a divorce settlement that I've heard of over the years, Robyn was very reasonable. We'd recently bought a new house at Bulleen for $42,000. Robyn sold that and, paid off the mortgage, which left her enough to pay cash for a townhouse at Pascoe Vale. Piri and I rented an old terrace house at West Melbourne. After some serious saving, we managed to scrape up enough for a deposit on a terrace at Carlton which was very trendy at the time.

Piroska was working as a teacher, so I had to fill in my days until I'd leave for the freight line at night. As there was no money to spare, the days stretched out a bit. To my shame, in hindsight, I should have learnt to be a better house husband, and taken care of some cooking, cleaning etc, but I didn't. I did become quite a good interior decorator, and spent time painting, making curtains, reupholstering old chairs, etc.

There were much that was positive from my time living with Piri. With her being a trained art teacher and quite a competent artist, I was exposed to art theory and knowledge of which I would otherwise be quite ignorant. We did several overseas trips, including to Germany where she'd been in a refugee camp as a child, and I was taken to many of the great galleries of the world to be taught some of the finer points of the great masters.

To compensate for the art training, I booked a camping and canoeing trip down the Murrumbidgee and Tumut rivers. It was a wonderful experience. It involved travelling in a group of several two-person canoes, along with a guide and we'd set up camps along the river at meal stops and overnight. The Murrumbidgee was slow-moving and quiet, but then we were transported to the Tumut, which by contrast, was very fast-moving. This nearly led to disaster. While our companions were often tipped out, Piri and I survived the rapids and obstacles well. Then, on a calm but fast-moving stretch we came around a corner and straight into a willow tree that had fallen across about a third of the river. Over we went, and Piri immediately disappeared as she was sucked down into the branches that were under water. I was stuck against the trunk with the whole weight of the canoe pressing on my back. I managed to get hold of Piri's hair, and tried to pull her up, but only managed to pull myself under. I had to let go. I managed to get around the end of the tree, and hang on to a branch downstream, stuck there like a boat with a bow wave, the river rushing past me, quite unable to move.

I was certain that Piri was gone. I couldn't see any sign of her, and a dread took hold of me. All of a sudden, there was a scream behind me. She'd become semiconscious under water, stopped struggling, and was washed downstream and bought to the surface by her life jacket. She was rescued by our guide further downstream. I, meanwhile, had to be convinced to let go of the tree branch and be towed to shore by our leader. We were lucky to get out of that relatively unscathed, but it was a very subdued camp that night.

A movie called The Green Book that I watched recently, about race relations in the Southern US states in the early 60's, reminded me of an event with Piri in Paris one time. I believe it was 1976 and a heatwave, which was terribly uncomfortable. There was no cooling, minimal refrigeration, and you couldn't get a cool drink or a cool room. We were walking back to our hotel after dinner one night, and became totally lost. I decided that I'd have to ask directions, so went into a bar. Unfortunately, it was a bar for Africans. There was a sudden hush when we entered, all eyes were on us, and the looks weren't exactly welcoming. Nervously, I asked the very large African barman, (my French wasn't too bad then) for directions. He responded by asking where we were from. "Australia," I replied, nervously. "OK," he said, "There's a lot of black people there."

"Oh yes," I said, "They're very popular!" Apparently, this was the correct answer, even if not exactly factual, as he ordered one of the patrons of the bar to drive us home. We probably weren't in any danger, but it was quite unnerving.

It was probably on the same trip that we caught up with some relations of Piri's too. They were a travelling troupe of entertainers (Gypsies again). They were well past their performing prime so could only get gigs in what I thought of as very ordinary venues. We went to see one of their shows in a seedy dive down by the river somewhere. It was a very rough crowd, who didn't think much of an elderly man and woman (Piri's uncle and aunt) in tights trying to do an acrobatic routine. They started throwing shoes, to indicate their displeasure. Some of the shoes came my way, and given my inability to catch anything, it was amazing that I caught most of them and so distracted the thugs sufficiently for us to escape. I never heard what became of Piri's relatives' entertainment career after that!

I remember Piri's relatives taking us to Verdun. This was the site of the World War I battle that destroyed hundreds of thousands of young French and German men in a matter of days. The history books say that was the battle that 'bled the German army white'. They had a great 'yank tank', as we called large American-made cars back then. It was too big for many of the narrow village streets, so we kept getting stuck, asking for directions, but not listening to the answers, so getting lost again. When we got to the monuments, I was very moved, but Piri's relatives didn't seem to understand the significance of it all, and just concentrated on putting on a show, even if the only audience was me. It was all rather surreal.

A fair bit of friction developed in our relationship, as I wanted Andrew and Simon to come and stay weekends, and Piri wanted to go and see her parents at Cowes on Phillip Island. With hindsight as a good parent, I should have stayed in town with the boys, and she should have gone to Phillip Island. Unfortunately, while perfectly comfortable for a working couple, with two children staying and without a spare bedroom in our Carlton terrace, it was overcrowded. We decided to move out of town and found a delightful cottage with a small pool at Black Rock.

I loved and admired Andrew, (and I still do) but he was a very difficult young person. He had every excuse for being so. His life had been topsy-turvy since I left the family home with Piri. Coupled with his highly strung nature, it made him very difficult to deal with. Not only for me, but his teachers, his mother, and the parents of his friends. I felt very strongly that his failure at the schools he was at, was because of the home environment, with his stepbrothers and the men in his mother's life. He was begging to leave there and come and live with me. Piri, as a no child woman, and with a very enjoyable career was totally against it, but I insisted. His mother Robyn and her partner Ian and I agreed that Simon would be her responsibility and Andrew would be mine.

Andrew came to live with Piri and I in Black Rock, and I enrolled him at Beaumaris high, but it wasn't a success! There were so many problems that I determined that he'd be better off in a country boarding school. I picked Hamilton College at Hamilton, the birthplace of Ansett Airlines. I assumed that there'd be less distractions there, he'd have to do his homework, and the other kids would be simple country kids that wouldn't be interested in grog, drugs, girls, etc. Unfortunately, it didn't work out like that, and he was very unhappy there, and failed each year.

Sadly, Simon's life was very unpleasant, due to his stepbrothers' bullying. I feel quite guilty that I didn't realise that he should have been the one to get the most support from me. He was the quiet one, and it was very much a case of the squeaky wheel gets the oil, so Andrew got the most attention. I admire Simon tremendously for the way he copes, and for his very successful family.

The owners of the cottage in Black Rock were Eric and Cathy Lomas – Eric was a 'film man'. We became good friends and still are to this day. Eric was a great practical joker. He'd catch people out with all sorts of tricks, and I was generally the sucker who fell for them. However, I did manage to get him back eventually.

He'd spent a long time and a lot of money renovating a house in Sandringham. It included a very large backyard pool. Being a perfectionist, he'd had the builders back over and over again in order to get it right. He was determined to be the first to swim in it, so I hatched a plan. One weekend I called in to see him, and I happened to be wearing a suit. The pool was finished and he was checking the chemical levels of the water. I said to him he'd be very cranky if someone used the pool before him. He certainly would be, he replied. With that, I dived straight in, suit and all. He didn't know whether to laugh or cry. It cost me a new suit but it was worth it for the look on his face!

Piri and I were married for eight years. She being a passionate and emotional Hungarian, much of that time our relationship was very fraught. Looking back, it probably had no future from the start given our entirely different natures and backgrounds. However, a wonderful part of human nature is that you only remember the good bits of the past and forget the bad, so I look on that period of my life with no regrets and overall consider it a positive experience.

I'm also very pleased that Robyn, who had done nothing to deserve such treatment, after going through many difficult twists and turns in her life, found a good partner and is enjoying a well-deserved and pleasant retirement. With the passage of time when I see Robyn at family functions etc, we get on very well for which I'm very grateful. She would have every excuse for carrying a grudge as so many divorced people that have been wronged do, but as a very sensible and practical person she moved on to a very successful life.

CHAPTER 17

Flying freight in an Electra

The Fokker F27 was a big success in Australian domestic service, while challenging to fly with its pneumatic brakes and steering. Over time I learned to play it like an organ. The route structure was quite varied compared to the jets, too. The Fokker serviced many regional towns, as well as the Bass Strait Islands, and the 'track trip' all the way to Darwin, as I've already mentioned.

I was looking forward to moving on to something bigger and faster, as well as eyeing off a higher pay grade. Pay rates then were based on a speed/weight formula for each aircraft type. The faster/heavier the aircraft, the higher the pay.

When a vacancy arose on the Electra (L188) I decided to take it, as it looked as though it'd be a long wait before I got a spot on the DC-9 jet. To stop too quick a rollover of crews, it was a requirement that you agree to stay for a minimum of three years on the Electra. In return, they said that the pay would be equal to the DC-9.

As it turned out I stayed on it for more than four years and became the fleet Training Captain. I enjoyed flying the L188 very much; it was a real performer with four 3,000 horsepower

(HP) engines, and a three-man crew. It was very manoeuvrable with a terrific rate of climb and was a delight to fly and land accurately. The L188 I flew had been converted into a freighter some time earlier, so all our flights were at night. Mostly the route I flew consisted of two trips to Launceston, which would take all night. By the time four nights were over I'd be very tired. With no passengers on board, we could take liberties that were impossible in the full light of day.

Occasionally, newspapers would have to be delivered to Hobart on a Sunday morning. We'd drop them off about 04:00/05:00 then return to Launceston to pick up freight for Melbourne. I'd fly at about 500 feet the 100 nm between Hobart and Launceston just as the dawn was breaking. It was incredibly thrilling to skim along at 320 knots, just above the beautiful Tasmanian countryside, watching the sun rise. Fortunately, no one ever complained otherwise it certainly would have been 'tea and bikkies' for me.

Night flying was generally very pleasant. The weather is mostly more stable and calmer at night, and there's not much other traffic around so to hum along with just the stars and the moon for company is quite a lovely experience. The pleasure was diminished somewhat once the time progresses past midnight towards 04:00 as it becomes a great difficulty keeping your eyes open. I've never enjoyed staying up all night, unless I had to, and it's always been a mystery to me why anyone would want to do so voluntarily.

Naturally, as in all flying over a long period, occasional challenges would arise. There was a range of low hills to the Northwest of Launceston airport which kept us at quite a high altitude until we got visual when approaching the circuit area. On our first trip down to Launceston the weather was foul, as only mid-Winter Tasmanian weather can be. It required a full instrument let down with heavy rain and a strong cross wind. It was way too much for the trainee I was instructing to handle at the time. We duly unloaded, reloaded, and departed for Melbourne.

On the next sector down to Launceston, at about 04:00 the airport barometric pressure was reported as having risen, and the visibility slightly improved. I decided to attempt a visual approach, followed by a low-level circuit, rather than the 20-odd minutes extra required for a full instrument let down. The hills were hidden in the dark and rain and by the time we turned onto final approach the whole perspective of the runway lights looked all wrong.

After we landed the altimeter showed us 200-300 feet underground. The three of us had misread the altimeter setting in the dim cockpit lights, due in some respects to the lateness of the hour and the stress of the moment. If we hadn't made an unusually steep approach, we'd have flown straight into the hills, and I wouldn't be writing this story. Of such events a lucky or unlucky life evolves.

Flying quite an old aircraft like the L188 that didn't do too many hours threw up quite a few maintenance challenges. It sometimes seemed that there were more people and events trying to stop the operation than helping to make sure that it proceeded. I always keep that in mind when I'm told that I can't do something.

Once I was flying to Perth after a very early start, with a Captain off the F27 under training in the left-hand seat, which was the Captain's seat, and I was in the right hand one. The sun was just coming up, and the three of us were feeling pretty sleepy, when suddenly the fire warning bell went off, along with a flash of engine no.3 fire warning light. I sat up, and the trainee Captain looked at me and asked, "How did you do that without touching the test switch?" We silenced the bell as per the procedure, and the motor kept on running normally. There were no windows in the cabin of the freighter, so the engineer couldn't go back to look at the engine out of the window. As a precaution, I ordered it shut down. We descended a few thousand feet and continued on quite happily.

Approaching the top of our descent, the fire bell rang again. We tested the fire warning circuits, and the no.2 engine didn't light up. It was running normally, according to our systems. What to do? As we were about to descend anyway, I shut down no.2 engine, just in case. The trainee continued on and did a perfectly good job of managing the approach and landing.

A memo came out later, to inform me that as it wasn't considered a full fire warning and that the engines shouldn't have been shut down. I was a bit put out by this, as it's always easier to judge after the event from the safety and comfort of the office. Hindsight, as they say, is always 20/20. We had a fleet Christmas party later, and one of the wags, David Ferguson, presented me with the Cowards' Asymmetric Award, due to shutting down an engine on each side, rather than two on one side, which is a lot more difficult and dangerous.

Quite often our cargo would be racehorses being moved around the country for breeding or to take part in major races. The boss of Ansett, Reg Ansett had a large interest in horse racing, and often his stable master would travel with us to look after the horses. He was an elderly, very quiet man, and I was amazed to discover he was Tommy Woodcock, who'd been the strapper for Australia's most famous horse, Phar Lap, who died under Tommy's care in the US during the depression. Phar Lap's stuffed body is held at the Melbourne Museum.

Another cargo that we carried often was gold bullion, along with used bank notes being sent to be destroyed in a reserve bank furnace. Our maximum payload was 14 tons, so you can just imagine how much our cargo was worth. The bullion would be loaded at a remote corner of the airport, and two Federal guards would travel with us to supervise. They always carried guns, but once the doors were closed, they were supposed to hand them over to the Captain for the duration of the trip. They were always very reluctant to do this, so I'd relent and tell them to just give me the bullets. I counted them one day en route, and discovered that they had kept one bullet each, just in case. Fortunately, there were never any accidents.

We had our regular guards, and over time became quite friendly. Eventually one of our regular guards turned up with a new partner. It took some time to get the story out of him, but it turned out that the missing guard was in jail! He'd been sneaking $50 notes out of the boxes of banknotes marked for burning before they went into the furnace. Over time he couldn't help but spend them, so when it was discovered that they were back in circulation, a secret investigation discovered the culprit. Very quietly, he himself disappeared from circulation!

All in all, I enjoyed being a freighter pilot very much. It had its challenges, not least of which was staying awake well after midnight. There was a line in one of the early Star Wars films that went something like, "Go to the freight line to get the best pilots". Even if the inference for the layperson was, "You're not good enough to be allowed to carry passengers", I feel it applies.

CHAPTER 18

Finally, the DC-9!

In 1978 a vacancy came up for a Captain on the DC-9 which I was very glad to accept. The DC-9 had been built by the venerable Douglas factory as a short range smaller two-engine jet for domestic service, which meant daytime flying for me! The DC-9 was a great performer and every pilot loved it. Its nickname was 'the pocket rocket'. The cabin was quite narrow, so passenger comfort was not so great, but it was a pleasure to fly.

The endorsement to fly it was in a simulator that only had vision for nighttime and was very basic by today's standards. I was trained on the aircraft by a very nice Dutchman, Fred Boomsma. After all the night flying, operating in daylight was a pleasure.

I did have some difficulty getting used to it at the beginning, which we called 'keeping up with the aeroplane'. Approaching the airport at 300 knots in the DC-9 instead of around 200 knots in the Electra was quite a challenge until you got used to it. The technique for landing was quite different too: as the engines were on the fuselage at the tail, the undercarriage was a lot further back than they were on a conventional aircraft with the motors under the wing. This meant that at 'the flare' on landing the nose couldn't be lifted too high or the wheels would be driven hard into the runway. Some of my landings must have given the passengers cause for worry, and poor old Fred some anxious moments, until I got used to it.

When it was time for my check out ride with a Check Captain, I set off with a very austere and distant character called Bill Baker. It was a two-day trip. He refused to meet for a beer at the pub on the route. He also had nothing much to say until the end of my check out ride in the debriefing room when he calmly advised me that I'd failed and would have to go back for further training.

The DC-9, in common with its big brother the B727, had very strict engine spin-up rules on approach. In the early days of jet airliner operation there were quite a few disastrous crashes because pilots were getting low or slow on approach, calling for power, and finding that there was no immediate response.

Once landing configuration was set, that is undercarriage and flaps down below 800 feet, the engines had to be spun up to a minimum power, due to the fact that from idle the response time was quite long. If you were a bit fast or high, this was a difficult thing to do. The Electra had instant power response, so the spin-up rules didn't apply on that aircraft. Apparently, Bill my check out Captain wasn't satisfied with my application of these rules, so a fail it was for me!

As I'm very averse to failure, it was quite a shock to fail the check out ride for the DC-9 and it took me a while to get over it. However, a bit more time with Fred fixed the problem. Baker eventually went off to be a missionary in New Guinea, which explained a lot, I thought.

Shenanigans, but no 'tea and bikkies'

There were a few events while I was flying the 'pocket rocket'. One in particular could have been catastrophic. One of the aircraft had been operating on one generator for a few days, which I thought was a pretty poor show on the part of maintenance. Taxiing out at Sydney, I decided to try a bit of trouble shooting. I had the FO taxi while I fiddled with the generator switches. We were approaching a corner of the taxiway, with a TAA DC-9 stopped at the holding point just before the runway. I checked that the FO could get around the corner ok on his steering, then he shouted, "Ken, no brakes!" I immediately applied my brakes, but the pedals went right to the floor with no effect. The anti-skid system had been activated to give full brake release! The DC-9 ahead of us was looming large, and our options were disappearing fast. I returned the generator switches to their proper positions, the brakes were activated, and we came to a very sudden stop. A few seconds later and it would have been a major disaster. I doubt if I would have survived for the 'tea and bikkies' that surely would have followed.

About this time OMEGA was introduced. This was a worldwide tracking device based on three very low frequency radio stations placed around the world. One was to be in Gippsland, in Victoria. There were public demonstrations against it, as the antiwar groups thought it would make Lakes Entrance a nuclear target. Installed in the cockpit, on the pedestal between the two pilot seats, were many instruments. Alongside throttles, engine controls and radio selection boxes, there was a small keyboard like a pocket calculator and a dial with a needle on it to give direction. The idea was that we could track direct to our destination rather than zig zag from ground radio station to the next station, as was necessary up until then.

The concept was completely foreign at first, so it took some time to get used to operating it. As a navigation aid it was far from perfect. If there was any bad weather around, it would have a hissy fit and give up navigation just when it was most needed. If by some error of programming, it would have a fence or gate between waypoints, the needle would turn through 180 degrees and try to take you back to where you came from. It just had to be ignored temporarily, reset, pick up its signal, and start tracking again.

I was with a trainee one day when we ran into the dreaded gate issue! He was dumfounded and looked at me for an answer. "Shut the engines down," I said, "Otherwise we'll be trapped in this nether zone forever." The shocked look on his face was a joy to behold until I assured him I was only joking!

Another time with the same FO as the no-brakes-because-of-the-generator-switches incident, flying into Canberra, we ran right to the end of the runway, and turned into the taxiway. Unfortunately, a TAA aircraft had entered the taxiway from the other end, so there we were, nose to nose, without enough room to turn around! There was no tug to push us out of the way, so we were well and truly stuck.

The manual, which was our Bible, specifically banned any attempt at backing using reverse thrust, but I didn't see any other choice. Back up we did, onto the runway, so we could turn around and go behind the aircraft coming out. It was well and truly 'tea and bikkies' stuff but fortunately I never heard a word about it.

The DC-9 route structure was pretty much up and down the East coast, as it didn't really have the range to easily make the distance to Perth. Occasionally there'd be an overnight at Mackay in QLD. Generally, we'd arrive at midday, so I'd hire a Cessna from the local flight school. The FO and I, and sometimes the cabin crew would join us, and we'd fly out to one of the Whitsunday Islands, do a bit of snorkelling and sit by the pool, then fly back later. It seemed quite a natural thing to do then, but looking back, it was quite exotic.

An amusing event took place on a line trip from Adelaide to Sydney one day. We were flying along minding our own business, when one of the flight attendants called to tell us that a delegation of Middle Eastern farmers were on board and they wanted to know when we were over the Riverina irrigation area. I said I'd call her when we were just about over Griffith, and she could bring them to the cockpit as they'd get a better view that way.

Unfortunately, before we'd departed, the senior hostess (who was a bit of a case) had given a mother with two children a hard time as she interrogated one of the children as to its age. The senior hostess had got it into her head that the child was above the age where she'd be eligible for a free seat. The Traffic Officer told me that was why we were delayed and the mother and child were in tears. I told him to get off the plane, close the door and we'd depart.

Later the chief hostess came into the cockpit to tell us that there was a strange noise down near the tail. As the engines were at the tail it would be very strange if there was no noise! Very bad in fact! We told her that everything appeared normal to us and she went away.

Being a bit facetious, we put our uniform hats on backwards to pretend to be Japanese, when she came back we told her we thought it was Japanese soldiers who didn't know the war was over and were hiding in the tail. She took offence at our childish attempts at humour and insisted that I come back and check.

Just for peace and quiet I went to the back door, and there was just a small pressure leak of no account, when suddenly I was seized from behind in an attempt for her to have her way with my innocent body. She was a big woman, so my options to escape were very limited. I let my knees buckle, dropped to the floor and scrambled up the isle to escape. I imagine the passengers in the back rows were quite bemused to see the Captain crawling up the aisle on his hands and knees!

On the way back to the cockpit I stopped at the Middle Eastern gentlemen and told them to follow me to see the irrigation area. They squeezed between our two seats to look out the front window, when all of a sudden they were pulled backwards out of the cockpit! It was the dreaded Senior Hostess again. She'd decided that they were a security risk and had physically removed them. I sort of expected some sort of diplomatic complaint and 'tea and bikkies', but fortunately nothing came of it. I asked the FO whether he got the impression that this flight was completely out of control. He nodded wisely and we completed the flight in contemplative silence.

Occasionally we'd have a fractious passenger, due to drink, drugs, or just an excess of emotion and tiredness. We were preparing to depart Sydney for Hobart one day when the Senior Hostess on that flight told me that a passenger was behaving very strangely, and she didn't think he should travel. I went back into the cabin to find a very large Māori man with a youngish Australian woman. He looked rather agitated and out of sorts, and she was at pains to explain to me that they had to get to Hobart. Being a bit of a sucker for a good story I was tempted to tell them to behave, and we'd be on our way. All of a sudden, he stuck out a very large hand and took a firm hold of my crotch! Of course, all the other passengers were leaning out of their seats to see what the fuss was about. It's very hard to instantly know, what the correct protocol is when a very large hand has you by the crotch in front of 100 people! If you jump back too quickly and squeal, it may appear that you're a bit too sensitive, on the other hand if you stand there too long it might look like you like it. I managed to disengage myself and instruct security that he would have to be denied travel, on my flight anyway. Fortunately, I never heard another word about it.

While I was a DC-9 Captain a friend bought an ultralight aircraft. It was effectively a tube with a seat on it, a small instrument panel and control column, with a framework behind the seat to mount the small engine on and the fabric wing on top of that. I was invited to 'have a go' one day, so went to the country paddock where it lived and was briefed on its solo operation. Most of the advice was to reduce power after takeoff otherwise the engine might fail. I took off toward trees at the far end of the paddock, but unfortunately reduced power too much. An ultralight means just that: it's ultra-light! It has very little inertia due to weight, and a lot of drag, so due to my excessive reduction in power it very quickly headed down into the trees. I managed to recover, but was a bit shaken, then climbed up to about 1,000 feet and realised I was sitting on a kitchen chair a long way above the ground. I landed as quickly as I could and decided that I'd stick with airline flying after that.

Trouble in paradise

Looking back, it seemed as though I flew the DC-9 for quite some time, and trained quite a few pilots on it, but in fact it was only for a few years until in 1979 a well-known Sydney businessman, Peter Abeles, mounted a raid on Ansett and took it over. It was the second attempt that he'd made. For the first one, the Victorian Premier, Henry Bolt, stopped it by making a law that banned 'foreigners' that is citizens from outside Victoria, from having a controlling interest in a Victorian company. Australia's Federal system works well, but as a leftover from Colonial days, the states still have some excess powers, in my opinion.

As human nature hates change, but at the same time needs it, there was considerable disquiet within the company. It wasn't long before Abeles announced a complete revamp of the Ansett fleet. We saw ourselves as 'Reg's boys' and felt we had loyalty to him, but when Abeles quickly announced a whole suite of new aircraft orders, we felt a little better at the prospect. This meant promotion, and the chance to fly the latest equipment.

The two-airline policy was still very much in operation, which meant that only two domestic airlines were allowed to operate, (at this time Ansett and TAA) and they had to each fly the same number of seats to the same places at the same time. TAA was government-owned, and Ansett was owned by Ansett Transport Industries (ATI), supposedly private enterprise, but the actual owners were very well hidden.

Ownership of ATI was effectively taken over by Rupert Murdoch's News Corporation and Thomas Nationwide Transport or TNT, which was controlled by Peter Abeles. Abeles had made his fortune in road transport and association with up-and-coming politicians including Bob Hawke, (the future Prime Minister) and Neville Wran (future Premier of NSW). Abeles was able to follow the two-airline policy to the letter but not the spirit, hence introducing a completely different fleet to that flown by TAA. The two-airline policy was that both airlines had to have everything exactly the same. Seats, prices, aircraft, everything. Reg Ansett, in contrast to Abeles, did that to the letter.

Abeles and Murdoch took over in 1979, and in late 1980 amid a blaze of publicity a huge order was announced for many new Boeing aircraft. This included being the launch customer for the B767, Australia's first wide-body jet; new B727's that we already had; plus B737-200s to replace our DC-9s. I didn't have the seniority for a good spot on the B727 so I elected to go for the B737. The idea was that a group of five Training Captains would go to New Zealand to train on the Air NZ B737 so that when the new aircraft were delivered, we could train the ex-DC-9 pilots after the DC-9 was sold.

Unfortunately, my marriage to Piroska was floundering by then. Andrew was not coping with living with his mother's new partner, Ian, at Croydon with his stepbrothers, and was doing very badly at school. So, when I was told that I was to go to New Zealand for training with Air NZ, I didn't complain too much. In fact, I was glad to escape.

Times have changed so much now, with men expected to do so much more domestically, that it would be considered quite irresponsible for a husband to duck out like I did. But back then it was entirely normal.

At home flying the B737.

CHAPTER 19

The B737

Christchurch

In 1981 I left for Christchurch to begin my training. My training partner was Geoff Henderson who turned out to be very entertaining, but very odd. Four of us flew to Christchurch in an Air NZ DC-8, in First Class. We were very impressed as the large seats had very comfortable sheepskin covers. The drinks were very liberal and free, so some of us may have overindulged. An Air NZ reception committee was waiting for us when we arrived, all very proper New Zealand gentlemen, well attired in suit or blazer. Unfortunately, our Brisbane colleague was well out of it. He was sick down the front of his shirt, and fell of his stool. The Kiwis weren't impressed.

The time in Christchurch was quite remarkable. As it turned out, the B737 was delayed so we were left there to our own devices for about three months. A separate wing of the Russley hotel in Christchurch was reserved for us, about halfway between the airport and town. We had our own bar with a dedicated barmaid and a company car for our own use. Air NZ had hired recently retired B737 pilots to be our simulator instructors and they were both very good and very flexible. Since there were no time constraints on us, if we felt like doing something else on a particular day, we'd just change our simulator booking time to suit our plans.

The simulator was one of the first built for the B737 and the movement actuators were air-driven, so there was quite a delay between moving the controls and getting a reaction from the machine. It took quite a bit of getting used to. Over time we adapted to it and got by, but not to a very high standard I expect.

My training partner, Geoff Henderson, a very weird character. His social life was pretty well way out there, he was quite a pickup artist in bars and pubs. It was all very entertaining, but I was at pains to just be an onlooker and not a participant.

We'd hang out a bit at the local aero club. We decided that we'd hire one of their aircraft, a Piper Cherokee, and do a bit of local flying. Geoff's girlfriend was visiting from Melbourne so with her in the back seat we set off for the mountains to the West of Christchurch. Based on the fact that I'd flown a Piper Cub to the mountains in Austria, I elected myself to fly. We were aiming for Mt Hutt, a well-known ski resort. The little Piper was pretty underpowered so getting up to the top of the mountain was quite a task and we ended up circling beside the main slope, which was very spectacular! The girl wanted to take a photo, so even though we were on the point of a stall, Henderson insisted that we go 'round again. We were very close to the steep snow field, the sun was in my eyes, so all I could do was hold the bank angle, balanced on a pin head, and hope. The situation inside that little aeroplane was pretty tense, so when Jan said she didn't know what button to press on the camera, so could I circle once more, I think I got pretty snappy when I answered.

I Think I'm Going to Be an Airline Pilot

We repaired to the bar on our return for a recovery drink, and another of our group who was a bit of a barfly was there and when he heard what had happened, he promptly attempted to tell me how I should have done it. As he was failing at the simulator and hardly ever left the bar, I think I got snappy again. We called him the 'Chief Pilot' after that. I think he had an affair with the barmaid, (she must have been desperate) and he ultimately died of alcoholic poisoning. His main claim to fame was that when he was a crop-dusting pilot for the Premier of Queensland, Joe Bjelke-Petersen, he flew into a windmill and wrecked the Tiger Moth crop duster, as well as the windmill! It's amazing he survived.

Eventually we finished the simulator, but there were some exercises that could only be done in the aircraft itself. In Australia we didn't do asymmetric exercises at night, and didn't shut engines down, just closed the throttle to simulate an engine failure. It was considered too dangerous otherwise, as there'd been several serious accidents during training in the past. One well known accident was at Mangalore when a TAA Viscount session shut down two engines during an asymmetric on takeoff. It crashed and both the pilots were killed. AirNZ had also had two tragedies over the years on training details.

Henderson and I were detailed to a Kiwi instructor for a night asymmetric session out over the ocean. We raised our eyebrows, but were only there to do as we were told. We set off in the pitch black, and our fearless leader descended to a very low level then attempted to demonstrate an engine-out low speed manoeuvre.

Unfortunately, it didn't work very well. The instructor reduced the power to almost nothing on one engine, and the test began. The aircraft looked very much like it was going to get away from us and dive into the ocean. I was in the pilot's seat so was able to concentrate on recovery, by bringing power up on the dead engine then levelling out and climbing away, but Geoff in the jump seat behind me was quite vocal as he was thrown around unable to do anything but hang on. We flew home very quietly after that.

Like all good things, our life of ease and luxury in Christchurch had to come to an end, so back home to Melbourne I came once I'd finished my training. Back home to a great deal of distress and confusion, too.

The early 80's; a fraught time

Piri and I had ordered a new project house from a company called Glenville Homes. They'd promised the world but unfortunately failed to deliver. Our Bayview Crescent house at Black Rock had been sold, so we were homeless!

The timing was ok for me as at the time, I was on my way to New Zealand, but relations between Andrew and Piri were not good at all. He went back to his mother's, and Piri and the cat moved in with friends a few doors up the road: John and Jenny Tebbutt, and their two young children, Sarah and Sam. By the time I turned up, relations were pretty strained between everyone, and with no house to go to things were messy.

Eventually, the house in St Andrews Court, Black Rock, was finished so we moved in. It was just a bare bones house, so there was lots of work still to be done. As I was waiting for our new B737's to arrive I fortunately had plenty of free time to build a garage, put in a pool, build a garden etc. As it was a new court, all the neighbours were in the same boat, so we all had quite a nice time helping each other.

Unfortunately, Andrew just wasn't doing at all well at school, and relations at home weren't going well either, so I decided the best thing for him would be a country boarding school. Based on the fact that he'd be locked in at night with monitored homework and no bad outside influences, I selected Hamilton College at Hamilton, about three-hour drive West of Melbourne. Coincidently, it was also the birthplace of Ansett Airlines.

However, a leopard doesn't change its spots, so Andrew didn't fit in very well there either. Meanwhile, Simon, who had stayed at home with his mother and stepfather, was in a much worse position. He was being bullied badly by his stepbrothers, but being very quiet, hadn't said anything to me about it at all.

The whole scene in the early 80's was far from pleasant. I did something that would be considered completely unacceptable today: I went with Geoff Henderson to Oshkosh in Wisconsin USA to the huge amateur fly-in there, leaving the whole mess behind. Henderson was very weird as I've said before. He'd leave notes here and there for me from a girl that was stalking me (which was totally fictitious), I believed it (being a sucker), so it was a very fraught time. It wasn't until many years later that I found out it was him, even though he denied it absolutely at the time.

On the way back from Oshkosh we travelled via Seattle, in order to have a look at the Boeing factory. We had a letter from the flight department identifying us as Ansett staff, so we presented ourselves at the factory office. We were allocated an executive to show us around. Ansett was the launch customer for the new, state-of-the-art B767 wide-body. When we were shown into the cabin, with a lot of workers on the job, our presence was announced, work stopped, and everyone stood up as we passed. It was very embarrassing! Later we were treated to lunch on the company boat and given gifts to take home. It turns out that the designated guide had the misguided impression that we were the actual customers, rather than just pilots!

A side issue with the guide was that Henderson (Captain Weird) started to regale him with his activities in Manila. I'll leave it to your imagination, but the stories included busses with blacked out windows, and a bar called the Angel bar. Our guide became very excited and for two bob would have followed Captain Weird to Manila on the spot!

Eventually, the shiny new B737-200 turned up. They were quite advanced compared to the Air NZ 737s which were basic models, so it was quite a shock working out the new systems on the planes that got delivered to Ansett that we hadn't seen before. They carried about eight more passengers than the old DC-9 but were quite a bit slower.

There was an event called the 'Great Australian Air Race'. The two airlines would depart at the same time to the same destination. Whoever could get away first would get the best cruising levels and win the race to the terminal. It didn't really matter to the passengers, but it was a lot of fun.

As we were still competing on the same routes as TAA in their DC-9s the company in their wisdom scheduled a shorter turnaround time for when we were on the ground. As we had to learn to set up all the new gadgets, this took us longer than it should have in the beginning, so we'd fall further and further behind. Eventually we got a handle on it all, but it was galling to watch the competition creep ahead of us all the time. Training continued apace to introduce the new fleet, and about this time Peter Abeles, in an attempt to break the monopoly that QANTAS held on international routes, started Air Vanuatu. He also started a route from Hobart to Christchurch, and later took over the management of Air Polynesia as well.

Venturing to Vanuatu

I very quickly became Mr. Vanuatu! An Ansett B737 would depart Sydney for Vila on Friday or Sunday. This meant that the crew stayed there either for the weekend, or from Monday to Friday. The flights took about three hours and were generally routine but sometimes the dreaded inter-tropic zone, (two weather patterns colliding) would set a line of thunderstorms for many miles along our track. Our navigation was via an OMEGA device. It unfortunately didn't work very well when electrical interference was nearby, like thunderstorms. Not only did you have to find a way between massive tropical storms without encountering severe turbulence, but there was no way to check our position over the trackless ocean without navigation information. It was necessary, while avoiding such weather, to continue on a compass heading until OMEGA picked up the signal again.

I found Vila to be a very nice place. The old French influence meant that there were a few classic French restaurants, and the hotel we stayed at, The Intercontinental, had lovely gardens right on the lagoon. The pace of life there was very relaxed and the crew and I would have a very nice time there indeed. An extra bonus was the allowance for duty free grog once a month on return. We had a little book that had to be filled in for Customs in Sydney.

Once, I'd bought my prized allowance, but when I stood at the Customs counter, the bottle tipped over and broke. The Customs officer still insisted on filling in my logbook. Against my protests, he said the grog was on Australian soil, so I'd used my allowance! That's the public service for you.

Being a very keen reader, I'd read a lot of the 'Tales of the South Pacific' and am not averse to flights of fancy occasionally. On one of my early trips there, I was invited to a local's house for a BBQ. Another guest was a native gentleman who'd been a skipper of a trading schooner that traded around the Islands. Sitting under the tropical stars next to the jungle listening to his wonderful tales of adventure was a particularly memorable night for me.

On another occasion on a trip to Tahiti with Piroska, we visited a Pacific Island trading schooner anchored on a lagoon. With the clear water down to the bottom and brightly coloured fish visible swimming everywhere it was very romantic. If stories of the South Pacific are interesting to you, I suggest you read Jack London, his tales of trading around the Islands at the turn of the 19th century are a great read.

A very nice problem to have was filling in the days while we were in Vila between flights. There was a local airline that had Britten Norman Islanders and Twin Otters that ran a daily service around the remote Islands. North of Vila was the big Island of Espiritu Santo. An Islander aircraft was based there, along with a Kiwi pilot and his Fijian wife, who was the local travel agent. Santo had been a significant US navy base during the war, and it was also the site for the book and film South Pacific. It was arranged for me to fly there, stay overnight with the Kiwi and have a look around. The chap was very pleasant, and his wife was away visiting family in Fiji. We walked through the jungle to a few wartime wrecks and in general had a very nice time.

When I got back, there was a reception committee waiting for me. "How did you go?" they asked in unison. I told them, and was very surprised to see the look of disappointment on their faces. It turned out that the wife, a very large Fijian woman, was prone to having her way with innocent male visitors like me. The story went, that if the visitor wasn't prepared to do his duty, rage at rejection and a good punching would follow! I had been set up, and counted myself very fortunate that she wasn't at home.

Another local trip was to the Island of Tanna. An active volcano well to the South of Vila. The cabin crew came with me. I sat in the right-hand pilot seat of a twin Otter. The pilot was a taciturn French man. We dropped the girls at Tanna, and I stayed on for a return trip to another remote Island. On the way back to Tanna, attempting to break the ice, I asked the pilot if he had flown these planes in Papua New Guinea. He just grunted. As we flew along, he indicated that I should fly. I steered for a while, and as we approached our grass strip on the side of a hill, cut out of the jungle, I kept expecting him to take over. He didn't! I did quite a creditable job of the approach and landing, but got stuck trying to select reverse pitch on the props. The result was that we went bounding down the runway until he took over and we stopped at the end of the runway in a cloud of dust. He looked at me, and said, "You flew these in New Guinea?" I'd never even been in one before. The girls waiting at the tin shed that was the terminal said that they thought the landing was quite spectacular!

Next morning, I thought I'd go for a bit of a jog along a track through the jungle behind the grass hut that was my accommodation. I was huffing and puffing along, quite isolated, rounded a bend, and standing in the middle of the track was a native man. He was quite naked, except for a penis gourd, a bone through his nose, and a clutch of spears in his hand. I couldn't see many options for escape, so just kept running, and raised a hand in greeting as I passed him, to which he nodded politely as I continued on my way. I had visions of me in the cooking pot as per the old Phantom comics. In the old days cannibal activities were normal among the tribes!

At this time the John Frome (cargo) cult was alive and well, as there was a large American supply base there during the war. The locals believed that if they worshipped aeroplanes, unlimited riches would be given to them, as had been delivered during the war years. The missionaries' message was obviously lost in translation.

The whole purpose of going to Tanna was to see the active volcano on the Island. Two of the girls and I were put in the back of a ute and bounced along a bush track for some time up to the tree line on the volcano. It was shanks pony from then on (that means that we had to walk). We were surrounded by bare grey sand and black boulders on a very steep slope. As we neared the lip of the caldera the pumice under foot was getting hotter and hotter. Being the tropics, I only had sandals on, which were not really suitable footwear for climbing volcanoes.

Along with our guide, we breasted the lip, a short slope down to a vertical drop into the mouth of the mountain. Puffs of steam were coming out of the ground all around us, and I judged it was very important not to get too close to the edge, as once you started to slip there was nothing to grab to stop the slide. Later, I did notice that the others had stayed on the peak, rather than moving down to look into the void below.

All of a sudden, there was a deep rumble and boulders the size of houses were ejected up from the bottom of the caldera! Some of them glowed red hot before they fell back into the void. Groups of smaller rocks started to pitter patter down on the slope around me, so I decided it was time to make a retreat. The feeling of having looked down into the bowels of the earth stayed with me for a long time. The UN, who provided a lot of aid to Vanuatu, were keen to make Tanna into a tourist destination, but as far as I know nothing came of it. Certainly there would have to be a lot of effort put into health and safety procedures before travel insurance would cover it.

However, it wasn't all beer and skittles! The approach into Vila by plane, always after dark, was quite challenging. The runway was in a valley with a hill at each end. This meant that a curved approach was required. We had to descend over the pitch-black sea, track towards a very low powered radio aid of only about 10 nm range and a green light on a small island off the coast. From the island there were strobe lights at intervals that curved towards the start of the runway. Unfortunately, the slope guidance lights were different to anything we had in Australia and the runway had a slope to it that threw out the perspective that we were used to judging for approach.

While challenging, with practise and concentration I could nail it pretty well. It was a different story though when the weather was unpleasant, with rain or fog the worst offenders. We arrived there one night and all seemed well, but on the approach the strobes were being reflected by mist. This made it very difficult to judge both rate of turn and descent. During the descending turn, trying not to be blinded by the reflected strobes, I called for full flap, only to have the indicator for a jammed flap turn on. This meant that the landing speed would be faster so the rate of turn had to be adjusted for the faster speed. Also, if we couldn't land we wouldn't have enough fuel to divert to Noumea with the flaps stuck out. Nightmare stuff!

I had no choice but to continue on. There was just enough runway visible to land on, but we ran straight into fog. I could only try to keep it straight, and stop as quickly as possible. Luck plays a big part in life, and on that occasion if I'd been a few minutes later my only choice would have been to land in the ocean in the dark. Fortunately, most of the Vila trips were routine.

We were so used to the very good organisation of the airline in Australia, sometimes it was quite a shock at the events that unfolded once we left home. The runway wasn't long enough in Vila to carry a full load of passengers plus enough fuel to reach Sydney – if we had a large load, it was necessary to stop at Noumea for fuel. The Sunday flight left at midnight, in order to have the aircraft back in Australia, ready for its domestic work.

Sydney had a 06:00 curfew, which meant no landings could take place before then, so the departure time had to be adjusted depending on whether we were going directly to Sydney or stopping at Noumea for fuel.

One Sunday, I told the airport staff, that if there were less than 40 passengers, (the maximum we could carry plus the weight of the fuel to fly direct) we would delay our departure and fly direct. So I told them that in this case they were to advise the pax (passengers) and call me at the pub to relay the delayed time. I heard nothing when I was at the pub, so slept soundly, until I was woken by a loud knock on my door. It was the security guard telling me the phone was ringing in the hotel office, and that it was the airport trying to contact me. I staggered to the phone in my pyjamas, half asleep, only to hear, "The pax are all on board, sir. How much fuel do you need?" It was a mad rush to wake the crew, get to the airport and depart. Fortunately, the payload was light enough for us to carry enough fuel to make Sydney direct, without much of a delay.

Another time, the aircraft was significantly over-fuelled for the payload, so we were well above our takeoff weight. There was a de-fuelling truck that was for exactly this purpose, but it was outside the airport fence and nobody had the key to the gate. My only option was to take off, fly around the Island for a bit to use up the excess fuel, land and pick up the pax to depart. I expected a 'tea and bikkies' call, but nothing happened. Fortunately, being 'out of sight, out of mind' sometimes had its advantages.

Eventually the runway was improved at Vila and the B727 took over, but my time at Vanuatu remains a very pleasant memory.

Training times

Meanwhile, the line training on the B737 continued, and I was pretty much engaged with a trainee full time. Then the B737-300 was introduced, it had about another ten seats more than the B737-200 and was a full glass cockpit. It flew pretty much the same as the 200 though. Over time I became the go-to guy for remedial training. That is, training the pilots who were transitioning to the B737 and having difficulties. I also trained new Captains who had failed previously, been permanent FO's and after pressure from the union were being given another go.

Sometimes, it wasn't in my best interests to get them through and help them pass, as they had a higher seniority number than me so when they checked out they could outbid me for other assignments. I learnt a lot about human nature while I was attempting to nurture, support and teach someone who was struggling with the tasks necessary to reach the standard to be checked out as a Captain.

It's very much the 'Peter principle', where people are promoted to a level at or above their competence. In general, they were quite good pilots, but when they had to think as Captains (make decisions under pressure sometimes) and fly the aircraft properly at the same time, they were found lacking. I would try all sorts of tricks to get their minds on the right track. Putting them under pressure to have to make decisions on their own without being able to turn to me was a classic technique that I used.

One of the chaps, a very nice Frenchman, would do anything he could to avoid taking decisive action. I'd tell him I was going to the toilet, leave the cockpit and not come back. I'd wait outside the cockpit door until past the descent point just to see what he'd do. It was very tense-making, as often as not he'd just keep cruising along, until I'd burst in, call for descent and have to force a much steeper descent rate than normal to get back on profile. He'd been a FO for so long he just couldn't seem to understand that now he had to work these things out for himself.

That particular man got through in the end, and promptly took a spot on the B767 that I would have got otherwise, which would have made a big difference to my superannuation. However, I got a great deal of satisfaction from helping him along the way.

Human factors

In the mid-eighties the air transport community worldwide was realising that nearly all of the accidents that were happening were due to what they termed 'human factors'. That is, events in which humans were bound to make errors due to the circumstances in which they found themselves. These errors could be due to the design of the systems, or the psychological environment at the time.

In other words, it was no longer considered good enough to just say an accident was caused by pilot error, then sit back and wait for the next one. As aircraft were getting bigger and more expensive, a way had to be found to reduce accidents caused by human factors. Ansett's training manager had a good look around the world and came up with the system used by KLM in Holland. He called for volunteers, of which I was one, to be trained by the British chap who ran the system there. It was a series of videos, followed by group discussion led by a facilitator/moderator, which turned out to be me. As well, we were sent to the Hawthorn Institute for a course on how to teach a skill to skilled people. It was very interesting. My class had police, nurses, firemen and pilots, and some very strong discussions resulted during the classes. I wouldn't have missed it for quids.

Running the day at the Ansett training school gave me insights into human behaviour that I wouldn't have otherwise had, and also gave me a day off flying which made for quite a nice change. I always had a monthly block of flying to complete in order to continue with the training that was required as new pilots came onto the type, or some poor soul needed a bit of extra time and TLC to get him up to the required standard. (I say 'him' as there were only one or two female pilots then.)

About that time, I was sent out to Apia in Western Samoa with FO Steve Mikonos and an Ansett aircraft to fly the Polynesian Airlines (Now Samoa Airways) routes around the Pacific as their aircraft went into the hangar for scheduled maintenance. We flew all night to get there, so by the time I got to the pub on the other side of the Island in Apia, it was mid-morning, I was exhausted, the air conditioning was very noisy, so the only way to get some sleep was leave the door open and the air conditioner off.

After a fitful few hours I gave up trying to sleep, called Steve to arrange lunch, and went to pick up my wallet off the bedside table. It was gone! Someone had come into the room, picked it up and gone on their way undetected. There was no way to replace the money, credit cards hadn't come to Samoa at that point, so my FO Steve had to pay for both of us wherever we went. I was like an aristocrat who never carried filthy lucre and left it to the staff to deal with such things. Steve, who was very clever, went on to great things a few years later as a management pilot with Cathay Pacific.

Operating out of Samoa was very different to the well-organised domestic operations in Australia – rather like flying out of Vila. The pace of life and the sophistication of life on a Pacific Island was very slow, compared to that which we were used to. After a suitable rest, Steve and I were scheduled for a trip to Tonga, then Auckland overnight, and a return to Apia the next day. We arrived at the airport earlier than usual and the Traffic Officers had a weather forecast for us. Unfortunately, it was several days old. We repaired to the control tower to see if we could do better. The control tower looked quite modern, and had been built with a United Nations grant, but there was a family along with chickens, dogs, babies etc, living in the entrance lobby and up the stairs. We managed to get to the top, only to find very large Samoan Air Traffic Controllers asleep on the consoles in the sun. As there was only one land line back to Australia, and it had to be booked in advance, the best we could find was a provisional forecast which was about 15 hours old. That had to do!

Back at the terminal, the local Traffic Officer asked me how many passengers we could carry. Obviously, I said the number of seats, 105 I think it was. Well, we have about 120 booked he said, and also told me that they were all travelling as family and refused to be separated. Quite at a loss, I said he'd have to sort it out as I wasn't getting between a huge Samoan mamma and her kids. When the load sheet eventually arrived, I chose not to look at the number of souls on board!

The next issue was that of alternate fuel for Tonga. As we had no up-to-date forecast, and there was no emergency power for the radio aids there, we had to carry enough fuel to fly to an alternate stop if we couldn't land at our destination. Auckland was too far away, there was no way that we could return to Apia, so the only suitable airport with the payload we had (which as I've said, was entirely fictitious) was an island called Niue. Unfortunately, there was no record of fuel being available there. I said to the Traffic Officer, "What if we can't get into Tonga and divert to Niue?"

"We'll send a ship with fuel," he said, deadpan! Imagine, being on Niue with more than 100 pax, plus crew, waiting for a ship to deliver enough fuel to depart. We set off well behind schedule, but Samoan time, and the timetables we thought we should keep, were quite different things. The local cabin crew's idea of schedule was Samoan not Australian. They were just wonderful, perhaps too wonderful, as later pilots got very involved with the cabin crew girls from Samoa, regardless of marital obligations back in Melbourne. But that's another story!

The cabin crew convinced me that they'd been working very hard and were very tired. I am by nature a sucker for a good story, so I believed them. I offered them a delayed sign-on time for the morning departure, provided that they promised that we could depart Auckland roughly on time in the morning. Looking me straight in the eye, cross your heart hope to die, they promised. FO Steve and I arrived at the airport at the required time, did what we had to do, but swiftly it became apparent that there was no cabin crew! With some difficulty, I found their motel phone number, and a phone, managed to get through to the seniors' room, and asked where on earth they were. A very sleepy voice answered, "Oh yes Captain, we come soon!"

"But you're still in bed!" I replied.

"Oh yes," she said.

"But you promised," I said.

"Oh yes," she said, "We come soon."

They turned up about an hour later, all smiles, not a worry in the world. We were very late departing and once again I expected 'tea and bikkies' but it was, after all, Samoa, so nothing ever happened.

CHAPTER 20

More change on the home front

Relations, breakdowns and dates

Meanwhile, relations between Piri and I had deteriorated to the extent that there was no point in continuing as a couple, so we decided to go our own ways. I stayed on in the project home and she went on to stay with Idun and Don Chip, whom we'd befriended via Geoff and Trish Robinson. Don was an ex-politician, who'd started a political party called the Australian Democrats. Their slogan was 'Keep the bastards honest', as they had no hope of ever forming government. It didn't work out very well for Piri, as Don would engage in actions that would be termed sexual harassment today. So eventually, Piri moved into a flat of her own.

Our separation was quite amicable until a young Hungarian 'flat mate' moved in with her, and turned her very much against me, so that lawyers became involved, which was quite a shame, but it all turned out ok in the end. I haven't seen her from that day to this, but time takes the rough edges from bad memories, so I only remember the good bits of her character. Towards the end of 2018 I heard that she'd died of cancer. Out of curiosity, and for old time's sake I went to her funeral, and all the right things were said. She'd married a German chap and apparently they'd had a good life together. Even if it was a character building experience for me, taken in total I can only look on that period of my life with affection.

After that, it was the life of a single person for me! I ended up selling the house at Black Rock and buying a duplex at Sandringham. Boarding school had proved to be untenable for Andrew, so at the end of year 11 he either had to repeat or leave. He was adamant that he wouldn't stay, so I then became a single parent. Our life together was not much of a success, I'm afraid. I wasn't as good a father as I could have been, and he wasn't as good a son! Fortunately, we survived and I'm full of admiration of him and Mary his wonderful wife. They are by any measure a very successful couple.

Occasionally I'd go on dates, but none of them would have been called a success.

A classic story is that a couple fall in love first, and then become friends over time. Jenny and I did it the other way: we became good friends, then as Jenny and John Tebbutt had run into marital difficulties, and decided to separate, we fell in love. I eventually moved into her house at Brighton, and we got married in 1987. We're just about to celebrate our 35th wedding anniversary as I'm writing this. It was probably the luckiest thing that's ever happened to me. It's been a wonderfully happy and successful partnership, and I hope it goes on forever!

Jenny's two children were pretty young back then, Sam was 10 or 11 and Sarah was 12 or 13. As a stepfather I had to adjust to belonging to a family where the children were 'fully cooked', so to speak. I had no trouble deciding to be fully committed to their welfare and happiness, but with hindsight I don't think that I took enough consideration of their willingness to accept a replacement father into their lives.

In an attempt to bond and blend a new family, I arranged all sorts of outdoor activities that we could do together. We hired a 'Gypsy Caravan' with a horse, to trek around the byways and bushland of Gippsland. It was a wonderful adventure. Jenny and Sarah slept in the wagon, and Sam and I in our swags under the stars. Bluebell, the horse, was tethered at night on a rope between two trees with her feed bag on. By the time we'd walked beside the wagon all day and cooked tea on the campfire we'd sleep like logs. Sarah, being the bossy one, (she still is) would insist on driving, and she did a good job of it too. Bluebell was so well trained that she didn't need much control, she pretty much knew what to do. But there was one spot that her owner had warned us about, where Bluebell imagined that there were monsters and sometimes shied, as she walked past.

Sarah was driving and Sam was walking beside Bluebell when the horse without warning leapt to one side. She whacked Sam, who tumbled off the road into the bush. The only thing hurt was his pride, and he took terrible umbrage to our hysterical laughter at him. He didn't think it was funny at all, but we did! Bluebell just resumed her steady gait as if nothing had happened.

Jenny in every respect is a very impressive person. She went to a selective high school, (MacRobertson High in Melbourne) the highest-ranking girl's school in Victoria, and held down a very good job at Rio Tinto mining company. One of her most endearing characteristics is being prepared to have a go at something new. I've never been any good at ball sports, something incidentally that she excels at, but I wasn't a bad sailor, so in the mid-80's

Jenny agreed for us to hire a bare boat at the Whitsunday Islands, South of the Barrier Reef.

Our first boat was called *Kepock*, an 8-metre yacht. It was quite small, but enough for the two of us. Unfortunately, it was full of cockroaches, which gave Jenny pause, but she took to self-crewed sailing like a duck to water. We'd sail island to island during the day, and anchor in secluded bays at night. It was just perfect. Some of the anchorages are in spots that are subject to 'bullets'! These are bays sheltered by hills from the prevailing Southeasterly winds. The wind would build up pressure during the night, then it would burst over the hill and down into the bay. We'd be sound asleep, when all of a sudden, a howling wind would lean the boat over and rattle the halyards and pull the boat up short on the anchor chain. There was not a light to be seen outside, so it was easy to believe that monsters were coming to carry us away or worse, until we got used to it each night.

On one of our trips, the boat that we'd booked wasn't available. The only other choice was the *Christiane*. It was more of a ship really, a 17-metre yacht, with all facilities and everything electric, including sail and anchor hoists. We just loved it, and because of its size we could go outside the main islands towards the reef. We spent a bit of time in a beautiful bay, snorkelling and fishing. Approaching cocktail hour, I decided to have another swim. We went over to the shore in the dingy, and Jenny stepped out onto a smooth sloping rock but unfortunately her wet feet slipped down to the waterline, which was covered in oyster shells. The soles of her feet were ripped to pieces. She was in severe pain, and almost instantly red infection started to spread up her leg. What were we to do? It was getting dark, and we were completely isolated. We bathed her feet as best we could, but it was a long night, and at first light we set off for Hamilton Island.

It took until about lunch time to get there. I took her straight up to the doctor's, who took as many of the shells out of the cuts as he could without anaesthetic and recommended that she get the next flight home. As it turned out, he'd done a good job, as he'd got all the foreign objects out of her feet and antibiotics stopped any further infection.

However, I was stuck on a big yacht that had to be delivered back to Airlie Beach. Fortunately, due to all the electric winches, I could operate everything from the cockpit solo. I set off, anchored at Hayman Island overnight, and next morning sailed up the Whitsunday passage, with a strong following wind, the stereo at full volume, a can of beer in my hand, reaching up to ten knots. It was a wonderful experience for me, but unfortunate for Jenny. Luckily, it all turned out ok in the end.

Jenny and I on my older brother's yacht in Sydney.

We did quite a bit of sailing in those early days. My brother Robert had a 12-metre yacht in Sydney that he was happy to lend us occasionally, so spending a few days on our own sailing around Pittwater or Sydney Harbour was just wonderful. Cottage Point and Clareville Beach are spots where we'd stay overnight and just loved to visit. A yacht hired on Gippsland Lakes with the kids was great also.

Work travel

I was rostered on a trip from Sydney to Alice Springs (ASP) and when I turned up for work, I was told that a Captain Ken Mulgrew from Air NZ would be riding with us in the jump seat. I assumed that he was from the new airline that I would soon be going to as an instructor in New Zealand, to be called Ansett NZ. However, it turned out that he was the manager of the Air NZ B767 fleet. As they had a trip direct from Auckland to Singapore, the New Zealand civil aviation department required that airports along the way that could be used to land in an emergency should be investigated and Ken was it.

Ken turned out to be quite a remarkable man. As well as being a management pilot he was a qualified ship's Captain. His brother Peter had climbed the Himalayas with Sir Edmund Hillary, and the brothers had also sailed the Horn of Africa on their own on a chartered yacht. His brother sadly was killed when the Air NZ DC-10 he was on crashed into Mt Erebus in the Antarctic in 1979. The FO was a graduate of the highly regarded California University of Music. Even though I was the Captain of the flight, I felt very mundane in comparison! When we moved to New Zealand later, Ken and I became good friends, but I'll talk about that in due course.

At around the time Ken and I flew to Alice Springs, Ansett was taking delivery of a new fleet of B737-300s. The fleet manager David James was responsible for their delivery and I was asked to join him in bringing one back from Seattle. Rather than going on my own, I took some leave and arranged to fly with Jenny to Los Angeles (LAX) on an Air New Zealand flight crewed by Ken Mulgrew. I went to the cockpit for the arrival at LAX and my eyes were like saucers. I'd never seen such complexity and amount of air traffic before. After a few days with Ken in LA we hired a car and set out to drive to Seattle. It was a wonderful trip, up the coast past Pebble Beach, inland via Yosemite National Park, to Lake Tahoe where the water is so clear that the bottom can be seen about 100 metres down. We drove back down to the coast via Portland, Oregon then on to Seattle. It took us about a week and was a wonderful trip. Better yet, it was all expenses paid.

The car we hired was a revelation. It was a Buick and it had all the warning noises that are normal now but weren't then. We found them very annoying. The most disconcerting thing was that when you got in and closed the door, the seat belt extended across you! It took a bit of getting used to – as well as driving on the wrong side of the road, of course.

Once in Seattle, we met up with David and he took us to a local restaurant for dinner. The waiter came out wearing a Melbourne Australian Football League (AFL) scarf. He'd heard our accent and wanted to tell us that he was a fan of the Aussie rules football that he watched on cable TV. It was a long time before cable was available in Australia, so it seemed very exotic to us.

Dave and I had to spend a bit of time at the Boeing factory for Dave to take care of the details of taking possession of the new aircraft. I was standing outside the hangar one day when a new B747-400 came in after a test flight. It only just fitted on the taxiway and I remember thinking, "Who are those men that can fly such a thing?" I never imagined that'd be me one day!

CHAPTER 21

Some time in New Zealand

Previous to our trip to Seattle, I'd been asked to be part of the team that was to move to New Zealand to help start a new airline there. The New Zealand airline market was very highly regulated, with the only operator allowed being the government-owned Air New Zealand (Air NZ). Peter Ables (Ansett's new owner) thought he'd found a way around this. He'd bought a bus company there that had a charter licence that allowed them to operate larger aircraft to fly tourists around the country. He planned to start an airline using Ansett expertise, New Zealand staff and the bus company licence, to compete with Air NZ. It was to be called 'Ansett New Zealand'. Deregulation had taken off in the US and was spreading around the world, so entrepreneurs like Ables were doing their best to take advantage of it. The plan was that a swag of Kiwi pilots who had been flying around the world would be hired, and five senior Ansett Training Captains would move to New Zealand to train them. Then, when enough locals were in place, the Ansett Captains would return to Australia.

I was very keen to go, but only if Jenny and the kids could come too. I put it to the managers that if they'd pay the equivalent of a room in a hotel for me, I'd rent a house and cover the difference with my salary. A Captain from MacRobertson Miller, a subsidiary company in Western Australia, was detailed to be in charge. He made it pretty difficult to arrange things that weren't run-of-the-mill as he had an ego problem and went to a lot of trouble to make sure everyone knew he was in charge. But we got it sorted out in the end, and were in New Zealand for about a year all up.

We did not get Sarah and Sam's father's permission to take them away, which was a mistake. This went on to cause some difficulties in the future, which could have been avoided if we'd been a bit more thoughtful at the time.

We duly arrived in Christchurch, found ourselves a delightful motel with a family suite, and Jenny settled Sam and Sarah in the local schools. New Zealand was very restricted on cars at the time. Tariffs were very high, so the only cars were English, and they were very expensive. I don't quite know how I did it, but I managed to have our Holden Commodore shipped over to Christchurch from Melbourne. This gave Jenny and the kids a great deal of mobility, so they could do some exploring while I was at work.

And boy, did I work. The powers that be had greatly underestimated the time it would take to train the locals. None of them had any jet experience, and the adjustment to mainline airline standards was a bit hard for them to grasp. For instance, my first trainee couldn't understand why he wasn't allowed to dive down through a hole in the clouds whenever he saw one and continue flying visually. That's just not what airlines do. Another trainee was failed by a visiting Check Captain from Melbourne as he didn't know that life jackets were required for crossing Cook Straight. Unfathomable.

I Think I'm Going to Be an Airline Pilot

This lack of competence amongst the trainees meant that I and my fellow instructors had to do nearly all the line flying at the same time as trying to get the new pilots up to speed. I ended up doing 600 hours of flying in six months, which was the maximum possible, and this with very short sectors as well.

Ansett NZ had built new terminals at Auckland and Christchurch, bought several B737-100s and had had them refurbished. The 100s looked great, with an all-white colour scheme and all new upholstery. Sadly, they were the first B737s ever built and mechanically they were very old and tired, with a big shortage of spare parts as well. After the aircraft in Ansett that were kept in perfect operating condition, it was a bit of a shock flying with multiple malfunctions going on, and a lack of spare parts to fix them.

Unfortunately, our new leader from Western Australia continued to have a bit of an ego problem, and decided he wasn't going to be upstaged by the mainline Ansett pilots, so there was some abrasion settling in. He got over himself eventually, and after a differences course and endorsement on the aircraft we were ready to begin. A 'differences course' is a training module on the differences between the model of aeroplane you're licensed to fly and the new one you're being trained on. That way you don't spend time repeating information you already know. This course was for us as pilots to get used to flying the 737-200 advanced, as opposed to the 737-100s.

As I was the senior instructor, and my main role in Australia was to do remedial training, I was responsible for training the ones who were having difficulties – again. As I mentioned earlier, I was allocated an Englishman for training. He was ex-Royal Air Force (RAF) who'd migrated to New Zealand and had been flying propeller aircraft there. Sadly, my English trainee turned out to be a dud. He'd migrated in the hope of a better life for himself and his family and was a very pleasant and urbane chap on the ground, but completely out of his depth in command of a jet. His errors were manifold. He would turn downwind at Auckland at about six thousand feet, (when it should have been about 1,500) I'd ask him how he thought he was placed, and he'd be perfectly confident that he was fine. He never seemed to 'get it' that in airline flying, certain parameters had to be met. He was oblivious that he wasn't getting anywhere near any of them.

Wellington was always a challenge for anyone, but for him it was impenetrable. Wellington was always windy; I think the most wind that I'd landed with there was about 70 knots, fortunately, mostly down the runway. It was nearly always night when we arrived there, and often as not, raining. Approaching one night in the rain over Cook Straight, when it was very black, I couldn't pick out the runway. My English trainee swore black and blue that he had it in sight. As we got closer, I saw that it was a row of streetlights running up a hill, quite some way from the runway! To complicate matters, there was a short delay when one radio aid was turned off before the one that lined up with the runway came on, so after me taking over, we were very much in the dark and heading towards rising ground. It was not a good situation to be in. Obviously, I'm telling the tale, so no harm was done. But it was not the sort of activity to be encouraged.

Another night, also in Wellington, after he'd made a mess of it yet again, we taxied in to the aerobridge, and about three metres short of where we were meant to stop, he just reached out and shut down the engines. He then just slumped in his seat, comatose. I managed to get a tug to pull us the rest of the way to the bridge but could get no response at all from my companion. What to do? The obvious thing would have been to call an ambulance, cancel the flight and leave the passengers who were on their way to Auckland stranded. You could imagine the publicity: "Pilot has nervous breakdown on new foreign airline!" His hopes of making a go of it in New Zealand would have been dashed, and the expense of keeping us all in Wellington for the night would have added to the indignity as well. For better or for worse, I moved his seat back as far as possible, locked his harness to minimise him thrashing about, and flew on to Auckland on my own. He walked to the cab and into the hotel on his own, and next morning came down as if nothing had happened. I was at quite a loss.

In the end, he gave up of his own accord and I think he became a co-pilot on the Dash-8, a 30-seater propeller aircraft. He couldn't do much harm there.

Quite a few years later, Jenny and I did a trip to Queenstown in New Zealand, and I said that if Alan Davenport was the pilot, we were getting off the plane. I think he was on a later flight where I heard they shut down an engine. To have been on that flight would have been most unsettling, and I'm glad I wasn't.

Inaugural collywobbles

I was rostered to do the inaugural flight from the new terminal in Auckland. The press, notables, and general freebies were gathered in the very plush lounge overlooking the bright and shiny new-looking but very old B737-100. Cocktails were flowing freely. We started doing our pre-departure checklist, only to have a leading-edge flap failure light came on. This was a no-go item, we wouldn't be able to depart! I called the ground engineer, he went away to investigate, and came back on the phone a short time later to tell me that the switch bracket had failed, and it was hanging only by its wire. There were no spares.

We went down and were standing in the dark under the wing, when I noticed the engineer had a steel rule in his top pocket. I took it off him, went over to a steel door, broke off the end of the rule, sent him away to get some Araldite (two-part epoxy adhesive/glue), mixed it with the remaining end of the rule, and used the broken bit to stick the switch back on the wing. That fixed that problem.

We were then delayed again. Just as we were ready to start, my remote reading compass came up with a fail flag, and again, there was no spare compass in Auckland. It could be transferred to the compass on the other panel, so I tried that, but the transfer caused them both to rotate 90 degrees off heading. What to do? Obviously, we couldn't depart with a failed compass, but transferring to the good one caused them both to read 90 degrees off. The engineer rang his boss in Christchurch, who said that was a special mod (modification), so you'd know that you'd transferred the heading information! I'd never heard of such a thing before.

The slightly tipsy VIPs were now lining the windows of the lounge waiting for us to depart with much fanfare. The chief hostess was telling us the passengers were getting very restless, so it was a stalemate. Much against my better judgement, I could see no other option than to depart with one operating compass rather than the two that were considered the minimum requirement. We found Christchurch in the dark just fine, so it obviously was the correct decision.

Auckland and back to Melbourne

We eventually moved from Christchurch up to Auckland, the kids settled very well into school there, and made new friends. One young girl called Vikki had parents who owned a bar down on the waterfront, a pretty rough area. Vikki's mother asked Jenny if she would like a part-time job. "Why not?" Jenny said, always ready to try anything new. She had a few eye-opening experiences as the local 'heavies' would come in with their minders and demand their usual from the very inexperienced new barmaid from Melbourne. It didn't take long for both the boss and her to realise that her talents lay elsewhere. When we moved back to Brighton, Vikki came to stay with us and did a term at Sarah's school, St Leonard's.

Simon came over to Auckland for a visit and we went down to Rotorua to visit the geothermal activity. Simon decided he'd like to visit the glow-worm caves at another place. The managers of the motel said they'd put him on a bus in the morning, so we left him there supposedly in safe hands and continued on our way. He turned up in some disarray in Auckland some time later. It turned out the managers had ignored him, there was some sort of riot from a group of Māori and he'd had to escape out the motel window.

My job was done by the end of 1987 and Air NZ was left to operate on its own. There was quite a bit of trans-Tasman politics involved in the airlines over the years. Air NZ took over Ansett Australia, News Corporation took over Ansett NZ and the company was sold in 2000 to New Zealand investors who operated it under the QANTAS banner until it went into liquidation in 2002.

Overall, our time in NZ was very profitable for the four of us, and we look back on our time there with very warm feelings. We returned to Jenny's house in Brighton and to normal life, and we were married in the backyard in March 1988.

Jenny's house in Shasta Avenue, which she'd bought as part of her divorce settlement for $100,000 which is hard to believe in today's prices, was a Californian bungalow with an extension tacked on the back. After we returned from New Zealand, we decided to sell my duplex in Sandringham, get a designer to draw up a plan and spend the money on a complete renovation.

Over the years, there'd been a bit of exchange of money between my older brother and me, first to help me buy my duplex, then in return from me to help my nephew David on a project. At the time we were ready to start renovating Shasta Avenue, Robert still owed me a bit, so we decided he'd do the project along with his offsider until he'd worked off the money owing. We, foolishly as it turned out, thought that we could stay in the front part of the house while work went on out the back.

As soon as Robert turned up, he told us that there was no way could we continue to live in the house while renovations were underway, and started to demolish things on the spot. At very short notice, Jenny had to find us a place to rent. In her usual efficient manner, she did, and we all moved into a vacant house that was waiting to be demolished. Unfortunately, it was full of fleas. We had to move out again until the place was deloused.

I managed to work a bit of a swiftie with the crewing department at Ansett. Because I was often rostered for a day running Human Factors classes, one section of crewing thought I was at the training centre, and the other section thought I was away flying.

Because of this, I managed to get myself a lot of time at home to work on the house.

Later, when we were involved in industrial action, Robert, who'd always been his own boss, and was therefore very conservative, was quite outraged that not only were pilots very well paid, we hardly ever had to go to work. That meant that he, along with many others, was no supporter of pilots closing down the airlines when the pilot's strike started, later in 1989.

Sam who was about 13 at the time, and quite work shy, thought that demolition and wrecking things was quite fun. He also thought actual work wasn't for him, though. And Sarah was about 15 and wasn't coping with the dislocation to her life at all well. I hired a local boy as a builder's helper, and suddenly Sarah's approach to the whole project changed, as she set her cap at Ian. However, despite the teens' efforts and lack of, we worked very hard and moved back into Shasta Avenue in Brighton about June/July 1989. We were very happy with the end result. Sarah and Sam each had their own bedroom with a built-in desk for schoolwork, and their own bathroom to share.

CHAPTER 22

The pilots' dispute

After some 15 years as a Training Captain, I was appointed as a Check Captain on the B737 in 1989. It was a requirement for an examiner from the Civil Aviation Safety Authority (CASA) to observe a line check. The examiner would observe me, checking the FO, on his bi-annual licence renewal. He simply had to fly to Launceston and back twice. Unfortunately, he made a mess of one arrival back into Melbourne. I had to take over, and as a result he had to be failed. I was approved to continue, but my next task was a new Captain's follow-up check after training. He wasn't up to standard, so I also had to fail him. I felt very bad, as I could see myself getting a glittering reputation as an impossible examiner, when in fact I intended to be very liberal and understanding.

Playing politics

But then, in August disaster struck. I'd been very unhappy with my treatment by the pilots' union when we were moving to Ansett NZ. It was compulsory to be a member of the union while employed by an Australian airline. They had been very successful in the past when standing up to the airline companies and had been instrumental in significantly increasing our pay and conditions. I realised there was no use just moaning about my treatment, so I joined the Victorian branch committee of the

Australian Federation of Air Pilots (AFAP). I joined thinking that perhaps I'd be able to have some influence on the occasional extreme behaviour of the union. What followed is almost a book in itself. I'll attempt to describe the events as I saw them unfold.

Australia was a financial cot case at the time. The Hawke government set out on a program of budget reform. Prime Minister Bob Hawke was an ex-union leader, and he managed to convince the current union leadership to agree to a wages accord with the Australian Council of Trade Unions (ACTU). This limited pay rises and benefits to a very small percentage increase over time. The pilots' union was led by a very feisty new Captain from TAA, Brian McCartney.

Brian was originally an army pilot, so he had a 'win at all costs' mentality. The TAA pilots' contract was long out of date, and he was determined that in order to catch up to their previous pay and conditions, the current accord was quite unacceptable.

The deputy president of the AFAP was an Ansett Captain, John Raby. He was from a Labor family and was also quite militant. He was also the training manager for Ansett. Peter Ables, who was effectively the owner of Ansett, selected staff for promotion from senior union members, hoping to continue to have influence in the union. It didn't work in this case, and Ables considered John a traitor, which didn't help our cause at all.

The pressure was building up industrially and there was talk of organising strike action amongst the unions, when I happened to be a passenger on the way back from Sydney, sitting next to Ansett general manager, Graham McMahon. I arranged to meet him in his office the next morning to discuss the situation. He was very affable and pleasant, but he advised me, in the strongest a terms, not to go ahead with any strike action. He was of the opinion that the forces aligned against us by the government and the companies were far too strong.

While we were talking in his office, he kept leaving the room to take calls from the US. It turned out later that these calls were very significant. He was arranging for American pilots from an airline there that Peter Ables had an interest in, to come to Australia to continue to fly for the airline if we went on strike.

I went to the union office to pass on this intelligence, but my information fell on deaf ears. The union leaders had the bit between their teeth, and they were determined to continue on their path to destruction. Unfortunately, previous threats by the AFAP had been very effective, but not this time.

While we were focused on the impending end of my wonderful career, the world was in turmoil. Not only had the Berlin wall come down, and Soviet era communism collapsed, but Chinese people were starting to revolt against the restrictions of Chinese-style repression.

A large student rebellion took place at Tiananmen Square in central Beijing. In June 1989, the Peoples Liberation Army (PLA) were ordered to clear the Square. This they did with tanks and machine guns. It was a bloody massacre. When the pilot's dispute came to a head in August, Hawke announced that all Chinese in Australia that wished to stay, could.

This was used as a ploy, to allow foreign pilots to take up residence here, contravening our migration laws, and allowing the airline companies to start operating again. This move left us local pilots out in the cold.

In order to force a back-down from the companies, the pilots' union instituted a 'work to rule' regime. This was never going to work, as the pilots would only fly in business hours during the week. The companies took the pilots to court. The union lawyers advised the pilots that the companies could claim all our assets, including our superannuation, so their advice was that our only option was to resign. The union tactic was to advise the pilots to all leave their roles, with the expectation that with no pilots left the companies and the government would have to negotiate.

Unfortunately, it was very bad advice, as the companies no longer had any obligation towards the now unemployed pilots, and were free to hire replacements from all over the world. They did with the assistance of the government. Prime Minister Bob Hawke was no friend of the pilots, and he was very friendly with the owner of Ansett. The other airline was government owned, so the government could do what it liked.

Unfortunately, the leader of the union, Brian McCartney, was very pig headed and was determined not to retreat under any circumstances. We were at a very bitter impasse. The people that suffered most were the businesses in the tourist industry, who through no fault of their own, suddenly found themselves without customers. Also, the younger members of the union, with mortgages and young families, suffered too.

I loved my job, and I was very fond of Ansett Airlines, so I found myself having to make a very difficult decision. Continue with the career I loved, breaking the strike, but suffer the hatred and disdain of my colleagues; or support the people that I'd worked with for so many years and join the strike action. Also, at age 49 I didn't have enough money yet to retire, so without experience in any other career, what was I going to do to make a living? It was very much 'Hobson's Choice'.

I decided that the only option was to continue to support my colleagues 'on strike' even though technically I'd left the company, and do everything possible to bring this madness to an end as quickly as possible and go back to work. I spent a lot of time at the union office, fielding phone calls, dealing with the press and generally providing what support that I could for the younger members who were really doing it tough. Jenny's support was wonderful, she understood the situation perfectly and never wavered even though the pressure was sometimes extreme. Her brother Max, who was a very senior TAA Captain, was a bit of a lost soul, and was under a lot of pressure to 'scab' and return to work. To our shame, we indicated to him that that'd be the end of our relationship with him if he did. It was bad advice, as his life just continued downhill from then on.

Along with another younger TAA pilot, I managed the welfare fund, which was set up to provide bare assistance to those who were really struggling to put food on the table. The trust was financed by contributions from pilots who could spare a little money. In that role, I very nearly made a fatal error of trust. An ex-Ansett FO that I thought I knew quite well, approached me for a major loan from the fund. He'd an importing business of some sort and needed money, just overnight (he said) to pick up a container from Customs. He said he'd replace the money the next day! The amount he wanted would have emptied the fund, but I trusted him and wrote him a check. Fortunately, the other trustee who was required to countersign the cheque refused. The FO then borrowed money from another colleague, who couldn't really afford it, and then did a runner.

That was a narrow shave for me, but it still didn't convince me not to trust people. I've been caught a few times, being a bit naïve with hindsight, but still believe that most people will do the right thing, I think.

I became more and more involved with office duties at the Fed's office (which is what we called the union office). It just seemed to be that people turned to me when there were problems to be solved. The media also got my number, so I was the one they called when they wanted a quote or interview.

Jana Wendt, a journalist, was very well known at the time on the ABC. Her staff called and asked for three of us to do an on-air interview. This was a new and novel experience for me. The first question she asked was, "What has the union achieved for you so far?" As the union had lost us our jobs and careers at that stage, it wasn't an easy question to answer. My first on-air performance was not a success, as I was struck dumb, without an answer. Fortunately, one of the others stepped in and gave what probably was a reasoned reply.

Another media request was for a radio interview and when I was asked my opinion of safety standards of the imported pilots, I suggested that it was a shame to throw away a system of training and operational excellence that had been built up over many years, just for the sake of industrial expediency. This led to me being sued by both airlines for defamation. Effectively, it was a stopper writ, designed to stop any further comments. If I made any, that would add to the penalty if defamation was proved in court. Naturally, I didn't have the resources to defend myself, so the advice from the lawyers was to keep quiet, and if I wanted to work as a pilot again, to leave the country.

The thought of long-range flying, especially at night, wasn't very appealing. And the added factor of a recalcitrant teenage stepdaughter who was making it very clear that she wasn't going anywhere, I decided for myself that this industrial madness would be concluded soon. It always had been in the past, and I thought I could go back to where I belonged. How wrong I was.

There were a number of abortive attempts from well-meaning people of influence to attempt to bring the two sides of the industrial action together. Each attempt was rejected either by our side or the other, meanwhile the AFAP influence was slowly being eroded as pilots from overseas came online and our own members that couldn't hold out any longer returned to their old companies.

I'd had a few connections with some politicians in Canberra. Specifically, Don Chip, who as I've mentioned, was the leader of a breakaway centrist party called the Democrats. They held the balance of power in the Senate, and used that power, along with the support of the Liberal party who were in opposition, to instigate a Senate inquiry into the pilots' dispute. An ex-TAA pilot Col Felton wrote the submission, and I arranged the terms of the inquiry. I borrowed a Cessna 172 and Col and I flew to Canberra for the hearing. The inquiry, like most Senate hearings, didn't have much of an impact, but activities behind the scenes did. Bob Collins, who was a sympathetic senator for the Northern Territory, took us under his wing and arranged meetings and phone hook ups with senior government ministers.

As an aside, Bob Collins who was the senator from the Northern Territory, turned out to be a paedophile. Many years later, when he was about to be exposed, he killed himself by running his Land Cruiser into a tree on an outback road. Sadly, Col Felton also took his own life after he retired from Singapore Airlines when he'd sunk into depression after an incident on the ground at Dubai airport.

Bob Hawke the Prime Minister listened in on a phone call – which meant he was on the line, and occasionally made a comment. Effectively, we were told that if the union would only make a proscribed statement, political face could be saved, and the problem could be solved. If they said they'd accept the wages accord then they'd be able to come back to work again, with all the uproar forgiven. We raced back to the pub to tell the leader of the union and his sidekick the good news, only to be dismissed out of hand. It didn't mean a thing they said, politicians couldn't be trusted anyway.

I returned to Melbourne very disillusioned. I'd realised by then, that even though I couldn't return to Ansett, the pilots' cause was lost. Ansett certainly wouldn't have wanted me anyway, so the future looked very uncertain to say the least. I'd spent all my working life in Air Transport, a very specialist skill that didn't translate to any other job. So the big question was: what was I going to do to support myself and my new family? It was a bit of a mystery.

Change in the air

The pilots' dispute eventually just fizzled out, and the airlines returned to normal operations, with mostly foreign pilots. The crazy part was that the replacement pilots were paid a lot more than the union was asking for anyway. TAA was taken over by QANTAS, and Ansett went broke and closed down about ten years later.

I Think I'm Going to Be an Airline Pilot

I did make several reluctant trips to Moorabbin to see if there was any chance of starting again as a mechanic, but there was nothing doing, which I wasn't very sorry about as the idea didn't appeal to me very much. Fortunately, I had my holiday pay in arrears from Ansett, and still plenty of work to do on Jenny's house at Shasta Ave in Brighton to keep me occupied. Jenny was working part time and Jenny's ex was paying a small amount of child support per month, so we were able to keep the wolf from the door, but obviously it wasn't ideal forever.

A part of the Hawke Labor government reform package for the Australian economy was to deregulate the airlines. Consequently, there were several groups that were trying to raise capital to start a new airline. I became quite heavily involved with one group, and it was quite interesting investigating aircraft leases, calculating rosters, costs etc. There was obviously very little chance of success, but it gave me something to do during a very difficult time. Later, when we'd moved to Singapore, Jenny made use of a lot of the information that I'd assembled in her presentations for a Graduate Diploma in Tourism Management that she did by distance education.

In the late 80's and early 90's Australia had slipped into a recession, probably not helped by the pilots' dispute, I felt that I had to invest what leftover pay I had, at the best interest rate available, to make it last as long as possible. There was a company based in Geelong called the Pyramid Building Society, that was paying 18% on money invested. I was going to invest all my money, but Jenny insisted that it was too risky, so in a fit of independence I put $10,000 in. Sure enough, the company went broke, and I lost the lot. Lucky for Jenny's common sense, or it would have been a lot more.

Even though Jenny and I were very happy together there was a lot of tension at home. Sarah had her first boyfriend, Ian, the helper on our building site, who was a bit older than her. He'd follow her home from school, and as I was there all the time being unemployed, I was considered a wet blanket as far as romance was concerned. The harder I tried to show her love and affection, the more resentful Sarah became. Both Sarah and Sam would go and stay with their father at Torquay down on the surf coast for the weekend quite often.

One Sunday, their father John rang Jenny and told her that Sarah and Sam weren't coming back. He was keeping them there, and driving them up to school in Brighton each day. This was devastating news for Jenny, who was losing her children. John refused to discuss it and Sarah was determined to not come back. Sam, who's always been the compliant one, felt that he had to go along with it to support his sister. Obviously, it didn't hit me as badly as it did Jenny, but I was rather hurt too, as I'd tried to do everything I could to give them a happy and loving home. Unfortunately, my efforts were misconstrued, and encouraged by her father, Sarah felt very threatened by my affection. Fortunately, we survived, and it's one of the great pleasures of my life to have Sarah and Sam as a much-loved part of our family now.

However, every cloud has a silver lining, as now whether we liked it or not, I was free to look for airline pilot jobs elsewhere. Not long after the start of the dispute in August 1989, a senior management team from Singapore airlines (SQ) had come to Melbourne looking to recruit pilots. SQ had embarked on a large fleet expansion and needed a lot of experienced pilots to fly their new aircraft.

At that stage I still foolishly expected that the dispute would be resolved and that I'd happily go back to Ansett. It also turned out that SQ required pilots who had experience on aircraft with a max weight of more than 50,000 kilos.

As I'd stayed on the B737 as a Training Captain I wasn't eligible to apply, the B737 being less than 50 tons weight. Unfortunately, by the time I realised that time was running out for me to get another job, all the SQ positions had been filled. I did fill in an application form and sent it off to Singapore. A confirmation letter arrived but then nothing more.

I heard of a new airline starting up in Germany. It was to be a subsidiary of Lufthansa, similar to Jet Star now. I applied. Lufthansa sent a Check Captain out to Sydney for me to do a demonstration on the QANTAS B747 simulator. It happened to be in a B747, an aircraft that I'd never seen before, but one that was to figure prominently in my life later on. This was a bit daunting, as I'd never been near a 747 before. The check pilot didn't overdo the required exercises, and only required standard manoeuvres, so very soon, I was on my way to Frankfurt for further checks. Nothing was confirmed at all. There was an understanding that I was considered suitable for the job, but no information about whether I actually had a job, or when it would start if I did.

On arrival at Frankfurt, I was told that I was going to Hamburg for a medical. The Lufthansa medical facility was a state-of-the-art laboratory, and the medical was like preparing for a space shot. I was poked and prodded in every direction by white-coated specialists who spoke only German. It was not at all like a visit to old doctor Lampard at Glass Street in Essendon, where if you could walk in, say you were fine, have a bit of small talk, he'd sign you off and you'd then walk out!

As all this is now considered 'the olden days' here's a bit of potted history: at the end of WW2, Germany was divided into East and West. The East was under the control of the Russians and the West divided between the US, UK and France. Berlin was in the middle of East Germany and was itself divided between the four countries. A communist government was established in the East, as well as in East Berlin. Conditions there became very dire. As a social experiment, communism was a failure. Thousands of people were fleeing the 'workers' paradise' to go to the democratic West. In 1961 the East German government built a wall dividing the city, to keep their people in. Many poor souls were killed by border guards while they were trying to escape to the West. That whole era of history became known as the Cold War. The two systems of government faced each other across the Wall, each one determined to destroy the other.

By the late 80's the East was facing economic and social collapse. East Germans were travelling to the West via Hungary which, while communist, was much more liberal. The East German government – almost by accident – announced that citizens could travel to West Berlin. Thousands attacked the Berlin Wall on November 9th, 1989, with whatever tools they could find while the border guards, who only a short time before had shot anyone trying to escape stood by. Germany was on the road to reunification.

Back in Frankfurt, the situation was rather fluid to say the least. The German pilots' union was very concerned about hiring foreign pilots, so had put restrictions on who could be employed.

I Think I'm Going to Be an Airline Pilot

Then the Berlin Wall came down and the government insisted that former East German pilots only should be hired.

Unfortunately for the company, the ex-communist airlines' operating standards made them completely unsuitable to fly modern Western airlines. Sud Flug, (the new Lufthansa subsidiary company) only had an office girl at that stage so finding out what the situation was, proved very difficult.

Eventually, I discovered that all the new airline could offer me was a one-year temporary contract. They were prepared to provide me with a hotel and an instructor to do the exams for a German air transport licence. However, it would be with no pay, and as the instruction was to be in German it was very daunting.

It appeared that my options were very limited, but on my return home I stopped off in Singapore to visit Geoffrey Robinson who had been wise enough to apply early to Singapore Airlines when they came to Melbourne looking for pilots. He had been trained and checked out on the B747-300. His training had been very difficult and stressful, and while he'd passed, quite a few of the newly hired pilots hadn't made it.

Airline house, the Singapore airlines office at Changi airport, was as hard to get into as Fort Knox, but Geoff arranged an appointment for me with the Chief Administration Officer. When I met him, I told him that I'd applied earlier but hadn't heard anything since. He sent a clerk to find my application, and after some time it was discovered in the reject bin. I then discovered the Singapore obsession with dotted I's and crossed T's. Apparently, I'd left a few boxes in the centre pages unticked, so off to the reject bin it went. On such small things one's whole life hinges. I was sent to see the Airbus chief pilot, one TK Pow.

A very stern gentleman, he gave me quite a grilling as to why I hadn't applied earlier.

Unfortunately, the administrative person felt that my answer made him lose face, so in the years to come he made it very clear of his low opinion of me whenever we came into contact. I returned to Geoff's flat in a state of shock, I required several whiskeys to recover from the Chinese shouting from Captain Pow. Later, I realised that the Chinese language spoken in English sounds very aggressive to our Western ears, and TK Pow wasn't as bad as I felt on my first impression. In fact, some ten years later when I was retiring, he offered me the use of his holiday home in Thailand.

CHAPTER 23

Singapore days

My introduction to Singapore airlines.

Getting used to Singapore

Singapore is the sort of place that everyone thinks they know about, but don't really. After all it's been the first overseas stop after leaving Australia on the way to the UK for very many Australians over the years. The fact that I'd been there before as a young mechanic helped me understand the local culture a bit better than some of the other expats.

Perhaps being a bit of a reject as a teenager had also made me sensitive to the debilitating effects of racism, so I was at pains to get on with my Asian colleagues. I made an effort not to be patronising to my younger colleagues, and to show due respect to my superiors. Unfortunately, this approach was not shared by all my fellow expats, especially the ones that were from a government airline. Fortunately, I was generally treated very well by most of the Singaporean staff.

In 1990 while Australia was sinking into the recession that it had to have, (according to Paul Keating, the Federal Treasurer at the time), Singapore was really hitting its straps on the way to becoming a major Asian economy.

Everything was shiny and new, and very much under the control of 'The Senior Minister' as the venerable Lee Kuen Yew was called. He was prone to making public statements about world affairs, which were generally not complimentary. He famously indicated that Australia was in danger of becoming the 'poor white trash' of Asia. Fortunately, as a country, we seemed to escape that position. As much as I hate to admit it, the economic reforms bought in by first Bob Hawke and then Paul Keating, as Labor Prime Minister and Treasurer, were vital in setting up Australia's strong economy as we know it today.

Singapore's population was about three million, which seemed very crowded then, but it's grown to about six million now. The population was mostly of Chinese heritage, with Indian, then Malay, and quite a few Eurasians mixed in, in order of frequency.

Each group mostly kept to themselves, but the government propaganda constantly insisted that everyone was 'Singaporean'. Capital punishment was very much on the statute books, with hangings carried out on Fridays at Changi prison. The number killed rose to 76 for the year in 1994 but has varied ever since. Murder and drug offences were the major reasons for the death penalty.

Without being a student of Singaporean judicial procedure, it appeared that if some poor soul appealed their sentence, it would be increased often as not, right up to capital punishment. I thought it barbaric then, and certainly still do now.

The government, under Lee's guidance, felt that Singapore was becoming too 'Western' and losing sight of its 'Asian Values', so five shared values were published by the government. These were to be taught in schools and followed by the general population and watch out if you didn't. These values, which are hard to disagree with, were:

1. Nation before community, society above self;
2. Family is the basic unit of society;
3. Community support and respect for the individual;
4. Consensus, not conflict; and
5. Racial harmony.

I feel that now most Australians would prefer that our politicians would follow number four. Every effort was being made in Singapore to educate the population to the highest level possible, especially in the STEM subjects. And it seemed that as long as the government line was followed, compared to the rest of Asia the average citizen could live quite well. Certainly not the middle-class standard that we enjoyed in Australia, but in the Asian context life was not too bad. However, no political opposition was allowed, and anyone foolish enough to try ended up either deported or in jail on charges that would be considered ridiculous in Australia. Probably due to the fact that I felt 'put upon' as a youngster, personal freedom has always been very important to me. When I hear Australians saying that we need a benign dictator, I feel they should try a Singaporean model, where if you follow the leader's dictates, you'll be fine, but watch out if you disagree.

Given that Singapore occupied a very small land area, was very much mixed race, and had nothing to sell but brain power, the country has done very well.

As expats, we were tolerated as a necessary evil, but it was made pretty clear by everyone official that they'd get rid of us as soon as they could. I accepted the fact that I was in someone else's country and culture and made a real effort to treat them with respect and friendliness. Generally, it was reciprocated, but quite a few of the expats, especially the ones who were ex-government airline, behaved very arrogantly and were patronising and superior to the locals. That didn't endear them very much to our local peers and higher-ups and often as not their contracts weren't renewed, much to their outrage. I believe that now, the Singaporean government has realised that expats are required to enhance innovation and entrepreneurship, so there's quite a lot of expats living there, and doing very well.

Changi airport was considered one of the best in the world, and still is and Singapore Airlines was the world's most profitable airline at the time. Singapore was full of the building of new towns and condominiums were popping up everywhere. Sand was being 'barged' from Malaysia to reclaim the seabed off Changi to eventually extend the airport. Last time Jenny and I went through there it looked as though Singapore extended nearly all the way across the Malacca straight to Indonesia. New towns were government-built high rises that could accommodate up to 20,000 people on a relatively small area of land. The occupants would be selected from the different racial groups in Singapore, so as no one group could dominate and therefore cause trouble with the others. Also, all the young men had to do National service in the army at some point. The main purpose of this was so they would be forced to live together in barracks with the other young men of different racial groups, so they would learn to coexist as Singaporeans in civilian life.

The A310: training

I was sent for a Singapore medical, which apparently was the sign that you were acceptable to the airline for work. The doctor gave me a once over, despite the 'space shot' very involved medical I'd just had in Germany. He told me that my ears were full of wax and that they must be cleared for me to pass the medical, which he could do for a fee. I wasn't in a position to argue, so he went ahead. My ears were fine afterwards, but I learned that sometime later that doctor was arrested and jailed for medical malpractice.

I was allocated to an A310 course that only started some time later, so had no choice but to come back to Melbourne and wait. It was a long and anxious wait, as the US invaded Iraq and all new staff were put on hold by Singapore Airlines. Eventually, I was given a start date, so off to Singapore we went again. We rented out Jenny's house at Brighton, stored the furniture, and then had a bit of a hassle because we had nowhere to live as Singapore had again delayed the course for a few weeks.

The company eventually put us up at the Paramount Hotel, which was about three-star but quite acceptable. I went off to 'school' each day and Jenny spent her time finding us an apartment to rent. Eventually we moved into Bayshore Park, which was an excellent condo not too far from Changi airport. It had lovely gardens, a big pool, and tennis courts. It also had quite a few Australian pilots, who like me, were victims of the 1989 pilots' dispute.

Fortunately for me, Jenny settled in very quickly and started playing tennis and Mah-jong with the other wives there. She also started a distance education course from La Trobe University in Melbourne, studying Tourism Management. She worked very hard at it and did very well. She graduated with very high marks after several years.

I worked hard at the A310 course and ended up with 100% in the final exam. SQ made a big thing of exam results, even though they had nothing to do with your ability to do the job. My name was put on an honour board at the training centre. I sometimes wonder if it's still there.

The really hard stuff came next, when it was time to start the simulator training. The Airbus philosophy was quite different to the Boeing one, so I just had to learn to think differently. The attitude of the instructors was also hard to get used to. Questions weren't welcomed, and if you asked one the usual response was, "You must know, you must know!" in a very aggressive tone of voice. I would spend hours studying useless information at night, just so I wouldn't be shouted at. However, I got through in the end, and as they say, anything worthwhile is not meant to be easy.

The next step was line training. My first flight with a Training Captain, (called a line instructor pilot, or LIP) and a safety pilot, both Chinese, left at midnight to Fukuoka in Japan, about a 6-hour trip. It was all a bit of a blur and I felt completely out of my depth. When we arrived at the pub in town, my fearless leader told me to get my Kimono (dressing gown) from my room, then come to his room. I did as ordered, duly arrived, and he proceeded to bring out the Black Label whisky. This was a bit of a shock as it was only about 07:00, after a night of flying. I ended up staggering to my room about 11:00 in my stupid Kimono, unable to get the key in the door. I remember feeling very addled and wondering, "What's happening, who am I, and what am I doing here?" My line training did get better after that, with some very good instructors, and some not so good.

I was ultimately checked out without too much more fuss, so went onto the line – that's when you fly to a roster. The Airbus route structure was quite varied, and covered a large area of the world, from Sendai in Northern Japan to Cairo in the Western part of the route map. The Kuala Lumpur shuttle was a regular, with four 20-odd minute legs on a day's roster. The Airbag as we called it could never be anyone's favourite aircraft, but over time I came to like it and accept its idiosyncrasies.

The A310: flying

The A310's route structure included quite a few regional towns in Japan. On one of my first trips the FO was a very affable young Chinese man, Eddie Foo. Eddie had brought his new wife Susan with him. We went to Matsushima, I think it was. The coastal scenery there is spectacular, with many small islets in the bay off the coast. Japan's most famous classical poet Basho had written a poem about its beauty. It was a one-word poem, "OH!" That's about as minimalist a description you can get, I think.

I invited them out for dinner to an Italian restaurant, not realising that they only normally ate a diet of Chinese food. Next day Eddie admitted that they'd both vomited later that night. The food was too much for them, but they were too polite to refuse.

Quite a while later while I was a supervisory Captain I was training a Singaporean Indian Second Officer. I insisted that he come out with me in Beijing for local food. He was reluctant, and it turned out that he'd only ever eaten Indian food, and had never used cutlery or chopsticks before either. Unbelievable to us now, but it was really the norm back then.

The international flying was quite different, as you would expect, to domestic flying in Australia. A quite remarkable destination was Mali, in the Maldives, about 4-5 hours from Singapore. On approach, descending in the pitch black towards the ocean was quite confusing. There would be radar returns everywhere, as well as lightning flashes from tropical evening showers. Then, out of the black, the string of lights that was the runway would appear. The airport took up all of an island, with just enough room for the tarmac and a small, open terminal. Behind the terminal was a series of jetties with a lot of the local Dhow-type boats that were powered by a putt-putt motor standing by, ready to take passengers and crew to their destination island.

My crew and I would climb into the little boat, and we'd set off into the dark across the trackless ocean, putting along at about eight knots. As we went, the boat would rise and fall on the Indian Ocean swell. After about an hour or so, a tiny light would appear on the horizon, we'd head toward it, and that was the jetty for our hotel which was our home for the next few days. The hotel itself took up just about all of the island, which you could walk right around in about 15 minutes.

The putt-putt we took to the crew hotel was eventually replaced with a speed boat. I remember the new boat was quite a remarkable design. All the passengers would be seated below in seating reminiscent of a minibus with no windows, and the driver would stand on top at the back. The advantage was that it reduced the time of transit to about 25 minutes rather than the hour it had taken in the past. The disadvantage was that it was pretty scary being stuck inside as the boat leapt from swell to swell with a loud crash as it hit the next wave. Occasionally, one of the young Singapore girls would get sick, and throw up. I made it my practice to stand outside by the driver. It was quite exhilarating, and I thought that if we hit anything in the dark, I'd have more of a chance of survival than being trapped inside. It certainly was a different form of crew transport.

Jakarta was also a regular destination. I recall that recently a London airport was closed down for hours as it was reported that someone may have seen a drone in the vicinity of the airport. A big hobby in Indonesia is kite flying. Flying downwind or crosswind at Jakarta airport getting ready to land it wasn't unusual to see a kite flash by the window. After I reported many kites on approach to the tower, response from the tower was, "We will pass on information sir!" As far as I know, there were never any collisions and nor was the information 'passed on' to anyone. But if it was today anywhere else in the world, the airport would probably be closed more than it was open.

I did have a rather dramatic trip to Jakarta once. Shortly after takeoff, climbing away from Singapore, my navigation screen went haywire. We transferred it to standby to try to fix it. As we climbed, all sorts of warning messages developed, and circuit breakers started popping. The cabin pressure started surging. The warning messages were coming onto the top of the screen faster than the FO could action them. I started the Auxiliary Power Unit (APU), which was only to be used on the ground, and everything suddenly returned to normal. The next day, I spoke to the ground engineer, expecting the aircraft to still be unserviceable. But it turned out to be a loose connection on a generator, which was bypassed by starting the APU. Pretty clever, I thought.

CHAPTER 24

Singapore-based, multi-country fun

Cairo and Saudi Arabia, Bangladesh and Kathmandu

Being a sensitive soul, I could never come to terms with Cairo. Its history was fascinating, but the dirt, pollution, and general degradation I found most off-putting. I generally spent several days there at a time when flying that sector.

The cabin crew had an arrangement with a local taxi driver, Tarik. He was a genial soul and would sit outside our hotel in his decrepit old taxi, available to take us wherever we wanted to go. Shopping was the cabin crew's top amusement, but sometimes the chief steward would arrange a tour of some sort. One particular trip was memorable. Jenny had come with me that time, so a trip to the pyramids had been arranged.

We squeezed into Tarik's cab with a few of his mates taxis carrying the rest of the crew, and off we went. Tarik took us the back way, alongside a filthy canal, and through a village where dead, partially-skinned camels swarming with flies hung from hooks outside mud huts squatting in the sand.

We were deposited at a compound with a few camels and handlers milling around. The crew, including Jenny, were allocated camels. Everyone seemed to have a local handler too. I looked on, bemused, because there didn't seem to be a camel for me. But wait: a scrawny-looking horse was led out, "For the Captain". I think I'd been on a horse before, perhaps as a kid at a fair or something. However, face demanded that I make the best of a bad situation. I mounted my horse in a most accomplished manner, or so I thought, and we set off into the desert, a little caravan straight out of the Bible. Well maybe, but we certainly were not the three wise men! We had our photo taken, and apparently I had a 'very good seat'. I thought at the time, "Yes I do, as long as the horse doesn't move much!"

It turned out to be quite an experience, plodding through the sand with the Pyramids appearing out of the haze over a sand dune. It was quite different to the usual approach that tourists made from a different direction, through chaos, disorder, and touts all trying to get money from you.

On another trip to Cairo, I was wandering along the Nile and came across local feluccas (rigged sailboats) for hire. I negotiated with the young boatman what seemed to be a very reasonable rate, and we set off slowly up the Nile.

After a short while he said, "You want photo?"

"Ok," I replied. He took the picture, then held out his hand and asked for two pounds. It was steep, but I paid. Later he asked, "You want Coke?"

"No thanks."

"You want beer?"

I Think I'm Going to Be an Airline Pilot

"No thanks."

He lifted his dress, "You want me? Ten pounds."

I was most put out by then, so I ordered him to make for the closest riverbank, threw some pound notes on the seat and stalked off. Unconcerned, he just sailed off looking for the next sucker/predator.

Fortunately, I only had one long stay in Dhahran in Saudi Arabia. I felt it was a benighted spot. We were put up in quite a nice hotel, but it was hellishly hot, you couldn't buy alcohol, there was no TV, and not much of anything else except for the Mullah's calling to prayers three times a day. When we arrived, while waiting in the terminal for our bags, I noticed a couple of baggage trolleys with a group of Philippino women on them. I asked the Station Manager who they were. He said they'd been there since yesterday, waiting for their masters. It wasn't safe for them to leave the terminal on their own.

I became very bored stuck in the hotel all day, so I went into town on the hotel bus. Unfortunately, everything had closed for midday prayers. While I was standing on the footpath, I was approached by a young Arab man who offered to drive me to where shops were open. Foolishly, I got into his new very flash Cadillac, and off we shot., straight out of town and into the desert. I quickly reviewed my escape options, of which there weren't many – none, in fact. I managed to convince him to take me back to my hotel. He insisted on coming up to my room, and once there, became verbally quite obsessed with sex in the Western world. I guess it came from living in such a closed society with lots of money and hormones going wild. I was physically able to throw him out into the corridor and lock the door. I considered it a very lucky escape.

I also saw planeloads of Russian women being brought into Sharjah in the United Arab Emirates to service the Arabs in the district. No doubt they'd been promised good jobs, but once there, they were trapped. It's a cruel world out there. Quite a few Westerners have told me over the years how much they love these 3rd world countries. The culture, the happiness of the people who have practically nothing. Obviously, they haven't seen it through my eyes, and I suspect, through the eyes of the women who have to grin and bear whatever 'their culture' throws at them.

The regular stay at Dhaka in Bangladesh was quite an eye-opener. Next to the Hilton hotel was a park, and as most of Bangladesh is a flood plain it was mostly swamp. I made the mistake of going for a walk there one day, only to find it swarming with people living there under old pieces of scrap. There were a hell of a lot of young girls, obviously pregnant. It seems that as soon as a girl reaches puberty in Bangladesh she gets pregnant, which explains their overpopulation problems. I soon discovered that even if you gave all of your money to the beggars it would make very little difference to the awful conditions that people lived in. My normal practice was to give whatever change that I had in my pocket, but obviously, it was never enough. It just became best not to leave the hotel.

A rather challenging and very interesting port to fly into was Kathmandu, in Nepal. The track would follow the Himalayas past Mount Everest – quite spectacular! The airport was at the bottom of a steep valley, with a mountain at the other side. It was also very polluted, so visibility was always poor. It took a great deal of care to make sure you didn't come to a sticky end on the hillside as had happened to plenty of other aircraft over the years.

Jenny came with me a few times, and she was most disconcerted by the funeral fires by the side of the river on the way into town. We spent one night in a hotel near a lookout that gave a view of the sun rising over Mount Everest. We had to climb the path to the lookout, a shrine of some sort, in the dark. It was very cold, but spectacular. Kathmandu was very poor, but had quite a 'vibe' to it, as it was the destination for the 'hippy' culture, as well as the starting point for Himalayan expeditions.

On another trip I went with the cabin crew on a rafting trip down the Ganges. Mostly, the river was wide and slow moving, with locals washing, bathing, fishing on the banks, just like old-fashioned picture books. There were very few bridges, or very little of anything really, so it was quite a sight to see a single wire stretched across the river, with a wheel and a harness on it. The village people, often with a baby on the women's' backs, would hang from the wire and pull themselves over the river, hand over hand. Obviously, you either braved the wire, which was quite a height above the river, or stayed where you were. It was quite a remarkable experience. Today's spiritual people would feel quite at home there as 'spirits' are supposed to live in the mountains. At least all the monks seem to think so.

Singapore keeps a Brigade of Gurkhas – who originate from Nepal – in Singapore, so we'd occasionally do a charter to Kathmandu for them to come home on leave. There was a British Major there to look after their arrival arrangements. I was chatting to him, when he told me a story about a Pakistani aircraft that had landed there, very fast and long so it needed very heavy braking to stop on the runway. When it taxied in, one of the wheels was on fire from overheated brakes. They had a fire truck, donated by the UN, but no one had maintained it, so it wouldn't start. What was he to do? Being an innovative soul, the Major ordered the lavatory cart, which is effectively a tank on a trailer, with a hose to connect under the aircraft to drain the toilets at the end of a flight, to be backed up to the burning wheel, and the contents dumped all over it. Unconventional and very smelly, but it worked. The fire went out, and if it hadn't been for his efforts the aircraft would have burnt to the ground. He deserved a medal.

Beijing too

I always found flying into China particularly arduous but felt that way especially about Beijing. Visibility was always poor due to pollution, the radio aids were nearly always out of service, the Air Traffic Control was just about impossible to understand, and all heights were in metres whereas in the rest of the world they were in feet. The Airbus just had a small single needle metric altimeter, and a chart to convert metres to feet so you knew the altitude.

One trip, after the usual trying arrival, we were held up in the terminal waiting for our passports to be returned by Immigration. No explanation was given for the delay. Eventually, a girl arrived with all our passports in a bag. She held one up and read out the name, "Jenny Tebbutt!" We'd been to Malaysia the day before to play golf and it seemed that inadvertently, I'd put Jenny's passport in my work bag instead of mine. I grabbed it, and quickly herded the crew onto the bus. I was in quite a state for the rest of our stay, as I didn't know if the error would be picked up on departure. Fortunately, it wasn't. Given the fact that in today's political climate when citizens of countries that China is cranky with are summarily arrested and jailed with only an excuse for a trial, I don't think I'd get away with it now.

I made a point of seeing the sights of Beijing; the Great Wall of China was particularly interesting. I also caught the hotel shuttle bus into town one Winter's day to visit the famous Tiananmen Square. This was the site of a dreadful massacre by the Chinese army in 1989, which I've described earlier. It was a clear Winter's day, and I had only light clothing with me. I caught a rickshaw to bring me back to the hotel, but as the temperature was only -5 degrees Celsius, I don't think I've ever been so cold.

I'd learnt of an aircraft museum a fair way out of town, and given my career of choice, I went there one day. It was a long, curved tunnel inside a mountain, with heavy blast doors at both ends, and a long straight road outside that could be used as a runway. Parked out in the open were many Chinese copies of Russian copies of Western aircraft. It was an Air Force base built to protect the aircraft in the event of a nuclear attack. The tunnel was full of Korean War era aeroplanes. Notices on them indicated the number of decadent invading Western planes that they had 'killed'. As a lot of Australians had been killed in the Korean War, I found it quite disconcerting to see this display.

Rockhampton, Taiwan and Abu Dhabi

Another interesting Airbus trip was flying military charters to Rockhampton from Singapore. The Singapore army had an agreement with the Australian government to use the large training area near Rockhampton for their own training. We'd have 200 young soldiers on board, and it'd be about six or seven hours direct from Singapore. Rockhampton runway was quite short for the Airbus, so I would always do the landing myself. It was important to be right on the numbers to make sure that a runway overrun didn't happen. I enjoyed the challenge. I think there was the odd overrun by the Singapore pilots who weren't used to being restricted by runway length. Luckily, the ground was hard, so they were able to get back on the taxiway again without getting bogged or having other difficulties.

Another regular overnight was to Kaohsiung in Southern Taiwan. It was there that I heard an interesting story about the 'green men'. Apparently, when Chairman Mao and his communists were winning the civil war in China, Chiang Kai Shek and his wife, who were the leaders of the so-called 'democratic forces' fighting the communists, were funded by the US in practically unlimited US dollars, also known as 'greenbacks'.

They were totally corrupt, and when, inevitably, they were forced to retreat to the island of Taiwan and were protected and financed by the US government, they included in their largesse their extended family. As the economy expanded, all promotions and public office went to people associated with the Chiang family. If you weren't in that clique, you might make it to middle management, but no further. The aim became to marry into the family, whereupon unlimited 'greenbacks' would be yours. Hence the moniker, the 'green men'.

I don't remember much about Abu Dhabi, but the trip from the airport to the city was quite an eye-opener. It was about 50 kilometres down a fabulous freeway. The limousine that took us to town went very fast. I noticed quite a few piles of twisted metal by the road. When I asked the driver what they were, I was told that the Arab drivers were going too fast, so speed bumps were put in. That didn't deter the drivers, who would hit the bumps at speed, become airborne and end up a pile of wreckage in the desert. Life seems to be cheap in the Middle East.

More human factors

It became the 'fashion de jour' for airlines worldwide to send all their pilots to a human factors course. The aim was similar to the Ansett one that I'd been a facilitator for while I was there, but the format was quite different. A group of us were sent to Bangkok, put up in a very flash hotel, and an expert from the US was bought in as our instructor. He was a very nice man, but not very worldly. Some of the FO's took him to the notorious Pat Pong night club district, which was a real eye-opener for him. I think he learnt more from his Bangkok trip than we did from him about human factors.

One of the exercises he set was very interesting. Three of us, a US ex-Marine, a South African and I were set the task of dealing with a situation similar to the Cuban missile crisis. The Cuban missile crisis was a situation when the Soviets were trying to station missiles in Cuba, aimed at the US. The South African said how he'd have a gun hanging on his fence post and if any of the local natives tried to take a short cut across his farm, he'd fire a burst over their heads, so that was the answer for the Cubans. The American said, "Nuke the bastards," and I, as the only moderate there, tried to get the message across that this wasn't the point of the exercise. Another task was a theoretical survival exercise. We were told that we'd crashed in the snow and ice in a forest somewhere. I knew that the only answer was to stay at the crash site and wait for rescue. The rest of the team didn't agree and decided to set out to find help. We all perished due to cold and starvation. My group were judged last on assessment, so I don't think the company got its money's worth from that course at all.

Supervisory Captain!

After a few years of line flying, I was surprised and flattered to be asked to take on a Training Captaincy, along with my friend Barry Deeth. Company policy was that only local pilots should have senior positions. In the past when the majority were expats, from most of the major airlines, each Captain insisted that the procedures of his old airline were the best and should be followed, and the Singapore airlines policies were to be disregarded. As standardisation is vital in airline operation, this caused a lot of upset to the trainees. Hence company policy was only pilots on national terms could be promoted as instructors.

It was quite a feather in our caps to be asked. As I'd always liked training, even though it's quite hard work, I was happy to accept. After some time at instructor school, I was installed as a Supervisory Captain (SUC). My role was to train Second Officers (SO), who had come from the training centre and who'd previously flown Lear Jets, as First Officers on the A310. This had its challenges as they had very little actual flying time experience. In general, they were very impressive with their attitude to learning, very disciplined and very respectful, if a bit hidebound by the rules, and fearful of using initiative. Singapore pushed constantly for promotion on merit. This was good in theory, but in practice it just meant that if a mistake was made, down to the bottom of the heap you went. Consequently, Singaporeans would avoid doing anything different or difficult, in case it was judged to be wrong and damaged their chances of promotion.

A case in point was the way they assessed visual approaches. In Australia, once the pilot judged that he could stay out of cloud or fog inside 30 miles from the destination, he would continue on visually and land. This just didn't happen internationally. Just about every approach was directed by radar until the instrument approach was intercepted. I would tell my trainees that they couldn't call themselves real pilots until they could see the airport in the distance and, without outside assistance, manoeuvre and land. Every chance I got, I would order a visual approach. In general, the FOs were very reluctant to take it on, as they felt something might go wrong and they'd be blamed. Years later when I was retiring, I ran into an ex-trainee. He wished me well and said that every time he heard of a visual approach, he'd think of me. I was rather chuffed by that.

To try to get them to be a bit introspective, rather than just avoiding trouble, I would sometimes ask after a trip, what did they think of their performance. Mostly they would attempt to not give an opinion. They'd just reply, "That's for you to judge, Captain!"

After a few very satisfying years I was delighted to be called to the office, and told that Barry and I were to be given a B747-400 course. Up until then, the 744 (As the 400-series was called) had been reserved for local pilots only, and expats were allocated other types. There was a fair bit of jealousy from some of my colleagues, which I ignored as I was very excited to be given the chance to fly the 'queen of the skies'.

I've just now while writing this watched on TV the final flight of a QANTAS 744 landing at Sydney. What a wonderful machine it was, and how lucky I was to be given the chance to fly it.

But what's your favourite city?

Over the ten years that we spent in Singapore, flying to many cities around the world, I was often asked my favourite city. I'd say that after a while, you feel like if you've seen one, you've seen them all. The first few visits to a place would be interesting, but after I'd done the tourist stuff, usually the local museums, art galleries etc, and had walked around the local parks, it just became another hotel room.

I enjoyed the climate in LA but wasn't too keen on the city. It was very spread out with little public transport, so it was very hard and expensive to get about there. New York was interesting, being considered the centre of the universe. The aircraft carrier Enterprise was always worth a visit, as well as the Museum of Modern Art (MOMA), Central Park, and other attractions.

Johannesburg was fascinating, but for all the wrong reasons. Our company hotel was in a very rich suburb called Sandton. I've never seen luxurious houses, cars etc. like it. However, the only people on the streets were black domestic staff, the houses had high walls and very high security. Luxury car dealers were on just about every corner, but the black people had only "shank's pony" – or their own two feet – to get about.

Occasionally, I'd see a white person shouting at a black person in a way that'd make me very uncomfortable. I even saw a TV commercial for a car hijack deterrent. It was for a contraption made of gas pipes under the doors on the side of the car. If a crook approached the car with a weapon and demanded the keys, you pushed a button and a jet of gas came out and was ignited. The attacker would be enveloped in flame. I'd say it was quite a deterrent, but I don't think it'd meet any health and safety regulations here.

I always liked Anchorage in Alaska too. There wasn't that much there, but just the fact it was so far North and so isolated from the rest of North America made it very interesting to me. It still had a bit of a backwoods feel about it. There's a lake next to the airport, which is the float plane centre in the Summer, but it's completely frozen over in the Winter. It wasn't unusual to see elk or moose grazing there in the Winter. The Iditarod, the world's longest and toughest dog sled race both starts and finishes there too. If I was lucky enough to be there when the race was on, I used to go to watch it, as it was really something to see.

There were both a stuffed Polar bear, and a stuffed Grizzly bear in the lobby of our crew hotel. Standing on their hind legs they were about four metres high. You sure wouldn't want to tangle with one of them. I was out at the local Anchorage golf course one day when a large brown bear ambled across the fairway. My companions said that if you got between him and his food, you'd be gone for sure. We just watched as he ambled past.

San Francisco was a bit of a favourite too. I thought it was very much like Sydney, with its bays and coastal environment. A ride on the cable car to Fisherman's Wharf was a treat. Although the smell from the seals was rather unpleasant. I loved the fish chowder though. There are a lot of Australian gum trees there, surprisingly. The bus driver I was talking to one day said the Australians had sold them to California as a source of building timber, for which they were unsuitable. "You clipt us!" he said, which was the standard joke about the eucalyptus trees, or so I understood. I was always distressed at the number of people begging in the city streets, often outside shops that had a 'staff wanted' sign in the window.

I guess that my overall favourite city though was London. After all, that is our British heritage, there's lots of interesting stuff to see and do, and everything, including the entertainment, makes sense to us.

Holidays

As a Singapore Airlines Captain, I got very reasonable staff travel privileges, so from very early on we took advantage of First Class travel and each holiday took a trip, mostly to France, as Jenny has a great love of Paris. Having grown up with boats, I got the idea that canal boat touring would be fun.

Originally the canals were built to carry farm produce across the country. They truly are marvels of engineering, and are mainly used now for tourists. For about 20 years we made it part of our holidays to hire a boat and travel the countryside. We'd pretty well covered most of France by the time we'd run out of puff to keep on doing it.

So, each holiday, we'd do a week or so on a different French canal, just the two of us. You'd think that'd be boring, but we didn't find it so at all. We were young and fit then (well, we were in our 50's and seemed young) and having a splendid time.

There were spikes and a hammer in the boat, so I'd find a good quiet spot, jump off, drive in the stakes, tie up, and that would be it. The serenity was wonderful. We always thought that we'd ride our push bikes to the nearest village for dinner. But by the time we'd have cocktails, shower, then Jenny would cobble together something good to eat, and we'd end up staying right there. We got into the habit of going to a village by the canal for lunch, then staying on the boat for dinner. Driving the boat, jumping off to work the locks, riding the push bikes to the local villages for food etc, filled in the days very well. Then we'd sleep like logs in the quiet of the countryside, just tied up by the canal.

I loved driving the boat, which was quite a challenge as they were rather underpowered, couldn't go backwards, and were very affected by wind across the canal. Modestly, I say I was very good at it! Often, we'd hang back and watch people that hadn't done it before getting in an awful tangle getting into the locks etc. Jenny was a wonder. Being very fit, she loved the exercise, and we developed our own system coming into the locks that worked very well. Depending on whether we were going upstream or downstream, the lock gate would be either open or closed. Later they became automatic, but when we started, they were all manual. If the gate was closed, we'd pull in to the bank, Jenny would jump off the boat, run up to the lock, lean on the bar and open the gates. This was very heavy work.

I'd drive the boat in and throw her the mooring ropes. She'd then tie up the boat and we'd go and close the upstream gates. I'd go to the downstream gates, open the valves that'd empty the lock and jump back on the boat. Jenny would ease the ropes out while the water dropped, then heave the downstream gates open. I'd drive the boat out of the lock and pick her up downstream. Sometimes, she'd ride her bike along the tow path to the next lock where we'd repeat the whole process again. We covered most of France this way. Travelling at a fast walking pace, it was quite surprising how much country we covered.

On one trip, our friends Allan and Aileen Reed came with us on a canal boat trip. Allan had broken his leg earlier, so it was in doubt as to whether he'd be able to join us, but he did. As moving about the boat was difficult for him, he did most of the driving. An as an ex-Air Force pilot, he drove it full bore all the way. He'd go full throttle into the locks, then full reverse to stop hitting the other end gate. He was mostly successful, but not always!

Jenny and I decided to ride our bikes to a local village one afternoon, leaving Allan and Aileen on the boat. We tried the local absinthe at a bar, and after only two small drinks, we were feeling no pain. We rode back in a wobbly mist, to find our companions sitting rather sheepishly on the deck. They were reluctant to say what had happened, but we wormed out of them that they'd attempted a bike ride, but in the process had dropped the bikes into the canal. But they'd retrieved them with the anchor rope, so no harm done, except for to their sense of dignity. Obviously, it was not safe to leave them unattended. My dear friend Allan died of cancer in 2021. We had a lot of good times together, and he's left quite a gap in my life and will do for a long time.

A couple of events from our canal boat travels stand out. We travelled up the Canal de Rhone, past Strasbourg, then headed West into the mountains. There were a lot of locks on this canal, and an 'ascencier', a boat lift. We drove into a large pool, with a gate and a red traffic light at the end. When the light turned green and the gate opened, we drove in along with two other boats, into a giant bathtub. The gate closed, then a giant gantry carried the tub and boats up a steep slope for 75 metres to the next level of the canal. On leaving the 'bathtub' we entered a three-kilometre tunnel that took the canal through the mountain, which was quite an experience in a boat.

Another time, we pulled up for the night near a small town. It was raining, and across from us was a very unsavoury looking fisherman, just sitting and staring at us across the water. Sometime later, a very loud alarm in a nearby factory started and went on for a long time. There was no way we'd be able to sleep if it went on all night, so even though the locks were closed from 17:00 and it was past that, we decided to move as far away from the alarm and the fisherman as possible. As we drove up the canal, the fisherman started throwing stones at us, some of which hit the boat, so we were glad to be away from there.

We were isolated in a forest, with just a tow path beside us, and had our pyjamas on, about to go to bed. Suddenly, there was an unholy racket outside. We were being attacked! The fisherman had come up the path and was attempting to break into the boat to get to us. He was screaming in German, kicking at the door, and jumping on the roof trying to pull the hatch open. Our options were negligible, as there was nowhere to escape to. Eventually, I opened the back door, ready to fight for our lives. He was an old bloke, and of course I couldn't understand what he was saying, but I got the gist that he wanted money. Apparently, we'd run over his fishing lines when we left the spot opposite him. He shouldn't have had them right across the canal, but we weren't in a position to negotiate. I gave him 100 Euros, just to get rid of him. So there was no harm done, but it was a shocking experience.

Most of our canal holidays were in France, but we did two in the UK, one in a narrow boat up from Shropshire where the White family originated, and on into the hills of Wales. The narrow boat had to be driven standing on the open rear deck with a tiller and the weather was particularly foul. The canal crossed a deep valley on a viaduct designed by Brunel, a famous engineer of the 19th century. The edge of the channel on the left-hand side was only about 30 centimetres above the water and well below the deck of the boat. Effectively, while steering with the tiller in the right hand I was standing right on the edge of about a 150 metre drop without any barrier to stop us plummeting to the valley floor. The other trip with our friends, the Culleys, up the River Thames from just outside London to Oxford. That was a wonderful trip. The river was beautiful, and the historic places we stopped at were marvellous. Pulling up at night next to famous historic spots, like Windsor Castle, Runnymede, Henley etc. was very special. Not only is it a beautiful semi-rural area, the Wind in the Willows Museum, which depicted many of the episodes that I grew up with, was marvellous. The fact that everyone spoke English was also a bonus.

CHAPTER 25

Flying the B-744

The Boeing 747-400
(Image source: Singapore Airlines media centre press release April 06, 2012)

Being trained on Boeing

I'd found it quite a culture shock, being trained on the Airbus. The French engineering philosophy of Airbus being so different to the American, it sometimes seemed that technology was used for the sake of it, rather than by its need. It was wonderful to become immersed in the good old-fashioned Boeing systems again; they all seemed to make so much more sense.

Right from the start of the Second World War, the US have developed transport aircraft, so each new model uses all that was good in the model before, and they just add the latest modern developments so the continuity of each new type makes a lot of sense. Back in my Ansett days I happened to be in Seattle at the Boeing factory when a new B744 taxied in after a test flight. I marvelled at the size of it, and wondered what sort of superman could fly those things. I never dreamed that I'd end up in command of one myself.

Ground school to learn to fly one was just a personal computer station at the training centre, where you worked at your own pace then were examined on whatever section you'd completed at the end. It was quite different, and a lot quicker, than the 'chalk and talk' schools of the past. I didn't get 100% on my exam this time though.

As one might expect, the training was quite intense, and Barry and I were partnered for the endorsement in the simulator. Simulators have always held a particular type of terror for me. My fear was quite unnecessary, as they couldn't possibly hurt anyone. But I couldn't stand the thought of failing. I never did fail, but I was never convinced that I'd 'got away with it' and thought I'd done so thus far, but maybe not next time. Looking back I can see it's foolish, really.

Unfortunately, I'd always been myopic – short sighted – and I was having more and more trouble in the Airbus simulator as it was a night-time simulation. Seeing the dials, switches, checklists etc. in the low light of simulated night flight was becoming more and more difficult. It was wonderful to move to the B744 sim, which was a daylight flight simulator. The original 747 had a three-man

I Think I'm Going to Be an Airline Pilot

crew: the Captain, FO, and a dedicated Flight Engineer who had a big panel which took up the whole wall behind the FO.

The 400-series was refined to the point that all the systems information as well as the flight instruments and navigation information was shown on two cathode ray screens in front of each pilot – the Captain and the FO. Even though by today's standards the computer power was very small it all worked very well and was quite straight forward to operate, once you knew how, that is.

All navigation was displayed on the nav screen in front of each pilot. The system was an inertial reference system (IRS), that was set and very accurate when the system was powered up at the parking bay. It would measure the direction and speed of the aircraft, and update itself when it flew over a ground radio aid. It's considered very old-fashioned now, as all navigation right down to ground level now uses the GPS system, powered by dedicated satellites.

We got through the simulation program without any major hiccups, although I do remember a particular attempt I made at a two-engine approach, which was the most demanding of the exercises to practice. Somehow it got away from me while turning crosswind before lining up on final. We stalled, but I managed a recovery, and somehow continued on to land. The instructor wasn't impressed and made me do a repeat – I felt that I should have got some marks for the recovery, but apparently not.

Pilots being endorsed who hadn't flown a Jumbo before were given a few circuits with an instructor and no passengers. Sitting some ten metres above the ground while taxiing took a while to get used to. As the aircraft was very light compared to its weight in normal service it took off like a rocket. On my first takeoff, Air Traffic Control requested an early left turn, which I was very happy to do. Just as the undercarriage was selected up, I started a 30-degree bank turn. Looking over my shoulder down that magnificent long wing just above the ground was a wonderful experience that I've remembered forevermore.

I was duly allocated to a Training Captain for the flying portion of my training. A rather quiet but pleasant Indian gentleman, Srinivasan was his name. Our first flight together was to Paris, leaving at midnight. He was the flight's commander, but with a Captain under training, he sat in the right-hand seat (usually the FO's) and the pilot under training (me) sat in the left-hand Captain's seat. Flights over 11 hours carried a relief crew, in this case another Captain and FO. How the system worked was that one Captain would be appointed the commander on the flight out of Singapore, then the other Captain would be the Commander on the return flight.

On my first flight, it was to Charles de Gaulle (CDG) with Srinivasan in command with me in the Captain's seat. The commander decided which rest he would take, which obviously included his FO, or in this case his trainee – me. He decreed that we were to take the first rest. I took off, set course, climbed to cruise over Kuala Lumpur, then the commander said to let the relief crew in. Out I got, put my pyjamas on, a new and novel experience while at work, and climbed into the top bunk in the rest area behind the cockpit. It was a wonderful feeling, drifting off to sleep snug and warm while this great machine hummed along through the night. About six or seven hours later I was called, somewhere over the Middle East. I got up, had a bit of a wash, changed out of my jarmies and sat back in the left-hand seat.

I'd settled down, looked around and there was nothing to see other than pitch black. Then my commander leant over and quietly informed me that I should have changed the linen on the bunk for the next occupant. I was mortified; it hadn't entered my mind. At the end of each flight the instructor was required to write a report on your performance. All I could think of was the note that would be in my first report: "Bedroom hygiene discussed." I was mortified! What a way to start on a new and wonderful component of my career.

If anyone has had to change the bedlinen on a bunk in a hurry as the cockpit crew wait for their rest, they'll know it's not easy. Just as soon as I'd got a sheet under one corner, the other corner pulled out. It all collapsed into a dog's breakfast. Not really what I had in mind for the start of the peak of my career, being trained as a B744 Commander, flying halfway round the world, in command under supervision. I came up with a system later, which was to put the clean sheets on top of the made bed when I boarded for pre-flight preparation. Then, when I got up from my rest I just removed the used sheet and pillowcase. Voila, a pristine bed, ready for the next occupant.

On another training trip the FO was a rather large and somewhat overweight Indian chap. On our rest, he was in the top bunk and I was underneath when we went through some quite strong turbulence. The frame of the bunk above me was bending and groaning with his weight. I was afraid that'd it'd break and I'd be squashed. I couldn't imagine what the training report would say about that.

On arrival on that particular trip, a careful study of the arrival charts for Charles de Gaulle airport in Paris showed the routes as similarly laid out as a tin of spaghetti. Try as I might, I couldn't get the dots to join up on the navigation computer to bring us in to land. Not wanting to show my ignorance to the great man supervising me in the right-hand seat, I reverted to basic flying from the old days. I maintained track on descent by using a small standby radio compass on the panel which was down by my left knee.

Who would believe it, I thought, here I am descending into CDG at 350 knots in a B744, secretly tracking on a fixed card radio compass. If my instructor twigged, he never mentioned it. He'd probably never used a fixed card compass.

As an aside, before I could be accepted at Singapore Airlines it was necessary to renew my Australian instrument rating. This meant hiring a light aircraft at Moorabbin Airport and flying to Cowes on Phillip Island where there was a radio beacon (that NDB I mentioned in an earlier chapter) and carrying out an instrument let down. A hood was fitted over the windows so there was no outside vision. That was to make it seem as if you were flying in cloud, so it was necessary to track on a radio compass. The examiner was surprised at the accuracy of my tracking. I didn't tell him that I'd been bought up in a hard school. In my early days on the DC-3 that was just about the only instrument there was, and the Captains were very fussy about our track-keeping ability.

Once I qualified, on my first flight to New York from Frankfurt, an amusing event happened. The first flight you took across the Atlantic once qualified, required you to accompany a Captain who'd done the flight before. The Captain I accompanied was quite a young Chinese man, and he bought his young son with him. It featured the dreaded visual approach at JFK airport, and he did an awful landing. In the car on the way into town, his son said, "That was an awful landing, Dad!" Out of the mouths of babes, as the saying goes.

Later, the station manager rang me at the hotel, which was The Grand Hyatt of Central Station fame, and asked if I could do the flight to Amsterdam the next day. I'd met the requirement of a crossing the Atlantic with another Captain so I couldn't think of any reason that I shouldn't. When the time came, I was duly escorted out to the departure bay, and proceeded to set up the navigation computer. It wouldn't accept the number that I was attempting to insert. The passengers were boarding, and I was getting more and more frantic, when the American ground engineer who was filling in the log sitting behind me, leant forward and said, "You're putting the figures in for JFK. We're at Newark." It was the first time I'd departed from a different airport to the one I'd arrived at in the same city. Fortunately, there was no harm done.

Later, on one of my first flights to Europe in command, I took the first rest, was called on schedule somewhere over the Middle East with about six hours to go. The crew that had been on duty told me that we were down five ton of fuel, and London was closed due to fog, and goodnight!

"Thanks a lot," I said. On those long-range flights, that sort of thing wasn't unusual. There was a complex set of equations to do to calculate the amount of fuel you needed for the flight, which included emergency reserves plus a percentage loading to cover any contingencies. You'd also have to calculate how much would need to be burned off for landing. You needed to make sure you landed with your reserve fuel intact. I had a bit of a time figuring it all out that night and we had to go on to London Stansted airport, which was another half hour of flight time.

Fortunately, it all worked out ok in the end.

Drama at the terminal

Another occasion, after I'd been on the fleet for a while, was to pick up a flight from LA at Taipei and continue on to Singapore, leaving about midnight. My crew were at the terminal awaiting the arrival of the aircraft, when I got a message from the Station manager. There was a recalcitrant passenger on board. It turned out that it was a young Pakistani on route from LA to Karachi to visit his sick wife. He was a chain smoker, who'd been without a smoke for a long time so was very jumpy, and he felt he'd been insulted by an Indian steward. As the incoming crew told the story, there'd been a bit of bad language, and some pushing and shoving. The obvious thing was for the airport police to detain him, and we'd be on our way. Unfortunately, they would have nothing to do with it as they had no facilities. It's a pretty normal thing with airlines: if the aircraft can be dispatched, once it's gone, any problems for the staff will go with it, so if they can get rid of the aircraft, it becomes someone else's problem. I went to interview the poor soul, who looked pretty dejected sitting on his own being guarded by a policeman.

I realised pretty quickly that he might make more sense if he had a cigarette, so had him taken outside for a smoke. He was obviously a complete addict. He begged me to allow him to continue, so I made him promise to behave, sat him on his own, handcuffed to the seat, and told the cabin crew to leave him alone. On route I sent a message to the company, that he was no problem and should be allowed to continue to Karachi. When we arrived there was a group of armed police who promptly arrested him. I attempted to intervene but was told very firmly to leave well enough alone. I heard later that he got six months in jail. So much for help from me, poor soul.

Flying freighters

The B744 was a mixed fleet of mostly passenger aircraft, but also several purpose-built freighters. It was quite a pleasure to fly the freighter, after all, I'd been a freighter pilot back in the 70's on the Electra for Ansett. The B744 was a hybrid of the 400 series 747. Our fleet were all brand new. I just loved the B744, it really was a magnificent piece of machinery.

The weight of it, some 400 tons, gave it significant inertia so once it was going one way, it took a while to change direction. The flexibility of the wing combined with the weight of it gave it a very comfortable ride in turbulence. It also was just a delight to land. Landing was still the area that had to be done by the pilot by hand and judgement. Certainly, under extreme circumstances, auto-land could be used, but most pilots get a lot of pleasure and satisfaction from a good landing – both then and now.

The 744 had a centre landing gear that was in the fuselage and was to the rear of the wing gear sets. As the centre wheels trailed lower than the other wheels, if the landing was judged properly, the rear wheels would touch the ground, slow the aircraft, and the aircraft would then settle onto the ground as smooth as silk. Self-praise is no recommendation I know, but I became so expert in landings that the passengers would hardly know we were back on the ground.

The fuselage of the B744 freighter was from the original Jumbo. It had just the small 'bubble' on the top for the pilots, with the whole nose opening up so freight could be driven straight in, as well as a large door where the normal rear passenger door would be. The wing and engines were 400-series, but there was no fuel in the tail plane, so endurance was less, but payload was bigger.

The cockpit had the normal two pilot seats, no cockpit door, a lavatory, a kitchen, six business class seats and two bunks. Most freight was carried at night, so cruising along over the trackless ocean with just the two of you plus no passengers or cabin crew to worry about was quite a pleasant experience. The main deck was all containerised freight, and a retractable ladder led up to the flight deck.

After I was checked out and officially a B744 Captain, my first line flight was a freighter to Anchorage in Alaska. It was mid-Winter and we arrived at the destination at about midnight. I'd set up for approach on the main runway when the tower gave us a runway change due to snow clearing. I manoeuvred to set up for the other runway, but found that intercepting final approach we had a strong tailwind. The tower then told us that due to ice on the ground, braking ability was poor. The operations manual was quite clear. Landing with poor braking, in tailwind conditions was 'not recommended'. We were at our maximum landing weight of 400 tons so our approach speed was in the vicinity of 160 knots. That meant that we were above the speed at which we could extend full flap, which would have meant less drag on landing to reduce the landing run. Add the tailwind to that, and we were really moving. Continuing on to Vancouver was our alternative, some three hours away, and we'd already used up some of our alternate fuel by circling for the changed runway.

I Think I'm Going to Be an Airline Pilot

What a choice: depart immediately for Vancouver, and arrive there with barely minimum fuel, or continue on and land, in not recommended conditions, as well as continuing to 'fly the aeroplane'. I continued on, set the auto brakes to maximum, touched down 'on the numbers' and the wonderful machine ran straight as a die, with the anti-skid system working perfectly, cycling on and off, on all 12 main wheels. We taxied very carefully to the freight hangar. When I came down the steps, snow was just about up to the hubs of the wheels, and an unbroken expanse of snow, except for where we'd taxied in, leaving wheel tracks, stretched back to where we'd turned off the runway. It was a most spectacular sight. I wish I had a photo of it. It was quite an introduction to line flying on the B747.

People in many walks of life have to make very important decisions in the moment. Sometimes, the longer there is to mull over a decision, the harder it is to make. I have no trouble now deciding what I'll have off a restaurant menu, for instance, and I get quite impatient when Jenny takes forever to decide what to eat. Compared to the many decisions that I and my ex-colleagues have had to make quickly and correctly, what to eat seems very unimportant.

This particular tale causes me to ruminate that no one likes being told what to do, me less than anyone. But it seems to me that as I get older, more and more people seem to need to tell me what to do. I'm sure that they mean well but they have no idea of the difficult choices I've had to make, and make sure I get right in the past. And as fortunately I've still got all my marbles, I don't need to be told how to make decisions.

A rather memorable trip that I did on a freighter, was from Auckland to Perth. Nothing special about it, except that from the moment we lifted off over the water at midnight, it was pitch black. Just nothing until we were over Hobart after about three hours. A very small sprinkling of lights, then it was pitch black again until we were descending into Perth after another four hours. There's a lot of nothing in the Southern Hemisphere.

Stressful moments

Charles de Gaulle airport

Charles de Gaulle (CDG) was quite a stressful airport for me. The taxiway design there was unique to France. The terminals were circular, with an inbound and outbound taxiway ring around them. If you missed the turnoff into the bay, there was no option but to go right around the circle to try again. Marry that up with the radio communications either being in very heavily accented English, or in French from the locals. Of course, they used French when they could get away with it, even though international aviation is officially all in English. They believed that it was their country so everyone should speak their language.

Much later, when I was approaching retirement, I just managed to escape an incident that would have ruined my career and left me under a cloud forever. I arrived at CDG at about 06:00 in the pitch dark. I had an Australian FO who I'd met for the first time as we did our flight prep to leave. First impressions were good, and the relief crew on the flight were Chinese Singaporeans. CDG was covered in taxiway works at the time, so there were red warning lights everywhere. Because of this, and the possible confusion that it might cause, I'd given a thorough briefing to my cockpit crew on where to go, and where not to go, after landing.

The normal procedure went like this: the Captain steered the plane, and the FO directed from an airport directory. Unfortunately, this FO, while good in the air, was not so good with directories on the ground. We left the runway and came to a fork in the taxiway. The right-hand fork was lit with centre-line green lights, while the left-hand fork was unlit. The FO directed me to turn right. "No," I said, "That leads to the freight terminal, we have to take the left-hand one that leads up to the passenger terminal." I told my FO to ask the tower for directions. The tower came back and told him we should go to the left. "Tell them it's unlit," I said. There was not a word from the relief crew sitting behind us in the plane. The tower replied in very heavily accented English, "You can take the one 90 degrees to your left." I judged that we could just make the turn in the dark.

The nose wheel on the Jumbo is some distance behind the cockpit, so on a sharp turn you go out over the grass, even though the nose wheel is still on the tarmac. I made the turn ok, but as we straightened up on the taxiway the aircraft gave a lurch like it had run over a bump on the road. I thought it was just a seam in the tarmac from the new works. At the terminal, after the passengers had disembarked, the ground engineer came into the cockpit and asked me what I wanted to do about the mud on the wheels. It turned out that the left-hand taxiway the tower had directed us to was an outbound, not an inbound taxiway. That meant that it had no left-hand turn fillet to allow the main wheels to cut the corner. (A turn fillet is an extra semicircle of tarmac designed to keep the wheels off the soft turf or mud.) When I turned left, because there was no left-hand turn fillet, the outboard main undercarriage truck had gone off the tarmac into the mud.

Fortunately, the centre gear took the load, the left-hand main gear sank into the mud and then came back onto the tarmac and we continued on our way. Imagine we'd gotten stuck, bogged, in the dark, with 400-odd souls on board, trying to get the passengers off the plane and the aircraft pulled out of the mud. There's also the possibility that the structure around the gear had been damaged.

The ground engineer was very cooperative, got a hose to wash the mud off, had a good look at the structure to make sure it was undamaged, and said no more about it. I lectured the rest of the crew, that they shouldn't ever mention what had happened in the pub or anywhere, as they'd be dragged into the investigation, even though I'd be the one held responsible. To this day, I consider it a very lucky escape, and I didn't mind a bit if I wasn't rostered to fly into CDG very often.

Berlin

I was in Zurich, scheduled to do a day trip to Berlin and back the next day. The FO, who I hadn't met before, rang me and suggested we meet for dinner. This was quite unusual, as the local (Singaporean) pilots generally kept their distance from us expats. However, I was glad of the company, so we had quite a pleasant time chatting. Even though I hadn't flown with him before, and he was quite a bit older than the usual national FO, I gave him the sector to Berlin. While the Captain on each flight is always in charge, they decide who's flying which leg of each flight on the route, as it was usual to take it in turns.

On the way to the cockpit, a young German man stopped me and said he was interested in aviation, so asked if he could sit in the cockpit for the landing. This was before 9/11 which of course changed everything. As it turned out it was fortunate that

I rejected him, regardless of how often we used to grant such requests.

The short flight sector was normal. The cloud base was about 200 feet, which would have been considered bad weather in Australia, but was not unusual for Europe. All went well until the landing, when the FO made a complete mess of it. He made completely the wrong control inputs, about a fraction of a second quicker than I could correct them. We bounced, he pulled the reversers even though we were about 50 feet above the ground, we bounced again, he pushed the nose down, and then we crashed to the ground on the nose wheel which is a big no-no. Then he tried to get the nose in the air again, so then the tail was in danger of scraping the ground!

It was the worst landing that I've ever been in. All I could do was apologise to the passengers and glare at him in anger. I was mortified, that even with all my years as a Training Captain I'd been unable to rescue what, except for the structural strength of a wonderful Boeing product, could have been a disaster. It turned out that he was a permanent FO, for a very good reason.

Lucky breaks

Luck has a big effect on most people's lives. Most people, at least in the Western world, stumble through life without any major trauma happening, but the odd individual has events happen that affect their life forever. It can't be explained; it's just bad luck.

I had an amazingly lucky run all through my flying career. The most difficult event on the B744 that I had to deal with was departure from LA flying to Taiwan at midnight. There was a curfew at LA that required all night departures to take off over the sea. This particular night we were within one kilo of our maximum takeoff weight. A young steward came to see me in the terminal in quite a state. He'd taken days off in LA but had to get on our flight to get back home for duty the next day. There were spare seats, but as we were weight limited he had to be left behind. He was frantic, as not reporting for duty was a sacking offence.

I told him to stand at the aerobridge and as they were closing the door, to hop on. Out of 400 tons another 50 or so kilos from a lightweight Asian man wasn't going to make any difference. He was very grateful.

On takeoff, well after our maximum stopping speed (called V1) had been reached, just as I started to rotate, the no.4 engine warnings all came on red. As all of my years of training kicked in, I continued on, retracted the undercarriage, and reduced the engine power to idle. We climbed away slowly, cleaned up on schedule, (accelerated and retracted flaps in stages) and all the warning lights went out. I slowly increased power, and all looked ok.

What was I to do? Returning to LA meant breaking the curfew, dumping some 100 tons of fuel, and finding accommodation for 400 people after midnight. Add to that, perhaps the engineers would find nothing wrong with the engine.

The alternative was continuing on for another 13 hours only to have the engine fail way out over the Pacific. That would have indeed led to 'tea and bikkies' for continuing on. This of course, is why the pilot in command is called Captain, and paid accordingly. Pilots are trained to make important decisions and get them right. Our flight plan had us looping way up North past Alaska and the Aleutian Islands to avoid the jet stream across the Pacific. There are emergency runways in Alaska and on the islands, though heaven help you if you had to use one, but it would certainly have been better than the ocean.

I elected to continue, much to the distress of the two FO's and the relief Captain, who was a very good Canadian pilot. In continuing, I decided to operate the engine manually by turning off its computer control. There was no way I could take my rest period, so I stayed on deck all night. Later I heard that they'd changed the engine in Taipei, but found nothing wrong with it. I never heard a word from the flight department, so there was no 'tea and bikkies' for me, just quite a few anxious hours.

Fortunately for me, my relations with my Asian colleagues were very good. Perhaps it was because I'd been to Asia as a youngster, so knew how to get on with them, or perhaps, as a 'reject' in my youth, I understood what it must feel like being looked down on by their 'Caucasian superiors'.

CHAPTER 26

Round the world for retirement!

I only had a short time to go to my 60th birthday and hence to retirement, when I was rostered for an around the world trip, mostly on the freighter. I met my FO in Europe, it was in Frankfurt I think, and we departed for New York. He was older than the normal FO, and made it pretty clear that he didn't appreciate being stuck with me, and would only do the bare minimum of his required duties. His attitude was churlish, I suppose you'd say.

The approach to JFK was the famous 'Canarsie approach,' which was a challenge, but doable (as the Americans would say). Being an expert at visual approaches, I nailed it. I gave him the leg from JFK to Brussels, which he did adequately, but in very bad grace. Fitting in on the taxiways at JFK is like peak hour traffic only worse and he didn't seem to understand, English being his second language, so I had to give considerable orders to him.

After that, he just refused to speak, so there were very long and uncomfortable silences as we flew. Often companionable silence is a blessing, while hostile silence is very hard for me to deal with. Keep in mind, there were only the two of us in the cockpit at the time, so we either got on or we didn't. There was no alternative.

Later we departed from Brussels for Sarjar in the United Arab Emirates, which was the Singapore Airlines (SIA) freight hub. It was the alternate airport for Dubai. On that flight, my surly FO was most uncooperative. I gave him the leg, he made a complete mess of the descent into Sarjar and I had to take over and climb back into controlled airspace. In the car into Dubai, I asked him what was wrong with his arrival. He launched into a tirade about my arrival into New York, which was perfect, and how he couldn't accept having to fly with an expat. I couldn't sleep that night in the pub in Dubai. What was I to do? As he was older, he had connections 'upstairs' in Singapore.

I felt I couldn't let his behaviour, and performance as a FO pass unnoticed, but I only had a few more weeks to go until my retirement, so I didn't want to have to finish my career facing an inquiry, knowing that an expat would always come off second best in a competition with a local. I got myself in an awful lather overnight in the pub, deciding to read him the riot act next day when we were to fly passengers to Singapore. Fortunately, he came up to me and apologised for his behaviour, so I was able to be gracious and tell him I'd be happy to not let it go any further but to lift his game. The whole episode left me with a very unpleasant taste in my mouth, and I was very glad that it was a rare occurrence and not the norm.

Jet lag, the constant companion

Unfortunately, most flights were East to West so I was always out of my time zone. Sleep became a priority. Try as I might, it was rare to get a full night's sleep. It was always good to be back in my own bed, with my wonderful Jenny, but unfortunately, as I was always out of my time zone, I rarely could stay asleep for more than a few hours. A trait that continues to this day.

I Think I'm Going to Be an Airline Pilot

Today, people ask, how did you cope with jet lag? The simple answer is, I didn't. When you're a pilot, you just have to accept that you're mostly tired all the time so just accept it. Keeping fit certainly helps a bit, as does sleeping when you're tired whatever the time of day it is. But for the long-distance traveller, it's just an occupational hazard.

The people who did the crew rosters were always very nice to me (I did suck up to them a bit), so they asked me what flight I'd like to do for the last flight of my career. I elected to just do a day turnaround to Bangkok, about two hours up there, then back. They then gave me a long trip to LA beforehand, so that I'd have days off to spend there, and that meant that Jenny could come with me. After we returned, I just had the Bangkok trip to do, and that would be the end.

When we got to LA, we elected to hire a car and drive up to Arizona to visit the Grand Canyon. We had a wonderful trip. The Grand Canyon is spectacular, and we had a couple of nights there, and also at a magical place called Sedona, where a lot of the old black and white cowboy movies were made. However, I seemed to be out of breath quite a bit. I had noticed that I was struggling to complete my gym routines earlier but just assumed that I was tired. On return to Singapore, I went to our usual aero-medical doctor to do an Australian licence renewal medical. He straight away sent me up to Changi General Hospital to a cardiologist and put me on sick leave.

That meant that the trip back from LA was unknowingly my last flight! I'd been a professional pilot for just over 36 years and had flown just under 20,000 hours incident-free (often luck rather than good management played a part). After starting on the DC-3 and then flying many different airline types and finishing as a B744 Captain, I felt very blessed to have had such a wonderful career.

People sometimes ask me about flying incidents. It's hard to find a suitable answer, because untoward events will always happen even within the best-regulated system. It's how the events are handled that stops them becoming something much worse, plus a bit of luck, which I seemed to be blessed with.

All in all, I was retired and looking forward to what the future held.

PART THREE

Retirement

The 1954 MG TF that I bought from Barry Deeth.

CHAPTER 27

Keeping up with fast-paced life

Sick leave? Cardiology? Me? I was gobsmacked.

After a bit of investigation, the cardiologist at the hospital said, in his very direct Chinese way that they were going to enter my heart via the left chamber and do electrical work on the right chamber. He told me to sit outside while he made the appointment. I sat in the waiting room with some very sick-looking Chinese people, in a state of some disquiet. Heart surgery out of nowhere, how could this be? Once the relevant appointments had been made, I went home to give Jenny the news. She was busy packing the apartment ready to return to Melbourne. The doctor at Singapore General Hospital said that he couldn't do the operation for a week or two, but that put us in a tight spot, as we were to leave our apartment in a day or so.

Singapore Airlines were great. The ladies at crewing had organised to meet me when I returned from Bangkok at Changi airport with a cake with which to celebrate my last flight, which was unfortunately not to be. They said they'd put us up in a hotel while we waited for the operation, but of course I wouldn't be paid as I was officially retired. I elected to come back home and be treated by an Australian specialist instead. By then I was barely able to put one foot in front of the other, so I could hardly do anything. My heart would run away and beat madly, then stop for as long as three seconds before starting again. Naturally, I'd stop whatever I was doing, too.

The Singaporean doctor had sent a letter to the Australian cardiologist, but unfortunately it got stuck in the system, so I had to wait quite a long time for an appointment. I wasn't in any pain, but moving with any speed, even standing was an effort. Jenny had insisted on throwing me a 60th birthday party. It was wonderful to catch up with many old friends and family, but it was very difficult too, as not collapsing took quite an effort.

Also, I'd bought a 1954 MG TF (see the accompanying picture) off my friend Barry Deeth who'd retired a few months earlier and who lived in Brisbane. He was into vintage motorbikes in a big way, and we'd arranged to join him and Ida on a trip to Tasmania, in the MG, along with the bike group. Nobody, even I, really understood the seriousness of my situation, so they kept urging me to keep up with them, which I found very difficult. On the overnight ferry back to Melbourne, I had to spend the night standing up due to the pain in my chest being too great if I lay down. I was lucky to survive! In fact, if there's a common theme of any kind to this story, it's luck.

Anyway, I did survive, and eventually made it to the long-awaited appointment with the cardiologist, a Dr John Kalman, who called himself an 'electrician'. By this he meant that he specialised in the electrical rather than the plumbing side of cardiology. He was very apologetic that I'd had to wait so long to see him, and promptly booked me in for an angiogram. This is a procedure where a radioactive dye is injected into the groin and tracked on a screen to see the blood flows along the arteries and through the heart. He wanted that done so that any unforeseen structural surprises would be discovered before he did his electrical work.

Unbeknownst to me, you're given a sedative so are perfectly relaxed during the angiogram process. I was lying on the table, chatting happily to the nurses, when a young man in a suit walked up. He introduced himself as Bill Wilson. "G'day Bill," I happily said. He turned, pulled on a white coat, then started to fiddle around with the equipment. He told me to look away from the overhead screen where I could see my heart beating happily away, and started doing something technical. "Oh no," I thought, "It's the great man himself, and I've just called him Bill." I was brought up to call people by their title, whether that's Doctor, Sister, Vicar, Captain, etc. Anyway, Bill whacked a few stents in, patted me on the arm, and left. It was rather a non-event in the end.

However, the ablation was a different story. I needed this procedure to restore my heart to its normal beat and that was the procedure to be done by the 'electrician', Dr John Kalman. An ablation is when the 'short circuit' in the heart is fused with a soldering iron (sort of), and then the scar tissue directs the electrical signals back to where they're supposed to go. Once again, I was on the table watching my heart with its associated plumbing thumping away on the big overhead screen while the medical team were pushing wires and things through my arteries. Suddenly, I started to feel significant pain. This is a no-no, as there are no nerve endings in the heart itself (or so I'm told). I was asked how severe my pain was on a scale of one to ten. I attempted to be tough, but had to admit to a rather high number in the end. As they were pumping morphine into me at a great rate to no apparent effect, I was very relieved when they decided to call the whole thing off, withdraw all the foreign objects, and send me back to the ward.

It turned out that all the wires and stuff inside me had set off oesophagus spasms, which are very similar to coronary attack pain. Unfortunately, that meant I had to go through the whole thing again. They managed to get it right the next time they tried, but I ended up with a side-effect called Brady Cardio. This means that my heart rate is stuck at a very slow, abnormal pulse. It won't accelerate under exercise as a normal heart does, so I run out of puff very quickly when climbing stairs, running etc. There's no treatment for it, so I just have to accept that I still can't keep up. Fortunately though, these modifications were going to last me another 13 years.

Travels: Darwin to Broome and more heart issue

After I'd recovered from the heart events, we decided to do a road trip with our friends David and Roz Brown through the Kimberley from Darwin in the Northern Territory to Broom in Western Australia via the back roads in a hired 4-wheel drive Toyota Land Cruiser. Despite all the years of flying over Australia, I hadn't really seen much of it from ground level. We didn't camp, but rather stayed at cattle stations and national parks with accommodation.

We made a point of avoiding the main highway, and followed the Gibb River Road, which was unpaved for most of the way, but gave access to many wonderful tourist spots that are only accessible by 4-wheel drive. The Bungle Bungles was a case in point. The track from the main road was 54 kilometres long and it took us about five hours to cover it. However, it was worth it. To think that this remarkable, worn-down mountain range was only discovered (by white man) in the 1970's is amazing. The isolation of these places is incredible. The population of the Kimberley even now is only about 50,000, spread over a huge area.

In my mind's eye, I can still see the amazingly bright colours of the sky, the rocks, and the landscape. Often the camps would be near a system of rock pools and waterfalls that ran during the wet season. They were just beautiful spots.

We did have an incident though. We set out on foot for a rock pool about five kilometres away in the middle of the day. The trail took us up onto a rocky plateau with no shade and the sun beating on our unprotected heads. I'd made sure that I had a bottle of water for Jenny and me, but David had no top (t-shirt), no hat, and no water. It was very hard to follow the unmarked trail, it was very hot, and Dave started to show signs of heat stress. He eventually collapsed to his knees. I had to pour our precious water over the back of his neck before he could keep walking to the shade and cool of the billabong. We cooled down in the water, and waited 'till the shadows lengthened to walk back to camp. It showed us just how easy it is for things to go wrong out in the wilderness.

After the Kimberley trip, we'd had a trip to Europe on the canals in 2013 as well, on 'our ship', the *Seaborne*. We had a stopover in Singapore on the way back home. Jenny went shopping, so I went to the famous Singapore gardens at Sentosa. I couldn't find a taxi, so I walked back to the hotel. I barely made it because I became so tired and my heart laboured so much, but I had a bit of a rest and recovered. On arrival back home at Melbourne, I found it very difficult to walk from the aerobridge to baggage retrieval, so I booked in and went to see Dr. Kalman again. I'd ridden into town on my motor scooter. Dr. Kalman said he'd admit me to hospital, so I said I'd ride my scooter home, then get a cab back. "No," he said, "You might drop dead on the way home!" That did get my attention.

Dr. Kalman passed me on to cardiologist Ronan Gurvitch who is a lovely youngish man who I like very much. He discovered some more blockages in my heart and fitted a couple more stents but there were some arteries blocked on bends where stents couldn't be fitted. Six months later the chest pains were back, so it was a quadruple bypass for me. Unfortunately, after they'd closed me up, my heart was labouring due to internal bleeding, so they had to open me up again to drain it. This caused my kidneys to shut down. The doctors expected them to start up again, but they didn't.

Each day, the physiotherapist would insist that I exercise in the corridor, which I found impossible. Even though I suffer badly if I have a 'man cold', nothing could compare with how bad I felt with a failed kidney. Eventually, a lovely Greek nephrologist came to see me and when I told her about my difficulties with the exercise, she said, "Of course you can't. You're 90% poisoned! Tell the physio to get stuffed!" I was very glad to do so. I was given a blood transfusion and gradually got better, but it was an experience that I wouldn't want to repeat.

Now, eight years later, except for my slow pulse holding me back, my heart is still working fine – touch wood!

CHAPTER 28

Cars and planes

The MG B that we used for touring with CHAOS.

The MG B

As I've said, just before leaving Singapore I'd bought an MG TF from my friend Barry Deeth. Jenny and I had joined the MG car club and had met a group there who'd become good friends. They'd formed an offshoot group that they'd called TITS, or 'Touring In TaSmania'. Every year they'd plan a tour somewhere in one of the Southern states and we'd go along and have a fine time. After that, when the leader of TITS moved to Somers, he started another group called Classic Heritage Automobiles Of Somers (CHAOS) and we enjoyed touring with them too and are still members of that group now. The MG TF soon proved itself inadequate for touring, so I replaced it with the MG B. This car lived happily at St Andrews Beach (where we were living) and we had many wonderful trips to places that we wouldn't have seen otherwise.

The Beechcraft Travel Air

A chap in Singapore, Reg Flanagan, would talk often of the Beechcraft Travel Air E95 (a light twin-engine aircraft) that he owned in Melbourne. He used to hire it out for flight training and charter. I was wondering what I'd do with myself back in Melbourne in retirement, so I decided in an attack of overconfidence to buy Reg's Travel Air, sight unseen.

I wasn't that interested in flying it but thought that helping with its maintenance would be an interest for me and keep me involved with aeroplanes. The aircraft turned out to be a bit of a dud. It looked pretty shabby and needed a lot of maintenance to keep it in the air. Also, I wasn't made to feel particularly unwelcome in the hangar, but as an outsider I wasn't included much either, so without any recent experience there wasn't much I could do to reduce the cost of maintenance. Later, I discovered that maintenance companies loved owners coming in to help, as they then could charge a lot more fixing the things that the owner got wrong.

There was one rather unpleasant experience I had while at the hangar. The Chief Engineer at the RACV hangar bought a camper bus. He left it at the hangar, but then disappeared. Calls to his house went unanswered. The police went round, broke in and found him sitting alone with his dog. He'd had a nervous breakdown and was starving himself, and the dog, to death. I don't know what happened to him after that, but it was very sad.

A service on the Travel Air was due every 100 hours. It included a check of the fuel filters that lived in the undercarriage wheel well, as well as various other checks. The aircraft had to be jacked up, which in itself was very difficult. The Beechcraft aircraft had a very odd jacking system, with a purpose-built jack. The wheels had to be half-retracted, and then I had to lie on my back to reach the filters in the wheel wells. They were always clean, but to reassemble them correctly was very difficult. One particular time, I got them all together, checked them for leaks, and found that all was OK. The next day an instructor from the club rang me, said that he'd been out in the training area with a student and that there was a very strong smell of petrol coming from the Travel Air. I twigged immediately as to what had happened, rushed down to the hangar, crawled under the wing, and sure enough the filter was leaking. Horror! Just a single spark as the wheels retracted and the explosion would have blown the wing off. The thought of it still causes me some distress as it would have very much been my fault.

I decided that I'd better learn to fly the thing, so I hired an instructor to do the required endorsement. I thought that as she was a woman, she'd go easy on me. How wrong I was. She was very tough. The fact that I'd been a B747 Captain meant nothing to her, so it was not an experience I enjoyed, and it was very expensive too.

The Travel Air was the only light twin-engine plane of its generation that could climb on one engine. That said, if an engine failed on takeoff, which was fortunately a very rare occurrence, the only chance of survival was to do everything right, and that very quickly. For training, just after lift-off, the instructor would shut the fuel off. Obviously, the engine would lose power, but the propeller would keep rotating. This caused tremendous drag on the 'dead side' – the side where the engine had lost power. This would also cause a large and fast drop in airspeed, a turn towards the failed engine, and only one way to go: down!

At once, the undercarriage must be selected up and full rudder put in towards the good engine. The failed motor had to be identified, the failed throttle closed, the feather button pushed, and the fuel shut off. All this had to be done at the same time as flying an aircraft that didn't want to fly any more. If all these actions weren't taken at once, a crash was inevitable. One lived in hope that it never happened.

It's not unusual for people to say that they think that single engine aircraft are too dangerous, but with two engines there's double the chance of a mechanical malfunction, and as far as light aircraft are concerned, if an engine is shut down en route, the operating engine only provides enough power 'to stretch the glide', hopefully as far as a suitable place to land. A reason that the Travel Air was so popular in its day was that as I've said, it could slowly climb on one engine. That was a claim that I certainly didn't want to try out.

After my instructor released me, I did a few trips in the Travel Air, including one to Adelaide to visit Geoff Robinson, but decided the whole exercise was too expensive, and too risky financially, for me. I managed to sell the plane for the same price I paid for it, but a condition of sale was that the aircraft came with a 100-hour inspection pass. Unfortunately, there was quite a bit wrong with the plane, so to pass the 100-hour inspection cost me some $20,000. It was an 'experience', but not a cheap one. I consider myself lucky to have found a buyer at the same price I'd paid for it.

In 2020 a Travel Air was destroyed by a collision with an aircraft that was climbing out of Mangalore, while it was descending. The two people on each aircraft were killed. It may have been my old aircraft, but nevertheless, what a dreadful end.

Navigation, GPS and otherwise

An unintended consequence of modern GPS navigation is its accuracy. Before GPS the chances of a head-on collision with both aircraft being exactly on the centre line were very slim. Even a ten-metre displacement off track would be enough to cause a near miss, but not a disaster. With GPS, when both were on opposing tracks, the chance of collision increased slightly as the tracks were so exact.

An event that amused me once, on the way back from Europe while I was flying the B744 over India in the middle of the night, I was sure that I heard Geoff Robinson's voice giving a position report, coming the other way. When we were junior co-pilots in Ansett, all navigation was via ground-based radio aids as I've mentioned elsewhere in the book. They weren't always very accurate, so the Captains that we flew with back then were very strong on staying on track. Any deviation by the FO would be picked up and dealt with very sternly indeed. I looked ahead for Geoff's aircraft beacon, which would be 2,000 feet below me, and saw it coming towards me. It passed directly underneath us.

Hopping on the radio I said, "Off track again!" However, it was a Swiss Air flight. And as everyone knows the Swiss are not famous for their sense of humour. The Swiss pilot replied very angrily that they paid very careful attention to their navigation and if anyone was off track it certainly wasn't them. I didn't bother replying that it was just a joke.

Not long after I retired, a Singapore Airlines B744 had a dreadful crash at Taipei. The weather at Taipei was often very poor, as it was on this night. There was heavy rain and wind, making visibility terrible. In Taipei, there were three parallel runways, but one of them had been turned into a taxiway only, however it was still lit as a runway. On the night of the accident there was a lot of heavy machinery left at the end of the taxiway which was lit as a runway. In the poor weather the crew turned into the taxiway thinking it was a runway and started to take off. As they got to takeoff speed there was a whole lot of obstacles in front of them due to the work on the tarmac. The pilot tried to pull the aircraft off the ground to avoid the obstacles, but the aircraft went over all the concrete blocks and machinery. Most of the passengers on the lower deck were killed. The upper deck passengers and pilots survived, though the pilots probably wished they hadn't. It would have been a very easy mistake to make, and I was just glad it wasn't me.

I heard that after the accident there was a complete shake up in the flight department, and all of the management pilots were sacked, and Air Force officers brought in. I would have thought that'd be a big mistake, as operating within the Air Force is completely different to operating in an airline capacity, but as I was long gone I never heard the outcome.

CHAPTER 29

9/11

The next significant event that happened was the dreadful events of 9/11/2001. Just about everyone alive at the time can remember hearing the news in the morning (Australian time) and watching those awful pictures of the towers collapsing, along with the unforgettable images of the 'jumpers', the poor people who'd been trapped with no way out of the buildings apart from jumping out the windows before the buildings collapsed. We all watched the TV show us the smoke, the buildings collapsing, the lost emergency workers, over and over and over.

Incidentally, when the towers were designed, they were made strong enough to take an impact from an aircraft flying into them, but the designers hadn't taken into consideration burning aircraft fuel weakening the steel building structure.

Watching this news, I remembered my first flight in command to New York. It was rather special. As the weather was perfect, I was given a visual approach down the Hudson, right past Manhattan, looking down on the twin towers (the World Trade Centre) and the Empire State Building, before landing at JFK. It's an understatement to say that it was spectacular. On a later trip when Jenny was with me, we stood on the lookout on the 101st floor of the World Trade Centre, next to the TV tower on the roof. It was quite an experience. When the hijacked aircraft bought them down, an event that changed the world, it was very easy to imagine the plight of the poor souls that were there on that fateful day. Years later, on a trip to New York we went to the site of the demolished buildings. In the memorial was the wrecked TV antenna that we'd seen sinking through the smoke as the building collapsed on the news channels on that day. Somehow, if you've been to a place where a dreadful event took place it makes it all seem so very real.

I often wonder if I'd been on route to the US when the whole US airspace was closed, how I would have dealt with it. That event changed history, as it started the 'War on Terror' that led to the invasion of Iraq and Afghanistan, both of which couldn't have been called successful by any means. In fact, there's a lot of evidence that Dick Cheney, the US Vice President at the time, had a large financial interest in oil companies that stood to gain a lot if the US took over Iraq. That's what happened, even though we know now that Saddam Hussein had no involvement in terrorism against the West. It's not drawing too long a bow to see that the division and upset that is bedevilling the US now started back then.

CHAPTER 30

A stint in the Rotary Club and becoming a 'Collins St farmer'

The Rotary Club

After the Travel Air was sold, I was looking for a replacement activity, so I joined Melbourne South Rotary club. Rotary is a wonderful organisation, and I'm really sorry that young people don't seem to feel the need now to join these volunteer organisations that do so much good work both locally and worldwide.

My task at Rotary was to arrange a speaker for each week's meeting, as well as recruiting new members for the Club.

I did well at the first, but failed at the second task. Getting a speaker every week was quite a difficult thing to do, but I decided that 'everyone has a story', so any time I met anyone I'd ask them to come and give us a 40-minute talk. Once I managed to draw people out, we had some amazing speakers. I also managed to arrange for a grant to be used to build a dam for villages in Cambodia so people could become self-sufficient in fish production and not have to just survive on hand outs, so that was something! As a result of my efforts, I was awarded a Sapphire Paul Harris medal. This was an internal Rotary International award, and each club had a few that they could give to particular individuals that they thought had made a significant contribution. I thought this was totally undeserved on my part, but I appreciated it very much.

Unfortunately, our attempts to recruit new members was a failure and a once-vibrant club slowly shrank to nothing.

Becoming a Collins St farmer

My friend Geoffrey Robinson bought about 12 acres of land in the Adelaide Hills after he retired, and decided to become a wine grower. I very much enjoyed going to join him and helping out among the vines. There were a lot of jobs like pruning, trellising, etc. Unfortunately, he had a bad divorce so the vineyard had to go and he moved back to Benalla where he grew up. I had a friend, John O'Conner, who had a farm near there too. In my single days I'd stay with him on the farm, help with farm work and enjoy the country life.

After Geoff moved back to Benalla after sadly losing his beautiful vineyard in SA, I had the bright idea of getting him involved with farm life again. I put it to John that we'd start a sheep company, 'The Acme Sheep Company'. John would provide the land, Geoff would look after the sheep, and I'd provide the administration and look after the finances. The three of us seemed to agree that this was a good plan, but unfortunately it didn't work out in practice.

Geoff and John's ideas of how to look after sheep differed greatly. John believed that a bale of hay had to be soaked in molasses to allow the sheep to eat it but Geoff didn't agree, and wasn't prepared to do the extra labour that it required. Eventually John removed himself from the whole process. There was then a drought so there wasn't enough feed on the land for the flock, and I was unable to get hay anywhere, so I decided to put ten acres of John's land into oats to feed the sheep. The paddock was quite weed infested, so walking up and down spraying by hand, before planting oats was a very arduous task.

I shouldn't have bothered, as I was hopelessly overcharged by the contractor to set the crop, and when it was harvested there was no longer any need for it as the long-awaited rain had arrived, wetting the stored hay, which attracted a plague of mice that infested it.

Without dogs, it was practically impossible to herd the sheep for crutching, and getting shearers to do the crutching was also impossible, so a lot of the poor animals became fly-blown and died. For ones that we managed to shear, Geoff and I became 'roustabouts', baling the wool and herding and penning the sheep for the shearer and his mate.

In a nutshell it was work that was beyond me. It was a tragic and very sad end to the Acme Sheep Company, John and Geoff didn't get along, the land was overstocked and the sheep couldn't be looked after properly. I decided to close the whole thing down, get the wool off the flock then sell them for mutton. I managed to get a shearer, but of course the drought broke, the sheep couldn't be shorn when wet, and they started to die from fly strike.

I never saw John O'Connor again, but I managed to sell the surviving sheep, so recovered some money. Seeing all those animals dying in agony was not a very pleasant experience. I'm still very sad about the dreadful deaths of the sheep, and not so thrilled about the cost of it all, but I'm very glad of the experience of being a 'Collins Street farmer'. I had the best of intentions but it didn't turn out too well!

I can't quite remember how it came about, but after Piri and I decided to go our own way, and Andrew had moved out on his own I was very glad to meet John O'Connor. He was on his own, so to go and spend the weekend with him working hard was a great diversion from a lonely life on my own in a cheap flat in Melbourne. John was a convicted Catholic so couldn't come to terms with the fact that his wife didn't want him anymore, but couldn't bring himself to ask for a divorce! It suited both of us to spend time at his farm, working hard during the day, drinking in the evening, and enjoying the country environment. At least I did anyway.

John had learnt to fly and had a Cessna 172, so I had the bright idea of making an airstrip on the front paddock. The drain beside the drive up to the house was a problem. I eventually found some plastic drainage pipes, dug a trench put the pipes in then covered the lot with dirt so the crossing of the road across the strip was smooth. I landed his Cessna there without a problem a few times.

John was very safety-conscious, so he was reluctant to allow Andrew to visit. I managed to convince him once to let me bring Andrew with me. There were motor bikes on the farm, and John was adamant they must not be touched. John and I were working in the top paddock on that visit, when I heard a distant noise. Andrew had taken a motorbike and was leaping the dam like Evil Knievel! John was distraught. I think it was the last time Andrew was allowed to come to the farm.

As a Catholic, John couldn't countenance abortion or interfering with the begetting of new life. Unfortunately, he always had a farm cat, which would regularly become pregnant. The kittens multiplied and became feral. It's attitudes like this that have led to the feral animal plague in Australia which is destroying so much of our irreplaceable fauna and flora. This is something that city dwellers know nothing about, but is a major problem in the country. Foolish animal rights activists won't allow culling of Brumbies, for instance, in the high country – to the detriment of much of the native environment.

CHAPTER 31

St Andrews

The house at St Andrews beach.

After the end of the Travel Air and the demise of the Acme Sheep Company, what was I to do? I had a think, then decided I'd like a small hobby farm. Jenny wasn't keen though, so eventually we found a suburban block at St Andrews beach on the Mornington Peninsula. Sea views were too expensive, but I could see that we could place a house on the block that we were considering that would face North to enjoy the Winter sun, with a view over open land that was due to become a golf course.

The golf course never happened, but seeing that we're lucky enough to live on the waterfront at Port Melbourne, the lack of a sea view was not a problem in St Andrews and the open and treed land looked good. Only once did we see a few kangaroos in the distance. The block of land had a slope to the street, so we could have a self-contained room underneath the house. It was also only a ten-minute walk to the coastal park and ocean beach. It was 100 kilometres exactly from Port Melbourne, so far enough to feel that we'd escaped the city, but not too far to drive to for the weekend. The land cost $164,000, which was quite a reasonable price in 2002. I think it'd be hard to find a vacant block anywhere now for that sort of money.

As I write this in 2023 it's hard to find any sort of reasonable houses in Melbourne for less than $1M.

Jenny found an award-winning designer and he came up with a wonderful plan for the house. I did a short course on being an owner builder, then we started work. It was a very fulfilling and entertaining project. At that time, in 2003, the economy was booming, and tradesmen were in very short supply. I had great difficulty finding a builder to start work. After quite a bit of red tape, environmental impact plans, pavement protection covers, etc., I managed to get the land cleared and the slab laid. The concreters were a pretty rum lot, their refreshment while working in the hot sun was warm stubbies of beer. They did a good job with the concrete, but they were supposed to also fill the concrete bricks for the retaining wall with cement. They said they did, but didn't, so it was a rather arduous job for me to do that work myself.

Over time, I managed to put together a team of experts who agreed to work on the project. The main man was Stuart the carpenter. He was a bit of a dag but highly skilled and a very hard worker. Fortunately, he and I got on very well together. The other trades were marvellous also. The plumber, the steel fabricator (for the supporting structure) the tilers, the plasterers, the earth movers, all were excellent and worthwhile men. I think that as an ex-apprentice I could talk their language and appreciated their skills very much. They responded in kind. We all got on very well, except for the electrician, who I didn't think much of at all, but all the lights and power points worked in the end so I don't suppose that it mattered much.

Driving up and back each day was tiring, and I was very grateful when my old neighbour from Black Rock, Don Moir offered me their spare room that was nearby to stay in overnight whenever I was working on the build. It sure saved a lot of driving, and I could be on the job nice and early when Stuart arrived.

I would joke that I was the most junior person on the site, going down to the shops for lunch, fetching and carrying, and generally assisting as required, except for Friday when I'd hand over the pay checks for the week. They couldn't boss me around then!

I became pretty expert on the shovel. There was a lot of dirt to be moved, and most of it I did by hand. When possible I'd hire a 'dingo', a little tracked earth mover vehicle which had a platform at the back that you stood on to operate the controls. It was a lot of fun, but like all machinery, care was needed otherwise accidents could happen. I overloaded the scoop one day, and the thing tipped onto its nose, leaving me stranded lying on top of it as it tilted at an angle. Stuart had to rush over and empty the scoop to stand it up again so I could clamber off. When the building was finished, I set to, to do the painting. Now that was a long and arduous job.

The design of the house was all glass along the Northern side, so in the Winter the living areas would be filled with sunlight and the open fireplace would keep it very warm after sunset. It did get a bit hot in the Summer, and the single-phase air conditioner struggled to keep a comfortable temperature, but the Winter was wonderful. We'd drive down most Fridays, and on arriving I'd light the fire, so by the time the sun set we were very snug and warm. We enjoyed St Andrews as we called it for some 14 years. We were very happy there on our own, but it was marvellous when one or other of the kids would come down with their families and stay over. There was a self-contained bedsit downstairs where they could stay, but they spent most of the time upstairs with us, which was just great.

Eventually, we got sick of driving up and down each weekend, Jenny got tired of looking after two houses, and I realised that there were some costly maintenance issues that would have to be taken care of in the near future, so we decided to put the property on the market. At the time there was a real estate agent who seemed to be very successful at selling in the area, so we engaged her. Naturally, she promised us a very large price, but in practice failed to deliver. It took her a while to get us an offer, which was well below her original appraisal, but by then I just wanted the whole thing done and dusted, so accepted it. With good old hindsight, we should have sat on it for a while. However, it's easy to be greedy. We doubled our money, and had had many wonderful years' use out of it. So overall it was a very good result.

CHAPTER 32

Money matters

One of the first things I did on returning to Melbourne from Singapore was to start a family investment company. I called it WTZ Pty Ltd. The idea was that the four kids and us would put in a minimum of $50 per month each and as the money grew, we'd invest it in shares, thus demonstrating the value of long-term saving and investing. It was a struggle for Simon to make his contribution, Sam could hardly ever manage, but Sarah and Andrew were able to put in more than the required amount each per month. We pretty well matched their total contributions ourselves too. The system worked well for some time, until Simon had a shortfall on his mortgage payments, so to help him out I took his share from the company. This was a mistake, as I didn't clear it with the other members. Andrew and Mary took out their share for an overseas trip after that, so we decided to close the company down. Sarah wisely kept her share as a share package, which has accumulated nicely since. The remainder we used to pay the deposit on a home at Coolum for Sam and his then partner. Sadly, that didn't end well. Overall though, it was a very worthwhile exercise but it would have been good if we'd been able to keep the investment company going.

Talking about money, I'd always been pretty frugal. Coming from a family that was austere, I suppose they had no spare dough to throw around, and as a very low paid apprentice, I was always aware of the need to save. At times, perhaps, I was a bit lousy at it, but in general I always tried to balance living a reasonable life along with being sensible about spending and saving. In Ansett there was a very good superannuation scheme, but not so in Singapore Airlines. I'd engaged a contact in the ANZ bank to advise me what to do with my super check that I'd got after 26 years' service with Ansett. Unfortunately, there was a recession about that time (1990) so a fair bit of it was lost. I then handed it over to a 'boutique' fund manager who promised the world, but by the time I retired, he hadn't been very successful.

At that point, I decided to take over the whole money management thing myself. At least I'd have no one else to blame if it all went bad. I look upon this task as my job, and in general quite enjoy it. I will say quite modestly that I've done quite well at it. It's impossible to say if a professional financial advisor would have done any better, but we've lived very well on our investments for the last 20 years.

The trick is to see through all the jargon and have a very simple strategy that works for you, and that you're able to stick with through the ups and downs of the market. The issue now as I see it, is to ensure that our money lasts as long as we do. Telling the future has always been a very inexact science, and you can only do your best. It seems now, as if there's more uncertainty in the financial world than ever. You'll never make money without borrowing, but being saddled with debt if there's a downturn, especially if you're not working, and the money lost can't be replaced, is very bad. Like everything else in life, striking the correct balance is the trick.

Occasionally, things go wrong like they did when I invested in Pyramid, against Jenny's wishes as I've said earlier. Even though the State Government had declared it was safe, sure enough it collapsed, leaving many people bereft. Once again, it showed the importance of listening to your wife. Sometimes, anyway! It's probably easier to remember the bad investments, rather than the good ones. That is unless the good ones were triple-bangers or something. (A 'triple banger' means tripling your money in a short time.) A good investment is one that slowly and steadily grows over time.

The Acme Sheep Company wasn't intended as an investment, but it certainly turned out badly. Another, (with hindsight) doozy was the Gold Coast bus company I invested in. I ran into an ex-Ansett colleague one day. We had coffee, and I asked him his retirement plans. He told me he'd invested pretty heavily into a Gold Coast hire car company. They were looking to expand into minibuses to transport tourists, golf groups, etc. The deal was that an investor – me – would contribute $50,000. This would buy a ten-seater bus, the company would operate the bus, and pay me $1,000 per month. I would own the bus and could sell it at any time. As this showed a return of some 24% and was something different to the share market, I took it all on face value, contributed my $50,000 and waited in vain for my $1,000 per month. It never arrived.

It turned out that the manager, a Kiwi with a diplomatic passport, had been selling the same hire car plates to different people, and when he'd accumulated enough cash, he fled the country, along with his Thai girlfriend. The legal advice I got was to hire some heavies and take the bus back, after all it belonged to me. Fortunately, it was free legal advice, and I know it's pub talk, but that's never been my style at all. It turned out that the bus had been left in a compound, and the Thai woman in whose name it had been registered had left the keys in a drawer somewhere accessible. I flew to the Gold Coast, turned up at the company, which as you can imagine was in 'disarray', grabbed the keys and took the bus.

The owner of the garage next door and the secretary were there. I asked how this crook had got away with it. They said he was charming, friendly and very believable. Any queries would be met with a very believable, "Don't worry about it! I'll look after it!" How many times has this kind of statement been used since? I did manage to rescue the bus, but what does one do with a minibus covered in company logos in Queensland?

I drove the bus to Alan Reed's house at Noosa, and it was quite useful for a while transporting family when they visited. But it was quite a task removing all the logos with a hair dryer in the meantime.

I put a 'For Sale' sign on the back of the bus, hoping that someone would take the bait and take it off my hands. Alan had some vouchers for a Seniors Lunch at a local restaurant, so we went there one day, in the bus of course. While we were lunching, my phone rang, I answered, and a man asked if I had a bus for sale. Very excitedly, I started on selling the virtues of this wonderful bus. Very aggressively he told me to move the f'ing thing as it was blocking his driveway.

I've always considered myself lucky that I became an airline pilot and not a salesman! Fortunately, I managed to get a buyer in Brisbane, and sold it for quite a substantial loss, but considered myself lucky to escape relatively unscathed from the whole mess. I promised to listen to Jenny before I took on any more wild investment schemes after that.

CHAPTER 33

More boating and a return to the canals

After the Travel Air, I bought a Farr 7.5m 'trailer sailor'. It was a lovely boat, although due to Melbourne's fickle weather we didn't get much use out of it. I did enter the Marley Point to Metung overnight race once, with Geoff Robinson and Peter McMahon as my trusty crew. It was a bit much for us though. The wind came up late at night, it was pitch black and we didn't know where we were, so I withdrew.

However, all was not lost. We'd bought a flat at Main Beach on the Gold Coast by that time, so I decided to tow the boat up there one year. It was a long trip with quite a large boat on the trailer, but the Gold Coast sailing was very pleasant. Eventually, after we'd towed it back home, I did a solo sailing trip from St Kilda to Portsea. Unfortunately, I misjudged the depth of water over the sandbank off McCrae so ran aground while still a long way from shore. The pounding of the keel on the sand caused a leak, so I decided it was time to put the boat on the market. I managed to sell it, and that was the end of sailing days for me. However, our grandson Oliver has taken up sailing in Brisbane, which I think is great.

I still was keen to keep up my involvement with aviation. I came across a group at Moorabbin Airport who collectively owned a Cessna 182 and a Piper Archer. I bought a share in the syndicate, and it turned out to be the best possible way to minimise the cost of operating a light aircraft, while still having the pleasure of ownership. Geoffrey Robinson by then had moved to Euroa, in Northern Victoria. There was a private airstrip nearby, so it was a very pleasant trip, in either the Piper or the Cessna to fly up and land there, and either continue on for lunch at Brown Brothers vineyard (no wine for me as I was flying) or stay with Geoffrey overnight, drink whisky, and talk aeroplanes.

The Piper was a very utilitarian aircraft; it flew well and was very easy to land well too. However, the Cessna was a favourite of mine. On one trip to a private airstrip near Euroa, the owner insisted that I park behind some trees out of sight of the road. Unfortunately, I left it parked sideways on a slope. The fuel in the wing ran out of the overflow overnight leaving the aircraft quite unbalanced for the takeoff next morning. They say that experience comes from the mistakes you make, and that was certainly true in my case.

Jenny and I did a trip in the Cessna to Merimbula to meet with Sarah and her family there. The weather was quite unsuitable for visual flight, and I'd not bothered with renewing my instrument rating. As I'd spent most of my life flying in cloud or at night, I was quite happy to continue with the trip. As a lot of the route was over mountains, wing ice was a real possibility which could have had very severe consequences. Fortunately, I managed to climb up to clear air between cloud layers, but it was an adventurous journey.

I Think I'm Going to Be an Airline Pilot

With the Cessna 182-S that I had a share in.

Due to the heart hiccup when I retired, I was on special medicals to renew my private pilot's licence. This required lying very still for ten minutes while being scanned, and enduring a radioactive dye injected into my heart to check its operation. I always found it quite an uncomfortable process. Eventually the doctor suggested that having this test wasn't doing me any good in the long term, I figured I'd had a good run flying until I was 72, so I decided to give it away. All things considered, my 'toy box' had been pretty full, so I had no regrets!

Sailing on the *Seaborne Legend*

After we retired, and I'd recovered from having the various stents put in my heart, we went back to canal boating, and we also discovered 'our ship'. This was a ship called the *Seaborne Legend*. She was very much a first-class ship that only carried 200 passengers, and she was just wonderful. The crew remembered us each time we sailed on her. Initially, we were the only Australians on board. Although from then on, *Seaborne* was 'discovered' here in Australia, so the proportion of our fellow countrymen increased. Each year after our trip on the French canals, we'd join 'our ship' for a voyage around the Mediterranean. Over quite a few years we'd been to most of the worthwhile places on the 'Med'. But we never felt the need to go to North Africa. The Greek Islands were marvellous, as was Venice, and I found Gibraltar very interesting too.

The ports of the Adriatic were fascinating, and Dubrovnik was of special interest to me as well. During the mid-90's war in the Balkans I was planning a flight from London to Singapore, and after submitting the flight plan for clearance from the areas we'd fly over, a reply came back from Serbia, in very unprofessional language, telling us what they'd try to do to us if we came near them. It didn't take any more convincing for me to pick another route. It was on a similar route that the Ukrainian rebels using a Russian missile shot down a Malaysian Airliner in recent years.

As part of our shore excursions when sailing around the Med, we'd sometimes do a Segway tour with a guide. The young woman who led us around the coast and outskirts of Dubrovnik was a teenager there when the Serbs bombarded the town from the hills surrounding it. It must have been a horrible experience.

Incidentally, I often flew with an ex-Yugoslavian Airlines (JAT) FO who was just about to finish his command training when he was told not to come to the airport, (he was Croatian) as it was held by the Serbs and he would certainly have been killed. He escaped to Singapore and was a FO on national terms, which to European eyes were very meagre. Pay and conditions were very low compared to expats. Along with his family they were sharing a very small flat with not a penny to their name. He was a first-class man, and I hope that things in Singapore turned out very well for him.

Eventually, the Seaborne company sold their small ships, and moved up to similar configuration ships with 400 passengers, but the same wonderful service, food, and entertainment. Sailing on those ships up the Fiords of Norway and the Baltic up to St Petersburg was just great. The palaces and museums are spectacular. It's easy to see where the Revolution came from in Russia. Palace after palace are just lined with gold, all at the expense of the people who lived in abject poverty. I think Russia is one of the few places in the world where there are more women than men, due to so many men being lost in the war, and the effects of excessive use of alcohol which caused early death.

The Hermitage gallery for instance has something like 3,000 priceless treasures on display. You need an expert guide to pick the eyes out of it for you to appreciate it. The battleship *Potemkin* is just there as it was in 1917 when it fired the first shot of the revolution, and I found Rasputin's palace and models of all the main players quite fascinating. The Czar's Summer palace, about 50 kilometres out of town, had to be seen to be believed. A military band was playing in the forecourt, cocktails were laid out for us on the lawn, an orchestra played in the great hall which was lined with amber and gold, and there were a couple of ballet dancers performing for us too. The grounds, which were huge, were laid out like an English garden, and had about 200 magnificent fountains that were gravity-fed from a lake about 20 kilometres away. The fountains turned on and off to a particular routine determined by a clockwork machine.

Russia is indeed a huge country, stretching across 11 time zones. The Western part seems very European, but under President

Putin, from our Western point of view, it seems a pity that it constantly attempts to be a 'disrupter' in the world order of democratic nations.

Other trips, down the St Lawrence to Boston, and from the UK to Iceland, were particularly special. The last one we took, from Vancouver to Anchorage in Alaska via the inside passage, was quite beautiful. In my working life, I'd flown the B744 to Anchorage from both Asia and LA so I was interested to see it again. The coastal scenery was spectacular, as were the coastal towns' history. The US bought Alaska from the Russian Czar for a very small amount once upon a time, so there's still a lot of Russian influence there. The Orthodox church is still popular, for instance, and Russian fishermen still come over for the salmon fishing season. The fiords were full of ice floes covered with mother seals and their pups, leading up to the glacier. Occasionally, we'd see a bear come out of the forest to fish, too.

We stayed at a hotel right on Lake Hood out of Anchorage. In the Summer the lake is literally covered with float planes. Instead of boats, the houses around the lakes have float planes. It was delightful to sit in the beer garden of the pub and watch the constant coming and going of the aircraft.

At a remote island called Icy Straights there was a zipline that ran from the top of a mountain down to sea level. The idea of it was too much for me, but Jenny gave it a go. You do the zipline in a harness, and at times you can reach speeds of 100 kilometres per hour. Jenny was very brave, I thought! She herself reckoned that it was one of the most exciting things she'd ever done, apart from a helicopter trip to the top of a glacier to go dog sledding. The zipline island was owned by a native Indian tribe, who set it up as a cruise ship destination after their fish cannery closed.

While I was waiting for Jenny to come down the line, an elderly English chap became quite aggressive towards a young Indian man who was manning the ticket office. This chap seemed to think he deserved some sort of special treatment, and was consequently quite rude. The young manager told him quite firmly, that his behaviour was not acceptable and if he didn't desist, he'd be forcibly removed from the island as he was one of the owners.

That was very well done, I thought!

Looking back, it's amazing that we always had fine weather, 'our ship' hardly ever rocked, and even in such notoriously bad weather places as Scotland, Iceland and Canada, it was always calm sunny and comfortable. I think of all our trips together, all over the world, and the only really bad weather we had was on our narrow-boat trip to Wales.

Jenny's been a keen bridge player for some time, so I've taken it up now. I don't expect that I'll ever progress to a very high level, but it's an enjoyable pastime, and exercises the brain. Also, it can be played just about anywhere. I like playing online where players from all over the world can log on and play to the same rules. We've managed our retirement very well, (so far) and I can't imagine a better person to be retired with, than my wonderful Jenny. As well as our many overseas trips we've always been very lucky to be able to head North each Winter to Noosa, and now, to stay in Brisbane and enjoy time with Sarah and her family.

CHAPTER 34

SarsCoV2 or Covid19

In February 2020 a virus called Covid-19 broke out in Wuhan, China. It quickly spread worldwide, something like 20 million people died, and many countries were devastated.

Fortunately, Australia being an island was able to close itself off to overseas travellers, so the impact wasn't as great here as it could have been. But it meant that states closed their borders to each other and enforced stay at home orders for many towns and cities.

As I write, we've had just about 18 months now of disruption due to the Covid-19 pandemic. There has been significant economic cost to many people, including Andrew and Mary's cafés and kiosks in the city. It also impacted Simon, who had unfortunately started out on his own with a new company that certified emergency equipment in commercial properties. Overnight, entry was prohibited. The jury's still out as to whether all the disruption has been worth it. It certainly has, to the people who are still alive, instead of the terrible death toll of other countries.

Years ago, I came across a local chapter of U3A, (Or University of the 3rd Age as they like to be called). I took over a class there that discusses 'current issues' each fortnight. Because of the Covid-19 pandemic lockdowns, we got together on the video conferencing platform Zoom, rather than in person. It took some getting used to, but the discussion was stimulating, and very good for the brain to be keep up with events and hear how other people have very different ideas about the same subject.

We took a trip in 2021 between lockdowns to our favourite Winter holiday spot in Noosa and visited Sarah in Brisbane too. Our drive back from Brisbane was quite eventful. Due to some impending Covid restrictions we had to cross New South Wales (NSW) within 24 hours. We left the Northern NSW border early on Saturday morning, and planned to overnight at a town not far from the Victorian border so that we could cross it the next morning inside the 24-hour limit. Unfortunately, we had a tyre blowout near Cootamundra, limped into town, only to find that our modern car had no spare at all, just run-flat tyres! It was impossible to get a new tyre late on a Saturday, so we ended up on the back of a tow truck at 04:00 on Sunday morning, in order to get to the border before it shut and stranded us in NSW for the duration. We just made it, and thanks to a very obliging tyre shop manager, got a replacement, so got home safely. As I write Melbourne is still restricted on movement, while the number of new virus cases increases daily.

Despite the pandemic, retirement life has suited both of us very well. We've had enough money to live well, but not so much as to overindulge. Most importantly, we've enjoyed good health, except for my heart malfunctions, and even that hasn't restricted me too much.

CHAPTER 35

Some advice and opinions

I like to say that getting older is an exercise in hope. Hope that any of the dreadful things that are possible to happen to the elderly, don't happen to us. I've had a good life, and below are some of the things I've learned along the way which hopefully can be good advice for young people, no matter how much the world changes.

Lessons from life

Demand respect, without aggression. Expect to be treated with courtesy and respect and always attempt to treat others the same way. Occasionally you'll have self-doubts, but always believe that you're worthwhile and deserve to be treated respectfully.

Be loyal and true to your friends. There will be times in your young lives when someone will try to pit you against another. Resist it, know who your friends are and stick by them.

Try to see the character in those that you're attracted to. Sometimes, just because someone is good looking it doesn't mean that they're of good character.

Be yourself! There'll be all sorts of marketing to convince you that some sort of a plastic role model is worth emulating. Resist it and be real to yourself.

Enjoy quality. Quality is remembered long after price is forgotten.

Lend a hand. Always be prepared to offer whatever help you can. The old saying, "Whatever goes around comes around," will always hold true.

Read History. If you don't know where you've been, you'll never know where you're going.

The older I get the more I think. And while, for better or for worse I'm as materially focused as ever, it's clear to me that all that really matters is who and what you love, the wellbeing and interactions of your family, and who your friends are. Of course, health and financial security are very important too.

Climate change/global warming

The big issue now is 'Global Warming'. There's no doubt in my mind that the world's population and industrialisation has had an effect on global climate, but whether the rate of warming is as bad as the doomsday forecasters are predicting is very moot. Due mainly to technology, Australia is slowly reducing its carbon emissions. Politically, the world wants more, but country people who make their living from coal mining are resisting.

As Australia produces less than 1% of global emissions, whatever is done here will have none or little effect worldwide, but as a rich country we have to be seen to be doing something.

Change is a fascinating thing. As far as society is concerned, due mostly to technology everything around us is developing at a faster rate than ever before. In theory, for the better, but in my opinion, it's very much two steps forward and one step back. Who would have ever thought that mobile phones would have become so ubiquitous that it's impossible to leave home without one, and the computing power would be so large that it's possible to run a company with just your phone. Unfortunately, personal communication seems to have suffered. How often do you see people sitting together, all on their phones, and not a word being said between them?

The power of science is to transform the world in ways that not even scientists can predict, but without the humanities, by that I mean ethics and behavioural structure, society tends to implode and collapse. The constantly increasing gap between rich and poor will one day have to be properly addressed by free market democratic countries if revolutionary discontent is not going to break out everywhere. Sadly, the dominant emotion of mankind is greed, and there will always be someone attempting to take more than they need from others.

Social media

Social media is a subject in itself. The original idea seemed simple enough, 'an easy way for boys to meet girls'. It always has been difficult for society to find an easy way for nature to take its course and for each sex to find 'the right one'. All sorts of cultural norms have been tried, from arranged marriages, to enforced slavery, with everything else in between. Who would have imagined that social media would lead to trolling, bullying, child grooming, and many other unmentionable social evils. I still can't come to terms with 'influencers'. People with no particular talents or skills, but simply by getting enough clicks on their profile can make a lot of money from advertising products.

On the plus side, much unethical and just plain criminal behaviour is now called out, and hopefully many instances of antisocial actions are being made public. Probably, the recent Royal Commissions into institutional abuse, aged care, and the financial industry wouldn't have happened without social media.

Feminism

Which brings me to the 'Me Too' movement, which has shone a light on very unsavoury practices in the entertainment industry. Whether honourable and decent behaviour by our leading lights in society has diminished, or bad behaver is just not as well hidden as once was.

I've always felt a strong affinity with the feminism movement from way back in the time when such views were far from fashionable. So, a change in our culture, that accepts the right of women to take on any task or position that they want to, resonates very strongly with me. There are still considerable headwinds for women to overcome; equal pay, glass ceilings, pushback from men who have always had the power to direct their own lives and can't come to terms with a perceived diminishing of their self-esteem and control. But sometimes the pendulum is in danger of swinging too far, with some companies, in an attempt to 'catch up' are promoting underqualified women over more experienced men just to be seen as socially responsible.

Domestic violence, just like many other ills that were well hidden once, is now being shown as the scourge that it is. There are many theories being put forward as how to combat it, but none seem very effective so far. I'm afraid that as long as men believe that having control of another person is admirable this bad behaviour will continue.

Epilogue

I'd like to quote from Winston Churchill to finish off, even though I expect that there are plenty of stories I've yet to tell.

> *"It's not given to human beings, happily for them, for otherwise life would be intolerable – to foresee or to predict to any large extent the unfolding course of events to come!"*

How you conduct yourself matters. How you treat your family, your friends, your lovers and to realise that just to have been here is a blessing in itself.

It has indeed been a fortunate life, and I did indeed become an airline pilot.

www.ingramcontent.com/pod-product-compliance
Lightning Source LLC
Chambersburg PA
CBHW070503120526
44590CB00013B/735